The **Chrysalis** Effect

"There's no other way to put it: 'The Chrysalis Effect' is the most brilliant *tour de force* of this decade. It is, and will continue to be, the most powerful and original analysis of this century's planetary vertigo. Without exaggeration, Slater's path-breaking illumination of our global 'state of mind' can be compared only with the work of a Gibbon, or Toynbee or Plutarch. It's that profound and should be the most widely read book for years to come." Professor Warren Bennis, University of Southern California, author of *Transparency* and *Judgment*

"Beautifully written, this wide-ranging book is full of fascinating information and trenchant insights. *The Chrysalis Effect* is an important contribution to the cultural transformation urgently needed today." Riane Eisler, author of *The Chalice and The Blade* and *The Real Wealth of Nations*

"Philip Slater has once again pointed the way to a more humane future by uncovering the cultural roots of today's discontents. His analysis of the waning Control Culture and the rising Integrative Culture is penetrating and all-encompassing, helping us gain insight into the biggest problems and the most intimate of family relationships. He brilliantly demonstrates the principles of Integrative Culture in action—that all things are indeed connected in the network age." Rosabeth Kanter, author of *Confidence and America the Principled*

"Philip Slater is always worth a good deep reading, and this time, though I have my differences, he is in fine visionary form, drawing on a huge range of material and experience to make a big statement about the main forces at work in the world. Among its other virtues, his new book is encouraging—not something that can be said about much in circulation these days. This book ought to launch a thousand necessary discussions." Todd Gitlin, author of *The Intellectuals and the Flag*, and *The Bulldozer and the Big Ten*

"Driving the political debates that dominate the daily news are deeper cultural choices that must be considered. Slater does so with lucidity that is engaging and wise." Jerold Starr, author of *Air Wars: The Fight to Reclaim Public Broadcasting*

"Philip Slater's *The Chrysalis Effect* overflows with gems of insight and surprise. Rarely have I dog-eared so many pages! Let this engrossing book cast its spell on you and you'll see the world anew." Frances Moore Lappé, author of *Getting a Grip: Clarity, Creativity and Courage in a World Gone Mad*

"Philip Slater is one of the most keenly observant, forward-thinking, and courageous social commentators of our time . . . or any time. He has an almost magical ability to alter the way in which we see and understand, and he does precisely that in his newest, and perhaps most provocative, book, *The Chrysalis Effect*. This is a transformative work that speaks the truth about the inevitable end of the dominant paradigm that shapes the strategies of organizations and nations, and of the emergence of an altogether new worldview—not because of some cataclysmic event, but because of the natural progression of living things. It's a wise, audacious, challenging, and unsettling work—but in the end, Slater offers a hopeful and sane alternative to the often bleak and unreasonable options that many suggest. This book will alter the nature of all your future conversations about leadership and organizations." Jim Kouzes, award-winning co-author of the bestselling book, *The Leadership Challenge*; and the Dean's Executive Professor of Leadership, Leavey School of Business, Santa Clara University

For
Susan Helgeson
and for
Gordon Slater and Milo Baker

The **Chrysalis** Effect
THE METAMORPHOSIS OF GLOBAL CULTURE

PHILIP SLATER

sussex
ACADEMIC
PRESS
Brighton • Chicago • Toronto

2 4 6 8 10 9 7 5 3

First published 2009, reprinted 2010, in Great Britain by
SUSSEX ACADEMIC PRESS
PO Box 139
Eastbourne BN24 9BP

Distributed in North America by
SUSSEX ACADEMIC PRESS
Independent Publishers Group
814 N Franklin St, Chicago, IL 60610, USA

British Library Cataloguing in Publication Data
A CIP catalogue record for this book is available from the British Library.

Library of Congress Cataloging-in-Publication Data
Slater, Philip Elliot.
The chrysalis effect : the metamorphosis of global culture / Philip Slater.
p. cm.
Includes bibliographical references and index.
ISBN 978-1-84519-311-9 (pbk. : alk. paper)
 1. Social change. 2. Globalization—Social aspects. 3. Metamorphosis—Social aspects. 4. Social history—1970– 5. Civilization, Modern—1950– 6. Social change—United States. 7. Globalization--Social aspects—United States. 8. Metamorphosis—Social aspects—United States. 9. United States—Social conditions—1980– 10. United States—Civilization—1970– I. Title.
HM831.S58 2009
306.01—dc22

2008029925

Typeset and designed by SAP, Brighton & Eastbourne
Printed by Independent Publishers Group, Chicago.
This book is printed on acid-free paper.

Contents

Acknowledgments

Writing this book has been a long and often interrupted process, for it has gone through a few metamorphoses itself. Thanks to Glenn Lyons and the late Al Adato, who made suggestions at the inception of the Wednesday coffee group. Thanks also to Warren Bennis, Todd Gitlin, Rosabeth Kanter, Felicia Eth, and Claire Braz-Valentine for early input. Later drafts had the benefit of helpful comments from Dick Vittitow, Gary Merrill, Jerry Starr, and Mike Vargo. Thanks are also due to Melita Cowie and my men's group—Mark Messer, Glenn Lyons, Andy Schiffrin, Ed Teitcher, Jim Mosher, Chris Tedesco, and Malcolm Terence—for their support and encouragement, and to Susan Schulman for her efforts on my behalf.

Above all, I want to thank Alfonso Montuori for his faith in the book, and Susan Helgeson for putting up with me during the long struggle.

Introduction

Elisabet Sahtouris, an evolution biologist and futurist, uses a biological metaphor to describe what's happening in the world today. It goes something like this:

A caterpillar happily eats its way through the leaves that surround it, consuming hundreds of times its own weight daily. Then one day it slows down and begins spinning a chrysalis.

Tiny new cells—what scientists call imaginal cells—now begin to appear in the caterpillar's body, and start to multiply. The caterpillar's immune system reacts to these new cells as foreign—as a disease, an infection—and quickly attacks and destroys them. Much the way a body will try to reject a heart transplant.

But more and more imaginal cells appear, and begin to link themselves together. Finally, the caterpillar's immune system is overwhelmed and the caterpillar is liquefied. The imaginal cells then recycle the liquefied mass into a new entity—the butterfly.

This is much the way cultures change. When old cultural assumptions are challenged, the innovations are not seen as mere novelties, but as a social ill, a critical moral infection, and attacked as such by the upholders of tradition. And when the budding culture replaces the previous one, it doesn't create a new way of being out of nothing, but merely rearranges old patterns to make the new ones. Just as the caterpillar has held the blueprint for the butterfly all along.

Today we're in the middle of such a metamorphosis on a global scale. We're in the resistance phase, when imaginal cells are being killed as fast as possible, yet new ones keep appearing with increasing rapidity. There's a feeling that both of these opposing forces are growing stronger, pulling us apart.

And we're just as confused by all this as the caterpillar must be.

The intent of this book is (1) to help understand the cultural metamorphosis taking place around us, (2) to ease the discomfort of living in a time of transition, and (3) to encourage adaptation to the change, which seems both inevitable and necessary.

PART I

THE WAY IT WORKS

1 In the Middle of the Bridge

A great complexity intrudes, tearing apart, piece by piece, all of
your carefully constructed denials.
MARK Z. DANIELEWSKI

What is now proved was once, only imagin'd.
WILLIAM BLAKE

Our entire globe is convulsed with change. There's confusion over
values, a loss of ethical certainty, a bewildering lack of consensus
about almost everything. Why is the world in such a mess?

Because, like the caterpillar, we're undergoing a profound metamorphosis. And, to put it mildly, not everyone is overjoyed about
it. Large segments of the population, both in America and
throughout the world, would just as soon go on chomping leaves.
Besides, it's a messy business being liquefied, even if you get to fly
at the end of it.

But why is this metamorphosis happening? When did it start? Is
it a good thing?

A better question might be: Is it a *necessary* thing? Jared
Diamond, in his study of failed cultures, observes that what usually
decides whether a society survives or collapses seems to be a "willingness to reconsider core values".

The good news is that the world has already been engaged in
this for over two centuries. The values and assumptions we've

been operating on for thousands of years—and which have brought our species to the brink of disaster—are all being challenged today.

The Decade of Sudden Acceleration

I've been impressed lately with how poorly people today understand the 1960s. To the media, of course, the decade was just about wearing funny clothes and long hair, taking drugs and protesting. It came and went, like all fashions. Because that's what media are about—fashions, surfaces, fads.

Others idealize the sixties. They seem to have forgotten that in the sixties what we now think of as a right-wing mentality characterized most of the nation. The sixties innovators were long on visibility but short on numbers. Despite all the huge marches and protests between 1967 and 1971, Richard Nixon won the 1972 election in a popular landslide.

The sixties were only a beginning. And while beginnings are fascinating and exciting, they only become significant if what has begun continues to grow. And in this sense, the sixties never ended. Did Jim Crow return to the South? Did blacks disappear from TV? Did women go back in the kitchen and stop going to professional schools? Did sex become taboo in the media and people start having to pretend they were married to live together or have children? Did interest in New Age ideas, alternative medicine, and organic foods suddenly come to an end? Did everyone revert to the environmental habits of the 1950s? Did people stop protesting foolish and unnecessary wars?

The truth is, all the trends that began in the sixties have flourished in the ensuing decades. If this weren't so, the fundamentalist backlash so familiar to us today wouldn't have occurred. It was the challenge to a host of basic cultural assumptions at once that horrified traditionalists the world over. As Joel Arthur Barker observed a decade ago:

> We're living in a time when fundamental rules, the basic ways we do things, have been altered dramatically. What was right and appropriate in the early 1960s is wrong and inappropriate today. And what was impossible, crazy, or clearly out of line in

the early 1960s is so ordinary that we forget it wasn't always that way.

Few people in the sixties recognized the common denominator to these movements, and the various groups involved—hippies, anti-war protesters, civil rights activists, feminists—engaged in loud and bitter arguments about priorities. But the Radical Right correctly saw in these movements the overthrow of an entire cultural tradition, and mobilized the antibodies. Yet despite their many political successes in the last two and a half decades they have been unable even to slow it down.

"The Center Will Not Hold"

We're used to riding the rapids of technological change, but social change, historically, has proceeded at the pace of a stream meandering through a dense swamp. The recent speed of social change has put a strain on our adaptive capabilities. We've had to adjust not merely to computers and cell phones and the Internet, but to the changing status of women and minorities, the sexual revolution, the decline of the nuclear family, the global economy, the increasing meaninglessness of national boundaries, the ecological movement, the bewildering concepts of modern physics, and so on. All in a few decades.

Consider the poor caterpillar again: it doesn't know it's going to become a butterfly. It doesn't even know what a butterfly is. It only knows it was perfectly happy crawling along and gorging itself when suddenly its world was completely turned upside down, and it found itself under attack from un unknown source.

As humans we have more awareness. We may welcome the changes that are happening and see in them a happier future. But it's also part of our human makeup to long for things to be simpler, to want something immutable and permanent. Which accounts for the increasing strength—in our largely secular, ecumenical society—of fundamentalism. It's as if people were saying, "I can accept that everything I own and everything I've learned and everything I enjoy is rapidly becoming obsolete, as long as I have these ancient dogmas I can hold onto amid the chaos". And who among us has not had days of wishing the world would slow down for a moment so we could get our bearings?

Obviously this isn't just an American response. The fundamentalists of the United States are mirrored in the fundamentalists of Islam, and the conflict between 'reds' and 'blues' in the United States is mirrored in the battle between Iranian ayatollahs and Iranian secularists. Everywhere on earth people are embracing change warmly and resisting it fiercely.

Some people talk about a 'culture war' between the West and Islam. But the real culture clash is taking place *within* Islam and *within* the West. This is not a conflict between nations, or between religions, or between left and right. The conflict is *within* every nation, every political party, every religious tradition, every institution, every individual.

Global Evolution

Incivility and chaos arise when an old system is breaking down and a new one hasn't yet fully taken hold. Today we're in that very spot, undergoing a transition between two global cultural systems with opposing values and assumptions: one of them thousands of years old and dying, but still tenacious, exhausting itself in ever more violent resurgences; the other in its youth, but growing stronger every day.

The change has been going on for generations, but in the last fifty years the pace has accelerated, creating the most rapid social upheaval in the history of our species. It has even led some fundamentalists to anticipate the end of the world.

And in a sense it is. The ending of an old world, the beginning of a new one. It's changing everything around us, from international relations to sexual relations, from how we arrange governments to how we arrange our gardens, from how we think about God to how we think about the atom.

And we're in the middle of it, trying to live normal lives.

An Example

The ongoing battle over evolution is usually defined as science vs. religion, but it goes far beyond that, reflecting two opposite ways of conceptualizing the world. Creationists and scientists are after all considering the same data—a planet full of living creatures of extraordinary complexity, coexisting in an ecological system of even greater complexity. The creationist looks at this and thinks, this could only have come about as the conscious creation of a humanoid intelligence—some sort of über-authority—since it would be impossible for this sort of thing to evolve on its own. He assumes that complexity presupposes intelligence. The scientist, on the other hand, would say the creationist has it backwards—that intelligence springs from organizational complexity. Mind inheres in any cybernetic system capable of learning from trial and error and becoming self-correcting.

Lewis Thomas points out that a single ant wandering about in aimless circles seems the height of stupidity. It's only when you're confronted with one of those long columns, running all the way from your garden into the house, up the stairs, into your cat's dish or honey jar and back again, that you can say intelligence is at work. But whose? There's no dictator ant. Alone every ant is as stupid as the next.

> Termites are even more extraordinary in the way they seem to accumulate intelligence as they gather together. Two or three termites in a chamber will begin to pick up pellets and move them from place to place, but nothing comes of it; nothing is built. As more join in, they seem to reach a critical mass, a quorum, and the thinking begins.

Creationism is inherently anti-democratic. It says order can only be imposed from above by some sort of dictator—that order can't evolve from interaction among equals. The great visionary Mary Parker Follett called democracy a form of *self-creating coherence*. This universal tendency toward spontaneous integration by living things is a deeply spiritual concept to many people, but anathema to mainstream religions like Judaism, Christianity and Islam, all of which are rooted in deeply authoritarian traditions.

Creationism, then, is based on a cultural principle of authoritarian control, while evolutionary theory is based on a cultural assumption of spontaneous integration. This difference underlies virtually all the social changes that have occurred in the past two centuries or more.

The Two Systems

The old system I call *Control Culture*. Its concern with mastery led to the creation of rigid mental and physical compartments, a static vision of the universe, a deep dependence on authoritarian rule, a conviction that order was something that had to be imposed, and a preoccupation with combat.

The new system I call *Integrative Culture*, because its guiding impulse is to dissolve mental walls and permeate artificial boundaries—to celebrate interdependence. It has a dynamic vision of the universe, a democratic ethos, and sees order as something that evolves, as it does in Nature, from spontaneous interaction.

Control culture was coherent. If your life revolves around getting and maintaining control over your world, you need to separate yourself—your mind, your ego—from Nature, from your own body and feelings. You don't want to think of yourself merely as part of the animal kingdom. You're outside all that—a separate, controlled, and controlling cerebral being. 'Human' is defined as 'not animal'. Nor is this world you've separated yourself from an organic, evolving whole. How could you ever control such a thing? So Controllers tended to view the world as fixed and unchanging, and liked to split it into paired opposites: friend/enemy, master/slave, material/spiritual, sacred/profane, good/evil. It was a worldview that fit the Bible and Newton's Clockwork Universe equally well.

Another problem for the Controller is that living things aren't all that crazy about *being* controlled. We humans were, after all, genetically programmed to be hunter-gatherers, and lived that way for 99% of our existence on this planet. So Controllers end up fighting a lot. Control Culture was a warrior culture—competitive, belligerent, macho. And a culture based on war has to be authoritarian. Slaves and serfs have to be kept in line, while fighting men—trained to be competitive and quarrelsome—have to be controlled. So rigid hierarchies with rigid rules of behavior became the norm. And because war was viewed as the most noble masculine profession, parents raised their boys to be 'from Mars'—that is, stoic, rigid, and aggressive. And since men were being trained to be unfeeling and insensitive, women had to specialize in what the men were being trained to neglect: love, cooperation, intimacy, nurturance. They were trained to be 'from Venus'. And since women weren't doing soldierly things—which were more highly valued—they wound up at the bottom of the social hierarchy. Even the lowest serf was expected to dominate his wife, and was looked down on if he didn't.

This demotion of women is the foundation of the entire system. You cannot have an authoritarian, war-like society unless women are devalued and oppressed. It is an axiom of Control Culture that a woman must not be allowed freedom of choice—not just about whether to bear a child or not, but about what she does with her life, who she sleeps with, how she looks—everything. Controlling women is fundamental to Control Culture, and women have the lowest possible status wherever Control Culture is dominant. We in the West are horrified that elders in a Pakistani village would order a woman to be gang-raped as punishment for her brother's crime, but in the Bible, Lot is considered noble because he offers his daughters to be gang-raped by a mob in order to protect his male guests. Misogyny is cultural, not religious or ethnic.

The Beginning of Control Culture

Prior to today's upheaval the most profound event in human history was the moment we decided not to rely on the earth's abundance, like other species, but to attempt to control it, by manipulating crops and flocks. It started us down a long, arduous, and frustrating road from which there is no turning back. Nor do we want to turn back. We're proud of our achievements. Yet we're occasionally made aware of the price. Most cultures have a tradition of a 'fall'—from a 'golden age', an Eden—to a life of constant toil and struggle (see Chapter 8). In other words, from the relative simplicity and ease of the hunter-gatherer life to the more stressful and laborious demands of agriculture. Trying to control your environment takes *work*.

This attempt to control nature was an addictive drug, requiring bigger and bigger hits. For before long it's not just plants and animals and insects that have to be controlled—it's other people. And ultimately, oneself, one's feelings (see Chapter 6).

Archeological studies indicate that Control Culture is only about eight thousand years old. For most of our existence as a species we were governed by very different habits and values. Control Culture is only a very brief phase in human evolution.

Yet we've been steeped for so long in this cultural system that many people assume its customs and norms are locked in our DNA. They think Control Culture is just 'human nature'. But what was human nature two thousand years ago is very different from what human nature was twenty thousand years ago, or what it will be a thousand years from now. Human societies have managed to persuade people to act in the most varied and outlandish ways, and to believe their odd habits 'natural'.

We're an evolving species. We're not locked into instinctual behavior. Nor are other species, entirely. Animal and bird behavior can be modified by environmental changes. Even fish, according to recent studies, are less bound by instinct than we used to believe— genetic factors are often modified by environmental ones:

> The environment—even social and cultural contexts—can switch genes on and off.

Nature and nurture are no longer as distinct as they used to be viewed. The old notion of the DNA as a "fixed 'blueprint' in each creature, altered only by accidents", has been replaced by a "new view of the DNA as a complex self-organizing system that responds to events outside".

Yet there's a grain of truth in the 'human nature' belief: a cultural pattern this deeply ingrained doesn't change overnight. It will take many generations for these habits to fall into disuse.

Integrating

Serious challenges to this cultural system came first in the 18th century, in the form of the spread of democratic ideology—triggered by encounters with hunter-gatherer societies in the new world. But Integrative Culture only began to make serious gains in the second half of the 20th.

The Women's Movement, the global economy, the ecology movement, the Internet, New Age philosophies, organic farming, the growth of international institutions and international law, the growing interest in understanding other cultures and in communicating with other species, the interest in telling old stories from new viewpoints—these things are all part of Integrative Culture. Integrative Culture is about embracing and integrating diversity. Control Culture was about eliminating it.

Whereas Control Culture viewed the universe as a gigantic, clockwork machine controlled from above, Integrative Culture sees it as a self-generating organism—a world-view more consistent with the revolutions in science brought about by Darwinian theory and quantum physics.

For modern scientists have been arriving at a vision of the universe that has undermined some of the Control Culture's most fundamental assumptions (see Chapter 4). Science, says Robert Laughlin, has now moved from an Age of Reductionism to an Age of Emergence.

> The objective of understanding nature by breaking it down into ever smaller parts is supplanted by the objective of understanding how nature organizes itself.

This shift in attitude is reflected in economic thinking. Kevin Kelly, former editor of *WIRED*, says that while "wars and battles were the allegories of the old industrial economy," the emerging network economy behaves like a biological community, growing and evolving organically, without centralized control (see Chapter 5).

Mary Parker Follett's concept of self-creating coherence has also become fundamental to our understanding of nature. J. E. Lovelock has described our planet as a self-organizing system. Janine Benyus describes nature's manufacturing processes as "self-assembling". And John David Ebert points out that the Gaia vision of the earth as "self-making" is "part of the same ecology of ideas as the self-organizing dynamics of chaos theory".

Dissolving Boundaries

Control Culture was obsessed with building walls—physical walls, social walls, mental walls. Between nations, between classes, between men and women, between mind and body, between mass and energy, between 'Man' and nature, and so on. Integrative Culture seeks to dissolve these boundaries, to stress their commonalities.

These trends are unsettling to the Controller mentality. The Controller hates the notion of the DNA uniting all of life. For the Controller, the prospect of entering a new phase of human evolution is terrifying rather than exciting.

Backlash against Integrative Culture has fueled the attack on science and the revival of creationism. The Controller is more comfortable with the idea of a static world, created all at once by a micromanaging centralized authority, than with the idea of spontaneously evolving life. In Controller thinking there can be no order without centralized control.

This obsession with control often leads to an inability to let go of the past. Hence the Controller preoccupation with avenging, punishing, repaying. "Remember the Alamo", "Remember the Maine", "Remember Pearl Harbor"—grievances fed and watered like horses, to bear more comfortably the burden of war (see Chapter 7). Perpetual revenge cycles are endemic in feudalistic societies.

But when Nelson Mandela brought about the end of Apartheid in South Africa, the African National Congress, rather than slaughtering their former oppressors, instituted the Truth and Reconciliation Commission to bring unity to the nation. This is a characteristic Integrative innovation.

For Integrators, grievances are hurdles to cross. Wherever there's an emotional or intellectual distance they want to bridge it. Integrating is an end in itself—an activity rather than a product. There is no ultimate goal toward which it tends.

Obsolete Habits

Relationships in Control Culture were based on what Riane Eisler calls the Dominator Model—a model that had meaning in a world where men were chronically engaged in physical combat. But since hand-to-hand combat has little relevance to modern life—even to modern warfare—the traits men are still trained in from birth have become maladaptive in the interdependent world we now inhabit. The cooperative skills women have been forced to specialize in, on the other hand, have become increasingly important to our shrinking world. The status of women has increased proportionately (see Chapter 3).

Integrative Culture even affects the way we think. Control Culture placed exclusive value on linear, left brain thinking, while Integrative Culture tends to value the synthesizing properties of the right brain.

These contrasts can be summarized as follows.

Control Culture	Integrative Culture
Universe split into opposites	Universe undivided, whole
World is static matter	World is energy, process
Authoritarian, hierarchical	Democratic, egalitarian
Competitive, macho, warlike	Cooperative, communicative
Women devalued, constrained	Women valued, empowered
Change ordered from above	Spontaneous evolution

Both of these systems are logically coherent. This is why the transition from one to the other is so difficult. They cannot logically be blended. Fortunately, as we'll see in Chapter 2, cultures are not, and cannot be, logical or consistent.

Not About Political Divisions

This cultural divide is not a Left–Right split. Communists and the Radical Right share many Controller values. And while the neocons in the Republican Party capture the fundamentalist backlash against Integrative Culture, more traditional conservatives, in their preference for spontaneous processes and deep distrust of centralized authority, embrace many Integrative values. Free-market capitalism, with all its flaws and abuses, is still more Integrative than a typical centralized Marxist state.

Progressives are also split. Controllers among them approach social change the same way they approach everything else—as a combat. There is only one 'correct' path to change, which must triumph over all other paths. This path usually puts a priority on gaining centralized political power, at which point change is to be imposed by force on a benighted populace.

Integrative progressives see change not as imposed from the top but as evolving from spontaneous, grass-roots movements. They tend to accept multiple approaches to change—those who work with corporations to achieve sustainability are not thought to have 'sold out', for example. There is no 'blueprint' for change, no party discipline, and leadership is seen as a quality that ordinary people everywhere can exercise in their own communities.

Why Now?

For thousands of years Control Culture not only dominated all the major civilizations of East and West, but also most of the cultures we call 'primitive'. Only a few islands of pre-Control Culture—like the Pygmies and the Bushmen—survived.

So why is it declining now? Why, after thousands of years of being second-class citizens, did women all of a sudden reject the role? Why, after thousands of years of accepting tyranny as the natural order of the universe, did people suddenly decide democracy was necessary? Why, after thousands of years of assuming war was just part of life—indeed the major way that men could prove themselves—did people start seeking peace and creating institutions to preserve it?

Their are four main reasons why Integrative Culture is growing so quickly:

First, a sharp increase in the pace of technological change;

Second, sharp increases in the speed and breadth of global communication;

Third, increasing ecological danger and awareness of our common dependence on the health of the planet we inhabit together;

Fourth, the decreasing utility of war.

I. The Pace of Change

Warren Bennis and I predicted in 1964 that democracy was inevitable and that the Soviet Union and other authoritarian regimes would either collapse or be forced to democratize within fifty years. Our prediction was justified. Since 1980, eighty-three nations have converted to democracy.

The industrial revolution was fueled by Controller needs, but it fed Integrative Culture by undermining the authoritarian hierarchies that were virtually universal when the industrial revolution began. Authoritarian systems are too rigid and slow to adapt in an age of rapid change. And authoritarian bosses—who tend to want only 'loyal' subordinates around them—are more apt to get locked into failing policies when those around them tell them only what they want to hear (see Chapter 5).

As the pace of change has accelerated, hierarchies in the corporate world have flattened, and ad hoc teams are replacing fixed pyramidal bureaucracies. As business analyst William Knoke observes:

> The behemoths that performed well in a static world are
> proving unadaptable to a changing marketplace, dizzying tech-
> nologies, and dynamic consumer tastes. . . . Hierarchy and
> centralized control are collapsing.

The reason for this, as Bennis and I pointed out, has nothing to do with idealism and everything to do with efficiency. Democratic systems, for all their apparent disorder and sloppiness, are better equipped to deal with complex environments and adapt more easily to change.

In his book *Six Degrees*, Duncan Watts points out that during 9/11 centralized emergency systems, like the mayor's emergency command bunker and the police command center, were immediately put out of commission, while informal networks all over the city responded quickly to the crisis.

Toyota's avoidance of a potential economic catastrophe in 1997 (see Chapter 5) exemplifies the value of decentralization in crises.

The man at the top of a hierarchy is supposed to have the 'big picture', but that picture is based on 3rd and 4th hand information, wildly distorted by the pressure to show loyalty to the boss and his ideology. The blunders of Hitler, Mao, Nixon, and Bush exemplify this problem (see Chapter 5).

In a crisis, as Alfonso Montuori points out, there is a strong tendency for people to seek a pretended homogeneity and a totalitarian structure, while attacking diversity at every turn. Ironically, this seems to be the worst possible way to deal with a crisis.

II. Communication

In 1900 a hurricane destroyed Galveston, Texas and killed 6000 people. It was the worst natural disaster our nation had ever seen. Yet most deaths could have been avoided. The Cubans at that time had an excellent tracking system and had predicted both the storm's intensity and its direction. But Willis Moore, chief of the United States Weather Bureau, a man with a "passion for control", couldn't accept the idea that the Cubans might have a better system than his. Just a month before the disaster Moore:

> persuaded the War Department to ban from Cuba's . . . telegraph lines all cables about the weather . . . this at the peak of hurricane season.

Since Moore's own predictions were wrong, Galveston was unprepared, and thousands were washed away. It's harder to achieve such stubborn isolation today. Data flies all over the world whether we like it or not.

In an executive training exercise, management expert Charles Handy would select two men from opposite sides of a room, place them in chairs facing away from each other, and auction off, one at a time, three five-pound notes, giving each man a turn at bidding first. Invariably the notes were sold at or above their actual value:

> There would be a rush of volunteers for the next round, eager to try out their theory of preemptive bidding. The result would

be the same as long as I was careful to pick them from different sides of the room.

Finally he'd choose a pair he'd seen whispering together. One would bid a penny, the other would pass, and they'd split the proceeds. Communication had transformed the situation. Without it:

Logical, sensible, mature individuals were competing to the point of lunacy.

In Control Culture value came from scarcity. In Integrative Culture it comes from profusion. A single telephone, modem, fax machine, or other communication device, is worth nothing. The more there are the more value they have. Communication transforms value.

III. Ecological Pressure and Awareness

The hunter-gatherers who covered the globe before Control Culture emerged saw themselves as part of Nature, and recognized their interdependence with all living things. Hunters identified with their prey, and felt their success in killing it was a gift. They would have been astonished to hear us talk about Nature as if we stood outside it. "Man against Nature" would have sounded as silly to them as "Toe against Foot".

Control Culture divided the world into a battleground of warring opposites. Everything had to be split into oppositional pairs: men vs. women, aristocrat vs. peasant, man vs. nature, good vs. evil. Mind was separated from body, spirit from matter, religion from sexuality. Even the unity of the human body was denied: The right hand became the 'righteous' hand and the left hand was 'sinister', as if the two halves of the body were enemies.

Today it's harder to make these splits. The world is shrinking. It's harder to avoid each other, harder to ignore each other, harder to deceive each other. Harder to deny our interdependence.

It's impossible now to take action anywhere in the world without it having repercussions for everyone. Factory emissions in Illinois cause acid rain in Massachusetts. Stock market prices in Europe and Japan affect those on Wall Street and vice versa. Insecticides from American farms leave deposits in the Arctic Circle. The greed of corporate executives in Texas destroys the pensions of widows in Vermont. Chemical weapons used against foreign enemies contaminate our own soldiers. Modern industry, modern chemicals, and modern weapons are all indifferent to national boundaries. We live in a woven world.

It's also a finite world. Our economic system demands perpetual growth, but we're already drowning in trash, and people have become frightened at the extremes to which the open-ended biblical precept to "increase and multiply" has been carried. Unlimited growth is, after all, cancer.

The only thing that can be expanded more or less infinitely is communication—relationships, linkages. And that's what Integrative Culture is all about.

IV. The Obsolescence of War

War as we know it, with standing armies, pitched battles, and large-scale slaughter, has only been around for six or seven thousand years, and for most of that time it had a practical value based on an agrarian economic system. Through war you could acquire land and the slaves to work it.

War also spread civilization. Both the Trojan War and the Crusades, for example, involved backward yahoos attacking superior civilizations and bringing their cultural advances back home, thereby creating new and even more advanced civilizations.

Today war doesn't buy you anything, even security. There's nothing you can get with war today that you can't get more cheaply without it. Any nation that makes war today is weakened by it.

Modern warfare also lacks the glamour of ancient hand-to-hand combat, being largely a matter of destroying infrastructures and slaughtering civilians, usually from a safe distance. The romance of war received a mortal wound when the gun replaced the sword, and was put out of its misery by Hiroshima.

Finally, in the global economy, it's hard to find a place to shoot or bomb where you won't hit parts of yourself—your own companies, citizens, and assets. War, in short, is bad for business (see Chapter 7). None of the world's most prosperous nations, in terms of personal income, ever engage in it.

It may seem odd to say war is obsolete when, as this is written, American soldiers are fighting in Iraq and Afghanistan, and there are wars all over Africa. After all, there hasn't been a decade since World War II that the United States hasn't bombed and invaded some little country. But to say something is obsolete doesn't mean it ceases to exist. Monarchy is obsolete, too, but there are still kings and queens throughout the world. People still ride horses, too, and take buggy-rides.

What does it mean, then, to say war is obsolete?

The 'War' on Terrorism

The invasions of Afghanistan and Iraq were defined as efforts to combat terrorism.But Al Qaida is a network, not a nation, its terrorists are drawn largely from Saudi Arabia and Pakistan—both our allies—but are found all over the globe, including the United States. Traditional nation vs. nation wars actually increase our insecurity, by inciting anti-American hatred in the nations we bomb and invade, by aiding the recruitment of terrorists, and by retarding—through the devastation of their infrastructures—the westernization of these nations. Before the Bush 'crusade', Iraq and Iran were arguably the most secular and westernized nations in the Islamic world.

The Bush administration's war on terrorism was an outmoded response to a modern situation—redefining an international problem (terrorist networks) requiring an international solution (pooling intelligence and police forces with other nations) as a national one (cherry-picking a single nation as the 'cause' of terrorism) requiring invasion of that nation.

Terrorism cannot be eliminated by military means. All the planes, tanks, and missiles in the world won't stop a single terrorist from poisoning a water supply or hijacking a plane. As John Arquilla, professor of analysis at the Naval Postgraduate School in

Monterey, California, points out, it takes a network to fight a network. The Bush administration's approach to terrorism was like buying grenades to rid your back yard of disease-carrying mosquitoes (and then throwing most of the grenades in the wrong yard).

Body counts provide a clear illustration of the difference between the two cultural systems. The Controller worldview sees enemies as isolated 'bad guys': each one killed is one less enemy, and if a few civilians are killed along the way, it's a small price to pay. Integrative Culture tends to see everyone as linked—each civilian killed as part of an extended family and community—so that every death may produce a dozen terrorists seeking revenge. In the Integrative view terrorism is not a war problem, soluble by mortar attacks and blowing up buildings, but a police problem—apprehending would-be murderers. This is the way European countries have successfully dealt with terrorists, and it has the added advantage that it doesn't cost a trillion dollars.

The habit of responding to any dilemma by making war on somebody is one that will persist for some time—in part because it provides an outlet for the frustrations people feel. But if American foreign policy fails to adapt to this changing world pretty soon, our nation will go the way of other obsolete empires (see Chapter 9).

Evolving

These are the conditions that have given rise to the evolutionary adaptation I've called Integrative Culture. Control Culture is declining for the simple reason that it is an evolutionary dead end. This doesn't mean that it will automatically disappear—both biological and social history are filled with examples of species and societies that failed to adapt to change. But it is heartening to know that the process of adaptation has begun. Mary Parker Follett said that the difference between competition and cooperation was merely that between a short-run view and a long-run view, and humans are the most cooperative of primates. Intelligence is largely the ability to take that longer view, and that's how we survived against more powerful and more aggressive species. A successful adaptation to the world of the future requires long-term, cooperative thinking, and that's what Integrative Culture offers.

Every aspect of Control Culture is being challenged today—and every aspect is being bitterly defended. The debate over which path to take is what makes our nation, and our world, seem so polarized. Paul Hawken lists 130,000 known organizations from every country in the world working to solve ecological problems and reverse our present destructive path. We can think of this list as an onslaught of Imaginal cells. And the fundamentalist, neo-con backlash is the immune system of the caterpillar, trying desperately to avoid having to change its ways and cease consuming several times its own body weight in energy every day.

We're so used to the intense debate today over Controller values that we tend to forget: it's only been a century or two since every one of those old values was accepted unquestioningly by all but a tiny minority. So we can see why fundamentalists are up in arms.

Fundamentalism is not really about religion. Between Islamic, Jewish, and Christian fundamentalists, what real cultural difference is there? They all have a static, dualistic vision of the world, with 'Good' battling 'Evil', they all enshrine primitive writings as the basis of all wisdom, they all want to control and enslave women, they all want rigid authoritarian rules and leaders. They cannot understand the concept of emergence, of an evolving universe, of self-creating coherence.

It's easy to overestimate the backlash. A hornet caught in a web, attacking furiously in all directions, sounds powerful and captures our attention, but it's only exhausting itself in futility. The political triumphs of the Radical Right in the United States in 2000 were impressive, much in the way the violent triumphs of segregationists impressed us in the 1960s, or Hitler's triumphs in the 1930s and 1940s. But Nazism was a brief 12-year backlash against the spread of democracy, and segregationist violence was a brief backlash against the rapid growth of the civil rights movement.

One Thing Leads to Another

Change is hard for everyone. A change we want may be less upsetting than one we don't, but all change brings unexpected and undesired consequences. Mixed feelings are the faithful shadow of social change.

There was a character in an old Hollywood comedy who liked to pull loose threads from other people's clothes. In the climax of this running gag he pulls a thread and a man's whole suit falls off. That's the way social change works. You think you're making a little adjustment—taking care of a loose end—and the entire social fabric comes apart.

Our left brains want to deal with one problem at a time, but real life doesn't allow it. An artist brightens the color in one corner of a painting and the whole composition is thrown out of balance. Some trees are cut down and a mudslide destroys houses and silts up a stream. A bypass is constructed and a town dies. Things are connected. Two centuries ago quite a few men wanted democracy. Most of them certainly didn't want the Women's Movement, and would have been horrified to learn it would someday result from their efforts.

If change happened slowly and smoothly we might be able to handle it more easily. But that's not what happens. A wall comes down in Berlin, but walls go up in Israel and on the U.S.–Mexico border. Old cultural systems are not abandoned without fierce resistance. As they sense an old cultural system dying around them, those who espouse it will assert its values more harshly, more stridently, more desperately.

An Awkward Age

The growth of Integrative Culture and the simultaneous rise in fundamentalism makes us feel the world's going in opposite directions at the same time: We've never been more concerned over our environment yet never more destructive of it; never more distrustful of technology yet never more dependent on it; never more opposed to violence yet never more fascinated with it; never more ego-driven and never more hungry to lose ourselves in something beyond ego; never more health conscious yet never more unhealthy. And while we've never had more ways of connecting with each other, we've never felt more disconnected.

These are the predictable symptoms of a society in transition. Old familiar habits have begun to seem irrelevant or destructive, while the emerging system still feels awkward and uncomfortable, like shoes that haven't yet shaped themselves to our feet. It will be generations before Integrative Culture achieves the universality that Control Culture enjoyed for so long.

It's as if we were in the middle of one of those shaky rope bridges in old Hollywood jungle movies, spanning a deep ravine. We're nowhere near the other side, and a long way from where we started. We're going to be in the middle of the bridge for a long time.

Some Good News

Integrative Culture enjoys an additional advantage in that it distorts our genetic programming far less than Control Culture has. We were, after all, hunter-gatherers for millions of years before the emergence of Control Culture, and our survival depended more than anything else on cooperation. It is our possession of superior cooperative skills—our social intelligence—that distinguishes us from the other apes. As Ernst Mayr points out:

> Any genetic contribution toward cooperative behavior would be favored by natural selection.

Two recent experiments underline this point. In one, the abilities of chimps and two and a half year old humans were compared in a variety of tasks. The two and a half year olds did no better than chimps in quantitative, cognitive tasks like adding, counting, remembering where things were hidden, but were far better at "communicating with others, learning from others, and 'reading the minds' of others". In other words, figuring out what others were doing and what they wanted the child to do.

In the second study psychologist Felix Warneken found that at 18 months a toddler would automatically come to the aid of an adult if the adult seemed to need help. The experimenter would struggle with tasks like pinning clothes on a line, or stacking books, and would drop a clothespin or knock over the stack. Within seconds, the toddler would come over and try to help him. This is without the experimenter asking or thanking or rewarding the toddler in any way. Furthermore, if the experimenter deliberately threw a pin or a book to the floor the toddler would ignore him.

These are genetic responses. But men in particular are often trained by Control Culture to suppress those instincts in the service of machismo, and both sexes will suppress them in the service of the capitalist values of individualism and acquisitiveness.

Integrative Culture is not only an inevitable development, it is a necessary one. While its ascendancy will not solve the world's problems—environmental destruction, climate change, overpopulation, economic inequality, terrorism, and so on—it will make an approach to their solutions possible. As long as Control Culture is dominant it will not only be impossible to come to grips with our most pressing problems, it will be impossible to keep from making them worse.

2 | The Way of Change: Purity Destroys

With every culture there are two sides. If you believe one thing to be true about a people the very opposite will also be true.

ANA CASTILLO

Without Contraries is no progression.

WILLIAM BLAKE

Before looking at the ways Integrative Culture is changing our lives we need to consider a paradox about the way cultures evolve.

Like the chrysalis, cultures don't start from scratch when they change—they build the new with the elements of the old—merely rearranging the raw materials, which, after all, lend themselves to infinite variation. Every new culture retains parts of the one that preceded it.

A culture provides us not only with a common set of rules and preferences for interacting with one another, but also a common definition of what we see when we look at something, or hear when we listen to it. We have no direct experience of the world he live in. We experience our world 'through a glass darkly', mediated, predigested, predefined by our culture.

Children in our culture, for example, are taught to define things by shape. They are told to give the term 'ball' to any spherical object, regardless of its size, color, texture, composition, odor, sound, taste, or function. These factors are thereby rendered less important in defining how we see the world. We will always tend to see it as a collection of discreet shapes. Those who don't see it this way are usually considered deranged, unless they're artists, physicists, or on psychedelic drugs.

The Rorschach 'ink-blot' test, designed to diagnose psychopathology, is based on these assumptions. If your responses are based on shape this tends to denote 'normality', while responses based on texture tend to set off alarm bells in the examining psychologist.

Yet we can imagine contexts in which form might be unimportant relative to other attributes. If you were being bombarded by objects, for example, you might prefer to know whether a 'hard' or a 'soft' was being fired at you. Whether it was a square or round 'hard' would be secondary.

Naming by shape distorts our perception in many ways. Since we feel most comfortable with forms, we create them by drawing lines around chunks of our environment—separating the inseparable with artificial boundaries. We draw a sharp line between the sea and the land, for example, and between earth and sky. Yet almost a third of animal phyla manage to squeeze themselves into that one-dimensional non-space with which we pictorially separate land and sea—the inter-tidal zone. Even our planet has a fuzzy boundary and is inextricably bound up with the rest of the universe.

Because of our language habits we tend to experience the world disconnectedly—to chop up our environment, and see these pieces, including ourselves, as isolated entities. Yet you are no more separate from the air you breathe, and the earth you walk on, and the trillions of bacteria that live within you and keep you alive, than your eye is separate from your brain.

So why do we name things by form?

Note that all other attributes, although they can be apprehended by one sense or another, cannot be physically *grasped* by the hand. They cannot be held, controlled, and directly *manipulated* (from the Latin, 'handful').

In other words, by our habits of naming we have created a world we can attempt to control and manipulate. This tendency is the basis of the complex civilization we inhabit, and of its many problems as well.

The Price We Pay

Every cultural system comes with a price attached. As Lewis Mumford once said, a system crams the complexity of life into an ideological straitjacket, ignoring much of what's natural and real. Similarly, every culture fosters and exaggerates certain human traits at the expense of others.

Every cultural system, in other words, is an oversimplification, a distortion, of our humanity.

A cultural system can make people believe the most bizarre ideas—even be willing to die for them, and to kill others for not sharing them. It can transform the most unpleasant kinds of behavior into cherished virtues.

Today we in the West find it hard to understand how men in some cultures could feel virtuous about killing a sister or daughter to "preserve the family honor," simply because a man had had sex with her. We're also appalled at fundamentalist parents who beat a child to death to "drive out the Devil" and ensure her entry into heaven.

Many foreigners, on the other hand, find it strange that Americans have elevated selfishness, discontent, and greed into our highest virtues, and that we seem pleased when we convert previously generous, considerate, and contented people to lives of competitive striving, status-seeking, and material accumulation.

All of us, everywhere in the world, from the day we're born, are indoctrinated with arbitrary rules of behavior, distorted images of reality, and value systems that demand that we pretend to be less than we are.

Safety Valves

But all cultures have safety valves that help release the tensions created by this twisting of our genetic makeup. Cultures survive only when they're impure—when they accumulate inconsistencies and contradictions like lichen on a rock.

Medieval Europe, for example, had a Feast of Fools, during which nobles and peasants exchanged roles, priests were the butt of practical jokes, and all the usual taboos and rules of deference to one's superiors were abolished for a day. Similarly, the Japanese

have a tradition that anything said while drunk must have no repercussions in their daily lives. Since people are more complex than any
system of ideas, these contradictions and inconsistencies are necessary for a culture to survive. As Mumford put it:

> This tendency toward laxity, corruption, and disorder is the only
> thing that enables a system to escape self-asphyxiation.

Some early Christian leaders, like Paul, portrayed celibacy as the
highest good. But if this principle had been enforced for everyone
the Catholic Church would have disappeared like the Shakers, who
never reproduced themselves. Mumford attributes the longevity of
the Catholic Church to its ability to absorb contradictory traditions:

> It is not the purity of Roman Catholic doctrine that has kept
> that Church alive and enabled it to flourish even in a scientific
> age but just the opposite.

It survived, he says, because of the many ideas and practices
"seeping in from other systems of thought and other cultures,"
especially that of the Greeks, and later, of science. Not to mention
the pagan elements (Santa Claus, Christmas trees, Easter eggs)
incorporated into the Christian religion as it swept through Europe.
    Similarly, Mumford argues, capitalism in its pure, bottom-line
form could not have survived without the "corruption" of child
labor laws, safety rules, product laws and other forms of government intervention. Since short-term profit is the sole motivating
force in pure capitalism, it would ultimately self-destruct from its
own shortsightedness—debilitating its labor force and poisoning its
customers. No viable society can be founded on a system that makes
greed the only operating principle, for such a system is self-extin-
guishing.
    Vast differences in wealth tend to generate enormous pressures
toward equalization, and if these are not expressed through progressive taxes or other forms of government intervention, they tend to
be expressed through crime. In Haiti, for example, the dominant
mechanism for spreading wealth is kidnapping.
    The neo-cons of the Bush administration saw in Iraq the oppor-

tunity to create a pure, free-market utopia. The idea was to dismantle all government institutions—including the army, utilities, and state-owned manufacturing companies—thereby creating a void that multinational corporations would quickly fill.

> Iraq was to the neo-cons what Afghanistan was to the Taliban: the one place on Earth where they could force everyone to live by the most literal, unyielding interpretation of their sacred texts.

Naomi Klein describes how this strategy backfired—creating massive unemployment, a collapsed infrastructure, and a bloody insurgency. Iraq quickly deteriorated to the point where the McDonalds and GMs and Wal-Marts of the neo-cons' dream wanted no part of it.

> In trying to design the best place in the world to do business, the neo-cons have managed to create the worst, the most eloquent indictment yet of the guiding logic behind deregulated free markets.

A society without government bureaucracy turned out not to be good for business after all.

Airholes and Packrats

Cultural systems force living things into boxes. Inconsistencies create air-holes that allow these living things to breathe. Every cultural system must have contradictions in order for its participants to remain human. Because human beings are inconsistent and have contradictory needs. We're active and passive, organized and impulsive, aggressive and gentle, cooperative and competitive. Yet every cultural system tends to suppress some part of that complex humanity.

So when a culture changes it eases the process if parts of the older tradition survive, even when—especially when—they contradict the values of the new one. Vestiges of the joyful celebrations of life and nature that characterized pagan cultures softened the impact of the death-oriented, otherworldly Christianity that was imposed on Europeans during the Dark Ages. Easter eggs, a pagan fertility symbol, helped Christians feel that there might, after all, be something to be said for life here on earth.

Healthy cultures are packrats. They don't throw away anything. They keep odds and ends of customs that contradict their dominant values. Communist bureaucracies could not have functioned at all without the system of official bribery carried over from Czarist days, and capitalists who are most dogmatic about free markets are the first to seek government subsidies and try to control prices through collusion. Ceremonious Brits adore making fun of pomposity, and materialistic Americans are addicted to sentimental movies proclaiming that the best things in life are free. In 1635 the intensely utilitarian Dutch went mad over tulips—the most useless of plants— paying astronomical sums for a single bloom and almost destroying their economy. And while the early 1950s were notoriously obsessed with planning for future success, the most popular song was "Che Sera, Sera."

Even at its height, Control Culture was softened by survivals from hunter-gatherer times, and Integrative Culture will be similarly leavened by Controller survivals.

Purity as a Sign of Decline

Throughout most of the Controller Age there was a strong sense of community, which had a moderating effect on the Controller system. But the industrial revolution devastated community life, replacing communities with sprawling, anonymous cities and suburbs. Relationships tended to become temporary and superficial. This change was a 'purifying' one—the competitive values of the Controller system were freed from the softening influence of community.

At the same time industrialism sliced the feminine mooring lines that held the system in place. When women lived in close-knit communities they could share tasks and commiserate with each other about the limitations of their lives. Their existence may have been harsh, but the presence of a feminine support system enabled them to tolerate their lives as "the way it's always been." The post-

World War II return to traditional gender roles, combined with the rapid spread of labor-saving appliances and the lack of community, isolated women in their kitchens and made their lives empty and emotionally bleak. A system that had been tolerable when women had a warm and intimate community to suffer in became intolerable when that community disappeared. Hence the feminist message of the Women's Movement resonated more strongly than it otherwise might have, and the decline of the Controller system was accelerated.

This particular bit of 'purification' was unintended, but often it's a matter of deliberate policy. When an old cultural system begins to give way to a new one its inconsistencies come under attack. There is an increase in fundamentalism—a call for ideological purity. These are seen as attempts to shore up the old system, but they actually weaken it further.

The Protestant Reformation in Europe was an attempt to 'purify' the Catholic Church of its contradictions and compromises with paganism. It sought to suppress the cult of the Virgin Mary and reestablish the supremacy of the Father—to make Christianity a more perfectly patriarchal religion and de-sacralize 'Mother' Nature.

The result of this new purity was to weaken popular commitment to Christianity altogether. Atheism and secular humanism grew rapidly, and European churches never again held the sway over public life they'd once had.

The power of kings, which in medieval times was limited by the nobles and hedged about by custom, reached a peak under the reign of France's Louis XIV, who detached the nobles from their land base and brought them to Versailles. As continued by Louis XV and Louis XVI, it was the purest form of monarchy that ever existed in Western Europe, and for that very reason was the beginning of the end.

Suicidal Purists

Centralized power achieved an even purer form in the 20th century dictator. The dictator had no limitations at all—no concerns about legitimacy, no traditional obligations attached to the role, no restrictions based on custom. The dictator was authoritarian power at its absolute purest, and hence an unmistakable symptom of its decadence. Nazi Germany's Third Reich—the purest and most perfect expression of Control Culture that ever existed—lasted only twelve years. And today the former Axis powers are three of the most vital democracies in the world.

The purest forms of a social system always appear as it decays. Often, when a system is ailing, its believers try to strip away its contradictions, leaving a system that is more pure, more rigid, and hence more fragile. Mao Zedong couldn't tolerate the "laxity, corruption, and disorder" in Chinese communism. By launching the Cultural Revolution—trying to strip away all traditional values and entrepreneurism—he smothered the system and opened the door to capitalistic and democratic reforms.

In a viable culture, customs, ideas, and myths may fall into disuse, but they're never thrown out. Cleaning out the cultural attic means junking the counterpoise that keeps the whole structure from getting too one-sided and collapsing.

The 'purification' efforts of fundamentalist ideologues are symptomatic of the terminal illness of Control Culture. Yet Integrative enthusiasts need to recognize and honor in themselves the same need for stability and familiarity that activates their foes. Radical leftists in the past have often crippled themselves through the same egoistic devotion to ideological purity, preferring to go down with the ship singing "nearer to the left than thee" rather than share a lifeboat with conservatives and compromising liberals.

Mumford's "laxity, corruption, and disorder" is an ironic phrase, but it's the way contradictions are viewed by ideologues. Purists believe they're trying to 'revive' or 'revitalize' a system when they call for a return to 'basic values' or 'fundamental principles', but since it's the "laxity, corruption, and disorder" that protect a system from self-asphyxiation, they're in effect smothering it. They are more committed to the *idea* of the system than the compromised reality. They are not only willing to go down with the ship, they're willing to sink it to prove their devotion.

Social Eversion

The effect of purism on a system is due to a process I call 'social eversion'—the tendency for a system, pushed to its extreme, to beget its opposite. Here are some examples:

- The space program was technology (with its preference for man-made environments over natural ones) extended to its fullest. It created space vehicles fleeing the earth in the quest for new worlds to conquer. But astronauts, looking back at the earth, saw its beauty. Their pictures of our blue planet created a new sense of global interdependence, and became a major symbol and inspiration for the ecological movement.

- The Crusaders, trying to destroy the Saracens and drive them out of Jerusalem—an exclusionary and parochial impulse extended to its fullest—ended by introducing Arabic culture and knowledge into Europe, laying the groundwork for the Renaissance, the expansion of trade, the voyages of exploration, and the unification of the globe.

- Linear, left-brain science, extended to its fullest, made possible the discovery of the Mandelbrot set, fractal geometry, and Chaos theory, which reinstated the value of right-brain thinking.

- The CIA—divisiveness extended to its fullest—trying to develop a chemical weapon for use against Russia, introduced LSD to Americans, creating a psychedelic culture that was strongly anti-war and produced a generation of seekers after spiritual oneness.

- The search for empire, for new lands to aggrandize the monarchs of Europe—authoritarianism extended to its fullest—led to the discovery of America and the egalitarian tribes who lived there, reports of which created the first stirrings of democratic and anti-authoritarian movements in Europe.

- Modern physics—materialism extended to its fullest—evolved quantum mechanics, forcing many materialistic assumptions to be abandoned.

- Modern industrialized agriculture—our need to control the

environment extended to its fullest—led us to an awareness of ecology, and the necessity of relinquishing control.

◆ Wartime research—militarism extended to its fullest—led to the Internet, one of the strongest forces in promoting international understanding, interdependence, and disarmament.

Some people misperceive social eversion as a 'pendulum' effect. But the pendulum—a static metaphor—applies only to short-term variations in fashion: the 'trends' that the media find interesting. The pendulum reverses when some process goes 'too far'. Social eversion happens when a process goes far *enough*. As William Blake said, "excess of sorrow laughs, excess of joy weeps."

The Ultimate Controller 'Purity'

Nazism was the purest realization of Controller values. The Nazis tried to maintain a tight control over every aspect of life, believed war was the fullest expression of German manhood, reduced women to near-slave status, and condemned their entire population to an oppressive authoritarian hierarchy. They were rigidly dualistic, exclusionary, compulsively secretive, and achieved solidarity by scapegoating Jews. Everything was sacrificed to product—the goal of a future Nazi Empire. There was no plank in the Controller platform to which they didn't subscribe—a purity that expressed nostalgia for a fading era. Nazism was both Control Culture's ultimate expression and its swan song.

During the 21st century there will be more Nazi-type movements around the world—more "cleansings", more shrieking about ethnic purity, more fundamentalist movements—as each segment of the world's population makes its last convulsive attempt to hang on to the Controller era.

But a 'pure' Integrative society would be equally non-viable. Attempts to create, on a small scale, such utopian societies have occurred from time to time throughout history but seldom lasted more than a few years. Attempts to suppress all competitiveness and ego, for example, usually produce explosions of both.

A Full Acceptance

What about the present, then? Why aren't we in an ideal state, since there's certainly plenty of 'impurity' in our present social system?

'Impurity' in Mumford's sense implies a level of consensus about what ought to be—a generally accepted framework within which impurities can be allowed. The Feast of Fools was permissible only when people accepted the status quo to which it was an antithesis. The Feast of Fools came into disfavor during the 17th and 18th centuries as the social distance between classes was being questioned. It was all right to play games with a system as long as that system was unchallenged, but when the system was no longer taken for granted its values had to be asserted more vigorously. It was no longer a joking matter. But in its prime the Feast of Fools, far from being a challenge to the system, was a measure of how utterly secure people felt about it.

What we have today is not a consensus with permitted impurities, but a lack of consensus. Control Culture and Integrative Culture are too equally balanced for either to tolerate the values of the other. There is no center yet from which these necessary exceptions can diverge. And until Integrative Culture achieves the kind of full acceptance that Control Culture enjoyed for thousands of years, there won't be.

While the balance in the world is gradually shifting from Controller to Integrative dominance, life will always be a mixture of the two. When Integrative Culture is fully established, traits such as competitiveness and the desire for control won't disappear, any more than cooperation and spontaneity disappeared during the Controller era. They'll merely become less dominant.

A new cultural system is often built around what was trivialized in the old one. Integrative values were never absent during the Controller era, they were simply assigned inferior status—something women concerned themselves with. Similarly, when Integrative Culture achieves a comfortable preponderance, Controller values will still have a niche—something men play with. The kind of consensus that will permit this is a long way off, but our descendants may enjoy it. Prophets of doom always attract an audience because people love drama, but the probable reality is more mundane: we can expect a long period of adaptation, during which violent flare-ups, like those of this decade, gradually diminish in frequency as more and more of the world embraces the emerging culture. Life on our planet will then settle into equilibrium—one that may or may not create more happiness, but will at least be more stable.

PART II

THE EFFECTS

All parts of a culture don't necessarily change at the same pace (see Appendix). Authoritarianism was the first piece of Control Culture to come under assault, and the passion for control will certainly be the last, at least in the West. The contradictions found in every culture often come about because people have especially strong attachments to some little piece of the old system—like the pagan fertility symbols still attached to Christian holidays. And in many countries where crucifixes are worn outside the clothes, Santeria beads or other traditional amulets are worn inside.

Different parts of the world also change at different times, and in different ways. The systems discussed in this book are global, but they are modified and adapted in accordance with the local constraints of each society's culture, just as each society's culture is modified by every subculture within it—urban culture, rural culture, youth culture, gang culture, drug culture, Red state, Blue State—the list goes on forever, down to small groups of friends and bizarre Internet niches. So while in the West democracy and feminism are close to achieving butterfly status, in the Middle East and Africa imaginal cells are still being successfully killed off by Control Culture's immune system.

The next six chapters consider examples of the impact of Integrative Culture (and the resistance to it): on gender behavior, on the way we think, on political and organizational structures, on the way we exercise control, on our approach to making war, and on religious ideas.

3 | On Gender Concepts: Is Stupidity Masculine?

Little girls seem so tough and confident now, knowing they'll inherit the earth. Whereas boys are left in a sort of prolonged infancy, lumbering about with dinosaurs, with . . . cars, with anything except what will help them get along in the twenty-first century.
AMANDA CRAIG

But I say, dot de women of today, smarter don demon in every way.
BLIND BLAKE

A great mind must be androgynous.
COLERIDGE

One day in early 2007 I was listening to Bulgarian and Rumanian students being interviewed on the BBC about having just joined the European Union. Most of the women were excited about the new opportunities this would open up for them, while the men were gloomy and pessimistic. And it struck me how familiar this seemed: women appearing confident and eager about the future, men doubtful and resistant. From American high school students to adults in many developing countries, women seem ascendant, men confused. While women are embracing Integrative culture with enthusiasm, Men seem to be mired in the caterpillar's liquefied remains.

With the possible exception of the spread of democracy, no trend in modern life is more indicative of the growth of Integrative Culture than the expansion of feminine influence during the past half-century. The change goes way beyond women's rights or male resistance. It's one of the main arenas in which the two cultures contend. Women are at the forefront of this new way of thinking, and for most women the path is clear. But for men the issue is complicated.

Do You Have To Be Dumb To Be A Man?

There's a new trend in the way men are portrayed in film and TV comedies today: they're getting *Dumb and Dumber.*

Comedies have always celebrated stupidity, but until recently there were certain rules about who could or could not look like an idiot. By and large you had to be unattractive, middle-aged or older, member of a minority, working class, or all of the above. The only exception was that an attractive leading lady could be ditzy—in the tradition of Carole Lombard, Lucile Ball, and Marilyn Monroe. But leading men could never be stupid. Lou Costello, the Three Stooges, Ralph Kramden and Morton could be stupid, but not Cary Grant.

Of course no red-blooded macho hero was ever a Mensa candidate. In old Hollywood action movies, men with exceptional mental ability were either mad scientists trying to rule the world or well-intentioned but doddering and ineffectual eggheads—often the heroine's father or grandfather. And the heroes of action flicks always *did* stupid things—so they could be captured, beaten up, and nearly killed to advance the plot—but they never *looked* dumb.

All this began to change toward the end of the 20th century. The dimwitted, loud, beer-swilling oaf—the hick villain or comic foil of earlier films—began to be treated positively. Films like *Dumb and Dumber, Dude, Where's My Car, Saving Silverman, American Pie,* and so on, are increasingly common and increasingly well-received. Beer ads, too, show men grunting like apes, repeating the same word moronically, and generally reveling in a kind of good-natured idiocy. While women are more and more often portrayed as smart, competent, motivated, and busy, today's every-day-life male protagonist (outside of action films) tends to be pictured as a brainless, lazy, unrealistic, insensitive, unreliable, and unmotivated slob.

This unflattering portrait fits the negative stereotype often voiced by women today, but most of these roles aren't created by women. They're written, directed, acted—and enjoyed—by men. And obviously men who drink beer like being portrayed as idiots, since it sells beer. Why are men so accepting of this unappealing image? It's as if they were saying: "Yes, we're dumb, and proud of it! That's what it means to be a real man! At least we're not women!"

Painting Themselves into a Corner

Men today seem to be struggling to define themselves. What does it mean to be a man? But those wrestling with this question all run up against the same dilemma: to define masculinity is to restrict it, for it means distinguishing it from femininity. To define 'man' as 'not woman' has the unfortunate consequence of eliminating a great deal of what it means to be human.

'Masculinity', in the Controller view, must include only what 'femininity' leaves out. To be 'masculine' is therefore to be limited. Defining masculinity negatively—as 'not woman'—typifies Controller thinking. If the right hand is good, then the left hand must be bad, and the fact that both are hands is best ignored. To be a macho man it was important not to do anything feminine. Men had to be content with leftover scraps from the women's behavioral dinner table.

So when women burst the bonds of gender constraint and decided to define themselves as complete human beings, 'masculinity' had to shrink itself correspondingly into a narrower and narrower corner. The 'dumb guy and proud of it' role so prominent in the media today is testimony to just how far the shrinking has gone.

This effort to find something specifically 'masculine' that will distance men from women shows that many men are still stuck inside the either/or box of the old Controller system.

In Search of a Role

The traditional male role—especially its demand that men repress all feelings except lust and anger—was as constricting and painful for men as its counterpart was for women. But the initiative for change came from women, and that makes all the difference. When one spouse in a bad marriage finally moves to end it, he or she will adjust to the split much more quickly than the one who's left behind, even if the two benefit equally from the separation. And so it is with the bad marriage of traditional gender roles.

The reason for all this male confusion is that Integrative Culture is one for which women happen to be better prepared and better suited than men.

The Feminine Renaissance

A poll conducted in 2003 by the National Association for the Self-Employed found that startups of women-owned businesses had grown by double digits annually since 2000. Between 1997 and 2006, women-owned businesses grew 43.3% (compared with 23.3% for all businesses). They generated almost two trillion dollars in sales and employed almost 13 million people. Women are advancing fastest in new industries, despite the fact that only 2% of all venture capital goes to women.

> If the male was the prototypical industrial worker, the information worker is typically a woman . . . Of the people whose job title falls under the category of 'professional' . . . the majority are women.

In 2002 the Employment Policy Foundation predicted that by 2030 women will outnumber men in professional occupations. Their estimate may be way too conservative.

(1) In the United States a few decades ago twice as many men as women went to college, but today women account for 58% of the bachelor's degrees and 60% of the master's degrees. Women are also winning a disproportionate share of honors degrees—in some public universities three-fourths of them.

(2) In 1963 female medical school applicants numbered only 8%. By 1983 the number was 34%. In 2003 it was 49.7 % and in 2004 women applicants outnumbered males.

(3) While in 1970 only 10% of first-year law students were women, by 2001 they were a majority.

That trend will affect the way law schools operate—perhaps making classes less adversarial, for instance—and change some-what the way law firms operate, lawyers and professors said.

And since legal training is often a prerequisite to a political career, we're also more likely in the future to see women in positions of power as this cohort moves up.

Women now earn the majority of all post-graduate degrees, and this educational gender gap holds for all social classes and ethnic groups. It is so marked, in fact, that colleges are routinely engaging in affirmative action for boys—admitting far fewer qualified girls and far more unqualified boys—to avoid having enrollments that are more than two-thirds female.

But women are outdistancing men in more than enrollment. Men get worse grades.

Male and female students alike agreed that the slackers in their midst were mostly male, and that the fireballs were mostly female.

It is impossible to escape the conclusion that this masculine fail-ing is the direct result of male gender training—what we consider right and proper behavior for young boys, which, while quite ser-viceable in preparing men to serve in a medieval army, makes them utterly unfit for any constructive role in the modern world of the 21st century.

Half of the world's countries now have no gender gap in educa-tion, and in eighteen countries, mostly Latin American, girls outnumber boys in secondary schools. Several Islamic countries and a few Sub-Saharan African nations are among those that have made the greatest strides.

In Iran, for example, well over half of university students are now women, and in the applied physics department of Azad University they make up 70% of the graduates.

This is important in the developing world, since educating women is associated with both economic development and population control. Furthermore, educated mothers—far more than educated fathers—tend to produce educated children.

The effect of this trend for the spread of democracy around the world can hardly be overstated. In *The Clash of Civilizations,* for example, Samuel Huntington attributes the scarcity of Islamic democracies to the lack of political values associated with Western democratic states, but Ronald Inglehart and Pippa Norris point out that the World Values Survey found almost no difference between Western and Islamic populations with regard to democratic political sentiments. The real differences, they say, are to be found in gender attitudes. In a questionnaire survey, 86 percent of Germans and 76 percent of Americans rejected the idea that men made better political leaders than women, while 91 percent of Egyptians endorsed it.

The authors found that agrarian societies in general haven't changed their gender attitudes since the 1920s, while industrial, and, especially, postindustrial societies have moved aggressively toward gender equality. As Jeffrey Sachs points out in his definitive work on global poverty, denying the rights of women is a major barrier to development.

Getting Together, Starting Early

As a fourth-grade student in Nashville, Tennessee, Melissa Poe wrote a letter to the senior President Bush, asking for help in her campaign to save the environment for the enjoyment of future generations. Since she was only a child she worried that her letter would never be brought to the president's notice, so she decided to get his attention by having her letter placed on a billboard. After a long, hard effort the nine-year old got her letter on a billboard free of charge and founded Kids for a Clean Environment (Kids F.A.C.E.).

Almost immediately, Melissa began receiving letters from kids who were as concerned as she about the environment. . . When she finally received the disappointing form letter from the president . . . she no longer needed thehelp of someone famous to get her message across. Melissa had found in herself the person she needed.

Within nine months more than 250 billboards across the country were displaying her letter free of charge. Today there are more than 200,000 members and 2,000 chapters of Kids F.A.C.E.

Trees

In 1987 Tara Church was 8 years old and living in El Segundo, California. On an outing with her Brownie troop a discussion about whether to use paper plates to save water during a drought led to the topic of deforestation, and the troop decided they wanted to do something about the environmental problems they had all been helping to create. They persuaded a local nursery to donate a tree and got permission to plant it on public property (by 1998 the tree was 50-feet high).

They then convinced the El Segundo City Council and the Girl Scouts to observe Arbor Day and began to examine city plans with an eye to planting more trees. They started to branch out, enlisting kids from other clubs, schools, and community groups. In 1990 they founded the nonprofit Tree Musketeers. They wrote articles for the local paper, spoke at conferences, and launched the city's first recycling program. By the time they were teenagers they had decided they were "too old" to keep the program going and began training middle-school children in leadership skills. The present CEO of Tree Musketeers is 12 years old.

When she herself was 12, Church approached a Forest Service representative and asked why they funded adult conferences but none for kids. He told her to submit a proposal and she did, scoring $100,000 in grants plus technical and manpower support for a three-day conference, with Tree Musketeers assuming all risks and liabilities. The conference was a success, with 425 kids and 175 adults from all over the U.S., as well as Guam, Jamaica, Sweden, and Russia.

In 1997 Church and Poe joined forces to launch the "One in a

Million" campaign: to have one million kids plant one million trees by the year 2000, with the final tree to be planted on the White House lawn. The campaign was enormously successful, exceeding its target well before the deadline.

The final ceremony on the White House lawn, however—originally scheduled for April, 2000—didn't take place until November. As Church told me:

> It was easier getting a million kids to plant a million trees than getting the White House staff to settle on a date.

Something to remember for people who think change comes from governments, or that you need to get into a position of power before you can achieve anything.

Women are Better Prepared

Today's women have a head start in Integrative Culture. Since young girls aren't trained to be compulsively competitive the way men are, the problem of clashing egos is reduced. It's a lot easier for women to join forces to achieve common goals.

And women in all fields of activity are getting together to pool resources and improve skills. They have writing groups, artists' groups, executive support groups, entrepreneur support groups, professional support groups, academic support groups—whatever women set out to do, they tend to do in a cooperative setting. In sports, in an era in which male athletes have become notoriously egocentric, women excel at team-building.

The Pre-Controller World

To understand why women are more comfortable than men with Integrative Culture we need to take a small detour and look at the role of women under the old system.

Before the advent of Control Culture—for most of human existence, in other words—women and men were equal. When humans lived in small bands of hunter-gatherers everyone needed everyone.

The cliché of the hulking caveman dragging a woman off by the hair is the invention of modern cartoonists. We who have lived for eight thousand years with war, domination, and competitive struggle have trouble imagining a world in which men would fail to take every advantage of their physical strength. But if strength were the key to success in evolution, humanity would have lost out to the mammoth and the saber-toothed tiger. As Richard Leakey points out, "cooperation and sharing was the basis of our success as a species." Ernst Mayr observes that one of the biggest evolutionary changes from ape to human was a huge *decrease* in sexual dimorphism. Forget Alley Oop—'apemen' were about the same size as their women.

If anything, stone-age women were more valued than men, because they not only gave birth, but as food-gatherers were "the steadiest providers of the most calories". The main deity everywhere in pre-Controller times was a goddess. Yet all signs point to equality—men and women seem to have shared almost all activities.

This is also true of surviving hunter-gatherer societies. Colin Turnbull reports that among the Pygmies:

> There is relatively little specialization according to sex. Even the hunt is a joint effort.

But with the evolution of war and conquest (see Chapter 7), size and strength became more important. Women became less valued, and were even viewed as impure and dangerous.

Turnbull compares the way Pygmies and their Controller neighbors handle a young girl's first menstruation. For the Pygmies the menarche is a happy event with much rejoicing—the women gather round the girl to celebrate, congratulate her, and teach her adult songs. For the neighboring Bantu villagers, on the other hand—a Controller society—the event is a kind of supernatural pollution, requiring humiliating purification rites to placate evil spirits. "The girl is an object of suspicion, scorn, repulsion, and anger."

A Sexual Dilemma

Whenever they conquered a new part of Afghanistan the first act of the fundamentalist Taliban army was to forbid little girls going to school. How did this fear of feminine power arise?

Women were valued in the Controller system only as breeders and sexual objects. Controllers wanted sons. In the Controller system having many sons put you automatically at the apex of a military pyramid. A man like the biblical Jacob with his twelve sons had a built-in gang to do his bidding. The more sons, the bigger the realm you could rule. A few generations gave you an army.

The earliest Controllers were animal-breeders, who knew that stronger parents produced stronger offspring. They undertook to breed themselves the way they bred their animals, and wanted to be sure of the paternity of their sons. It was fine to have women as sexual objects, but what if the mother of your sons was someone else's sexual object? How would you know the sons were in fact yours?

So Controller cultures have always been obsessed with virginity—something their predecessors cared little about. Virginity gave the Controller husband a greater feeling of confidence. He wanted exclusive ownership of his breeder—to know that she had never experienced another man and couldn't make comparisons.

In traditional Controller societies being a man meant having an active sex life, while being a woman just meant getting married and having children. This Controller mindset—still present in much of the medical world—may be why Viagra was immediately placed on most insurance approval lists when contraceptive devices were not. Viagra *enabled* men to fulfill their traditional Controller role, while contraception *prevented* women from fulfilling theirs.

Controlling Women's Sexuality

In Nigeria, a sixteen-year-old girl was condemned to receive 80 lashes for getting pregnant after she was raped by three middle-aged married men. When they denied her accusations she was given 80 more for accusing them.

In Israel, a woman cannot unilaterally divorce her husband for any reason unless the divorce is approved by a panel of elderly orthodox rabbis, which it seldom is. On a state-supported bus line servicing ultra-orthodox neighborhoods, men have harassed and beaten women for their Western dress, and forced them to sit in the back of the bus.

The harem, the purdah, the veil, the chaperone, and all the other constraints of Mediterranean and Middle Eastern cultures are expressions of this anxiety about female sexuality. Some sub-Saharan cultures have gone a step further with clitoridectomy, so that women would have difficulty enjoying sex at all.

When we say a society is puritanical we're talking only about how women are constrained. The restrictions rarely apply to men.

The notion that women are 'naturally' monogamous and men 'naturally' promiscuous springs from the same Controller anxieties. An ocean of ink has been devoted to this proposition, which, if true, wouldn't need to be so loudly asserted. In Controller thinking, women can be normal sexual beings only by being 'bad women'.

In our own society women's sexuality has become more acceptable in books and on television, but Hollywood is still fumbling with the buttons of changing mores. In horror films we still expect the monster or maniac to strike whenever a woman takes her clothes off or begins to have sex. And columnist Stephen Holden observes that women in films who are openly and avidly sexual usually come to a bad end. Frankly sexual women tend to be portrayed as predatory, scheming, or just plain crazy.

Trying to control female sexuality tends to infuse the male sexual impulse with hostility, and vice versa: the whistles and obscenities directed toward women in the street, for example, as well as the double meaning of the verbs "fuck" and "screw". And Frances Conley observes that the most common form of harassment women doctors suffer from senior male surgeons is being groped while working, or being propositioned in front of their patients.

Women at the Bottom

Control Culture prided itself on having 'risen above' necessity, so the less needful, practical, or useful an object, person, or activity was, the more earnestly, strictly, and violently its importance had to be asserted.

Anything attached to survival had low status. The useless metal, gold, became more valuable than food; the idle aristocrat was valued more than those who produced necessities; and the ability to kill was valued more than the ability to give life.

Those at the upper end of the social scale often went out of their way to demonstrate their uselessness (and hence, superiority) by wearing long flowing sleeves that inhibited use of the hands, or growing ultra-long fingernails, or having wives with bound feet. Even today those who deal with pieces of paper are seen as 'higher' and paid much better than those who produce necessities. Much of our food in the United States has traditionally been sown, grown, and harvested by people who weren't even supposed to be here and were paid accordingly.

High heels are another survival. They showed that a man's wife was incapable of engaging in physical labor, proving he could afford to maintain a useless and expensive appendage. Now that women have come into their own, high heels are becoming obsolete. A 1999 survey found only 24% of women wear them on the job—down from 37% in 1990—and those who do tend to be less educated.

So women wound up at the bottom of the Controller pecking order. A man, however humble, was master in his own home. Angry serfs or workers could always go home and beat their wives— behavior that was encouraged by the upper classes. "A man's home is his castle," they were told, and a wife was to obey her "lord and master." A study by the World Health Organization found that even today spousal abuse of women is worldwide, although far more prominent in rural areas, where Control Culture values tend to be stronger. Women everywhere are at far greater risk of violence from a husband then from a stranger.

To facilitate this domination, men have often insisted on marrying women who were much younger. In many cultures, notably in Ancient Greece, the Middle East, and India, the wives of adult males were still children.

Western observers have been appalled at the sweatshop conditions under which women from agricultural societies are forced to work. Yet the women themselves are often delighted at the opportunity to escape being farm wives, i.e., unpaid personal slaves and baby machines. In the factory they have independence, income, and hence, power. And the working conditions are comparable to what they've known.

There are two reasons why women today are better adapted to Integrative Culture:

First, they were less committed to the Controller system—profited less from it.

Second, the role they were relegated to under Control Culture actually prepared them for the new one—trained them to be Integrators.

1. The Advantage of the Outsider

In 1964 Warren Bennis and I made an observation that has become an axiom of organization theory:

Innovation comes from outsiders. Those most deeply committed to, and successful in, an old system will be the last to notice a radically new idea, and will be most resistant to it. When change comes, it's the outsiders—those uncommitted to the status quo—who are poised to catch the wave. History teaches the same thing: the barbarian tribes of one era become the imperial rulers of the next. "The last shall be first" isn't just an apocalyptic prophesy—it's an historical fact. There's a saying in the business community, "nothing fails like success". Corporate leaders today are taught that success is dangerous, because it blinds you to the wave of the future—and those waves are coming in a lot faster these days.

Fresh Eyes

Outsiders have fresh eyes—they aren't hampered by old status-quo ways of looking at things. It was the untaught child who saw that the emperor had no clothes.

The legend of Parsifal carries the same message. Raised in isolation by his mother, Parsifal grows up to be a complete innocent, which makes him the ideal candidate to win the Holy Grail. But he's taken in hand by a well-meaning uncle, who shares Robert Bly's concern that the boy's manly education has been neglected. The uncle teaches him to be more macho and not go around asking everybody naïve questions. So when Parsifal comes to the Fisher-King's Castle and encounters the Grail he fails to ask the simple questions that would give him the Grail, free the Fisher-King from his terrible wound, and bring peace to the world. Parsifal is the outsider open to a new paradigm, but he gets trained in the old one before he can take advantage of his fresh eyes. He's like the newly hired company man who's taught "how we do things here" before he has a chance to create a better system.

This is the first reason women are better adapted to Integrative Culture: they're more open to it than men because they're less committed to the old one and its Dominator values. They were outsiders in the old system.

2. The Advantage of Integrative Training

The second reason women are better adapted to Integrative Culture is that it demands precisely those skills that women developed and honed during their long travail as Controller pariahs.

Since men in Controller Culture were hampered by the strait-jacket of macho competitiveness, it fell to women to take care of those human needs irrelevant to combat. Women in Control Culture had to become skilled at negotiation and compromise, at recognizing and anticipating the rights and needs of others, at mediating ("Your father really loves you, dear, he just doesn't know how to say it"). Because of their lowly position women were able to preserve the cooperative habits of pre-Controller societies.

This gives women an advantage in a shrunken world in which communication and cooperation are again vital to our survival as a species. As a group women are better attuned to the demands of a modern democratic society than men are. Men talk constantly about 'being firm', 'standing tall', and 'standing up to' people, as if working collectively on a problem were a matter of maintaining an erection. But rigidity is not a virtue in a democracy, and solving collective problems is not a form of hand-to-hand combat.

The rise of women, in other words, can be seen as an evolutionary adaptation by our species.

Men tend to have more developed 'left brains', women more developed 'right brains'. In the past this difference was seen as an indication of female inferiority—the right hemisphere was intuitive and artistic but not really IQ-smart. But linear, left hemisphere intelligence is easily automated. What traditional IQ tests measure a computer can do 100 times better and 1,000,000 times faster. So now the scorned, right-hemisphere intelligence of women has become the key to the future (see Chapter 4).

> We've progressed from a society of farmers to a society of factory workers to a society of knowledge workers. And now we're progressing yet again—to a society of creators and empathizers, of pattern recognizers and meaning makers.

Better Leaders?

Deborah Tannen finds that women often make better managers than men because they tend to involve employees in decision-making, leading to more enthusiastic implementation. Women in business, says Carol Frenier, have less need than men to have their egos stroked and their ideas copyrighted. And while there are always a few women managers who try to 'out-male' men, most women managers want primarily to be acknowledged for "carrying their weight."

Leadership maven Tom Peters believes women will lead most companies within 20 years, partly because:

> Women have traditionally been stronger than men at such things as forming relationships, using intuition and not being threatened by strong people . . . all qualities that leaders need.

Connected to Life

Women are also compelled by their biology to recognize the limits of control. Menstruation, pregnancy, and childbirth, tie them to nature.

There are certain episodes in the life of a female that are guaranteed to be boundary-dissolving.

While men have tried to dominate their environment and make it predictable, women have always had to live with confusion and chaos. In traditional households they had to adapt daily to the unexpected, between active small children and the whims of demanding husbands. Women are also used to being involved in several activities at the same time, of functioning in the midst of chaos. As Tom Peters says:

These are crazy times and you have to be able to do 11 things at a time . . . And guys can't.

This ability women have to attend to several things at once may have to do with brain functioning. Studies have shown that women can listen to two conversations at once, and that they use both sides of the brain to do it, while men use only the left side—the linear, logical side. It seems likely that the gender training men receive leads to a partial atrophy of the intuitive, synthesizing part of the brain. The inability to focus on more than one thing at a time may reflect their extreme need to feel in control.

And while men under stress are limited to fight or flight responses, a UCLA study showed that women have another option—under stress they tend to bond with other women, which not only has a calming effect but increases the resources available for solution.

Futurist Women, Retro Men

As part of a "Women, Sex, and Power" workshop—one of the many psychological fads that swept the nation during the 1970s—several hundred women were placed in a large room and told not to leave for any reason. Within fifteen minutes the women had ironed out an agreement to send a delegate to the workshop leaders with an ultimatum to come to the room or refund their money. Among the men who were placed in the same situation the struggle for leadership was so intense that fistfights broke out.

Research confirms these everyday observations: women try to maintain equality in relationships while men tend to compete for status—a difference well-entrenched by the 2nd or 3rd grade. Women focus on community, men on competition; men boast regularly, women do not; women tend to seek out the wishes of others, men do not; men tend to take suggestions as being ordered around, women do not. In short, a man tends to see himself as a competitor in a pecking order, while a woman sees herself "as an individual in a network of connections."

There are, of course, many women who are wedded to Control Culture and live by its precepts. And there are many men embracing Integrative Culture. But on average, women find Integrative Culture more comfortable than men do. And it's this difficulty in adapting to a changing world that has left so many men confused and angry today.

> Women have spent a lot of time preparing for a world that's different. Men have not done that . . . We don't know what we want to be.

"What About Us?"

So women have a head start in Integrative Culture. But what of men? Will they be left behind while the world moves on to better things? It wouldn't be the first time such a thing has happened:

> Certain superficially weak organisms have survived in the long run by being part of collectives, while the so-called strong ones, never learning the trick of cooperation, have been dumped onto the scrap heap of evolutionary extinction.

Men, of course, won't become extinct. But what role will they play in the emerging system? That their competitive Controller skills are becoming obsolete creates tough choices: do they turn into cultural Luddites? Or try to retrain themselves, to evolve? And if so, how?

To answer that question we need to ask: what is it in the

Controller conditioning of men that makes adaptation to our new world difficult? And how can men overcome this handicap?

Making Men

For eight thousand years, whether a society was actually at war or enjoying a peaceful spell, war has dominated male consciousness:

> The male psyche is, first and foremost, the Warrior psyche. . . .
> All men are marked by the warfare system and the military virtues.

When Shakespeare described the seven ages of man and wanted to define young adulthood—between his adolescent lover and his middle-aged judge—he chose:

> A soldier, full of strange oaths . . . jealous in honour, sudden
> and quick in quarrel, seeking the bubble reputation even in the
> cannon's mouth.

And Henry V, encouraging his soldiers before Agincourt, ties masculinity to war in the same competitive way:

> And gentlemen in England now a-bed
> Shall think themselves accursed they were
> not here,
> And hold their manhoods cheap whiles any
> speaks
> that fought with us. . . .

Being a soldier was the masculine ideal, and men whose young adult years occurred between wars often felt cheated and emasculated.

To distinguish themselves from women, the creators, men were trained in Control Culture to be killers and destroyers. This is why men who were artists, writers, musicians, etc., have traditionally been considered effeminate. To be manly was to be ready to destroy, not to create.

So what qualities would you want to instill in men who were going to devote their lives to war? Especially war as it existed when military training began—that is, hand-to-hand combat?

First of all, you'd want them not to be easily intimidated—you'd want them to be insensitive to the boasts and threats of their antagonists. You'd also want them to be pitiless—to show no mercy in battle. Finally, you'd want them to be unquestioningly obedient to their leaders.

Part of military training even today consists of what Lt. Col. Dave Grossman calls "seemingly sadistic abuse and hardship"—browbeating, frequent and degrading punishment, humiliation, pointless tasks, and so on. It's often claimed that such practices will 'make a man' out of someone who could not otherwise lay claim to the title. "Boot camp was awful," some men say, "but it made a man of me." And while it certainly won't make a man for all seasons, it definitely makes a soldier-man.

Learning to accept abuse and not react produces the numbness needed for physical combat. It helps the soldier deaden himself to feeling, and hardens him to suffering—both his own and (since he witnesses the abuse of his fellow soldiers) that of others. This is important in warfare since the soldier is primarily engaged in inflicting suffering and shouldn't go around feeling bad about it.

This is what we want in a soldier—an unfeeling, obedient man who can kill designated opponents on cue and without remorse.

An Instincual Snag

But this last requirement poses a problem. While it's in vogue to believe that human beings are 'naturally' homicidal, the facts, says Grossman, are quite the reverse:

Normal humans have an instinctual, genetic reluctance to kill members of their own species. This reluctance has to be trained out of soldiers.

In World War II only about one-sixth of the soldiers ever fired their guns in combat. And according to Grossman—a former paratrooper and military trainer—most soldiers in most wars have fired over the heads of their opponents. His examples are drawn from the Napoleonic wars, the Civil War, and the two World Wars; and his conclusions hold for all the nations involved—French, Germans, Japanese, Russians, Americans.

> The media's depiction of violence tries to tell us that men can
> . . . kill casually and guiltlessly in combat. The men who have
> killed, and will talk about it, tell a different tale.

More soldiers suffer psychiatric disorders than die in battle. And Grossman shows that it's not fear but the stress of killing. Those who don't have to kill at close range, or who don't have to kill at all, are not as prone to psychiatric disorders *even when exposed to greater danger.*

See No Evil

Killing in war today is usually done at a distance, so that those who kill and maim are protected from seeing the result. At close range, the butchering of civilians is considered an atrocity, a war crime. But at a distance it's merely "acceptable collateral damage." The casualties in a heavy bombing raid are primarily women and children, and their horror and suffering are just as extreme as if they were hacked to death in person, but the crime is sanitized by distance. If President Truman had ordered our troops to enter Hiroshima and Nagasaki and slaughter all the women and children by hand, he would have been considered a war criminal rather than a statesman. Yet the suffering would have been no worse.

Most primitive tribes also show extreme reluctance to kill face-to-face. And this is also why, Grossman says, gangland executions are carried out by a shot to the back of the head, and why men are blindfolded when shot by a firing squad. Hostages and kidnap victims are far more likely to be killed if blindfolded.

There are, of course, exceptions to this reluctance. In any armed force, Grossman says, about 2% are sociopathic—men incapable of empathy who enjoy killing.

What is it We Want in a Man?

Some people expressed surprise that Timothy McVeigh, the

Oklahoma City terrorist, felt no remorse for killing so many men, women, and children, since he had been a Marine and was 'a good soldier.' But this is exactly what a good soldier is trained to do—kill large numbers of people without hesitation. If the building had been in an enemy country, many would have considered him a hero.

We still seem confused today about whether we want men in modern society to approximate this military ideal. We generally want more complexity, a wider range of values. Yet we still— judging from movies and TV—admire the man who kills, and all men are infected to some degree with macho values. Particularly when other men are around to enforce conformity through ridicule and shame. This is another reason why the Controller male has to have an enemy: he needs something on which to project all the parts of himself that don't fit his narrow concept of how he should be— an enemy that can represent the aspects of his own nature he can't understand or doesn't want to deal with.

We've been indoctrinated with Controller values that train us to associate manliness with domination. The media refer to significant events in human history as 'conquests': the 'conquest' of the sea, the 'conquest' of polio, the 'conquest' of Everest, the 'conquest' of space. Many men never feel they're winning in life unless someone or something is losing.

Yet some men feel that Integrative Culture offers advantages— freeing us from the role behavior that abuses us—the competitiveness that isolates and stresses us, the status-hunger that separates us from loved ones and keeps us from enjoying what we have, the belligerence that turns the world hostile, the stoicism that prevents relief.

Men's studies departments grew tenfold in little over a decade, and over 500 colleges offer courses in men and masculinity.

All this has been lumped together as "The Men's Movement", which makes sense only if it's understood that 'movement' doesn't imply direction. The only thing men agree on is that they should get together. What they think they should *do* together seems to depend on how they feel about the Women's Movement. Some see only threat in it while others see opportunity.

The Threat Response

Even though they still run the world, many men today express feelings of powerlessness. They're angry that women are invading previously all-male domains, and upset that women aren't as dependent on them as they used to be—especially since most men still feel dependent on women: sexually, emotionally, domestically.

This sense of loss—of uselessness, of vanishing function—echoes the feelings of skilled 19th-century craftsmen displaced by machines. Like those craftsmen, modern men have been trained in macho skills over many years and at severe cost, only to discover that those skills are no longer of any use to anyone. Strutting, boasting, fighting, destroying, and killing just don't seem as important to the world as they used to.

Some men respond to this loss by clinging desperately to ever-shrinking definitions of masculinity. As women have expanded into 'male' arenas, for example, there has been a huge increase in body-building and steroid use by men—part of what Harrison Pope calls the "Adonis Complex"—a growing male preoccupation with body image. He suggests that men are retreating to gyms as a way of asserting their manhood:

> The courts can decree that girls must be admitted to the
> Citadel, but they cannot decree that a woman can bench press
> 300 pounds. The male body is becoming the last refuge for men
> who are trying to hang on to certain masculine distinctions.

The Opportunity Response

In a 1993 survey three-fourths the men polled said more time with their children was the most desired change in their lives. Seventy percent were willing to slow their careers to bring this about. Warren Farrell found that out of 10,000 men asked, 80% would prefer to take six months to a year off work to be with a new baby full time, while only 3% would prefer to keep working full time.

There are three million children in the United States today living only with their fathers. And in one out of five intact families the husband is the primary parent. Men are suing corporations like Microsoft for discriminating against those with families.

Such men have welcomed Integrative values. But they're pursuing an uncharted course with little support from others. Women who gather with their children in parks are often as unwelcoming of 'Mr. Moms' as firemen are of women firefighters. And I've seen women intrude with astonishing arrogance and officiousness into the parenting of men who have been a child's primary caretaker since it was born. Women, too, have trouble giving up old patterns.

Making Yesterday's Men Today

It's easier to prepare children for the future than it is to change your own ingrained habits. Immigrants have been doing it for centuries. Carole Gallagher, who studies successful women executives, commented in an interview that male CEOs who have been blind to discrimination against women quickly regain their sight when their daughters encounter it.

But few parents are as forward-looking when it comes to their sons. Men have a horror of their son being seen as a sissy—despite the fact that so many of the 'great men' of history were called sissies or mama's boys when they were young. There are five times as many boys as girls classified as "Gender Identity Disorders."

Women, too, seem nervous about this, and often—against their own instincts—encourage their sons to be exactly the insensitive, selfish, inconsiderate, and boorish men they're always complaining about.

Basic Training at Home

It isn't just in boot camp that men are trained in Control Culture ways. "Be a good soldier", a male child is often told when asked to deal with an unpleasant, painful, or tiresome situation. Traditionally, young boys are not supposed to cry, show fear, or be quiet and studious, or emotional, or nurturant, or play with girls. They're expected to be tough, stoical, competitive, noisy, boisterous, not too bright, and enjoy destroying things. This is what will earn them the proud honor: "he's all boy." It's what William Pollack calls the 'Boy Code', and it's still prominent today. Boys, in our interdependent, shrinking world, are still being trained—by parents, schools, other adults, and older children—as if they were destined to spend their lives engaging in hand-to-hand combat. Much of the world's constant slaughter can be attributed to the fact that men simply aren't being trained to share power.

Children who are abused tend to become abusers. So it's no surprise to find that boys, who commit the majority of violent acts, are treated more harshly as children than girls are. They're half again more likely to receive corporal punishment at home, and six times more likely in school.

Some people believe these 'male' traits are in the genes, although they're entirely absent from many cultures. And if they were 'natural' you'd think boys would be happy and comfortable in their assigned roles. Yet eighty-five percent of teen suicides are boys.

And in fact nothing about the "Boy Code" is natural or genetic. David Gilmore, who looked at cross-cultural studies hoping to find some universals in male behavior, was compelled to admit defeat, and research efforts to find a biological foundation for male aggression have failed repeatedly, despite the immense popularity of the idea.

Biologically men are no more prone to aggression than to nurturing or generosity or any other trait in the vast repertory of human impulses. Male babies are actually more emotionally expressive than girl babies, and until the age of four or so—by which time they've been thoroughly indoctrinated with the Boy Code—boys are just as interested in infants as girls are. In some cultures nurturance is considered as much a masculine trait as a feminine one. Infant males in our own culture, moreover, are just as empathic as females.

But by four or five years old, in most cultures, emotional intelligence, tenderness, and empathy have been largely squelched by the Boy Code. Boys are being systematically deprived of many of the right-brain qualities Daniel Pink says will be most needed in the future (see Chapter 4).

The toughness and stoicism that are supposed to be genetic in men turn out to be easily discarded when permission is backed up by strong enough group support. When Robin Ely, a Harvard Business School professor, studied workers on an oil rig in the Gulf of Mexico, she was shocked to discover that these men, who rode Harleys, went hunting, made crude jokes, and did all the other things 'real men' are supposed to do, were completely open in expressing emotional and physical vulnerability. They told the others when they didn't feel safe, or wanted help and support staying focused because of an emotional problem at home. This openness was the result of a safety campaign initiated by the company, and was successful partly because of the very real dangers on the rigs, and the fact that the men worked and lived so closely together. Older workers told Ely that before the program was instituted the rig had had just the kind of competitive atmosphere she had expected to find, with workers continually trying to out-macho each other.

"Do What's Natural Or I'll Whup You!"

Efforts to demonstrate biological gender differences are often based on studies of children several years old, when gender training is firmly entrenched. Deborah Blum, for example, cites the fact that boys five years old are rougher and tolerate much louder noises than girls of the same age as evidence that boys are genetically from Mars. But if you tell people an infant is a boy they'll treat it more roughly and talk louder to it, which renders Blum's observation meaningless.

Louann Brizendine has written perhaps the most comprehensive survey of innate gender differences, but even she fails to take into account the powerful impact of gender training. She places great emphasis, for example, on the fact that the communication center is bigger in the female brain, and that it "develops a greater ability to read cues". But if people talk louder to infants they believe are boys, and treat them more roughly, obviously their ability to read cues is going to be less highly developed.

There are, of course, hard-wired gender difference, but at present it is impossible to tell how much the differences we see are created or exaggerated by gender training. Brain growth is not a simple genetic unfolding, but is part of an open loop. The brain develops in interaction with others (see Chapter 6)

Those most insistent on a biological origin for gender behavior are the very ones who get most upset when it isn't manifested. One young girl was confined to a mental hospital for several years for not being "feminine enough". But if gender behavior is based on biology, we should all be able to sit back and let nature take its course. Instead we see hordes of otherwise intelligent people forcefully imposing traits on children who are supposed to already possess them.

In reality, gender indoctrination begins at birth. The very first question people ask about a newborn is whether it's a boy or a girl. They want to know how to behave toward it—how to train it. People will get upset if you dress a child in the wrong color or give it a gender-ambiguous name.

Adults watching an infant crying will interpret it as anger if told it's a boy, and fear if told it's a girl. If they think an infant is a boy they'll talk about its firm grasp; if they think it's a girl they'll comment on its softness and fragility. Parents of newborn boys will describe their offspring as stronger, larger, better coordinated and more alert than will the parents of newborn girls, even when no differences exist. Infant boys and girls will be given different clothing and toys and their rooms will be decorated differently.

Sociologist Dane Archer found that merely dressing the same infant in pink or blue would elicit different responses. Dressed in pink, the infant was always said to be beautiful; in blue, almost never. In blue, many career choices were prophesied; in pink, only one—Miss America.

Training for Obsolescence?

Today many people are asking about the use of traditional masculine gender training in the modern world. Will it help a boy become a manager, teacher, or film director? Encouraging insensitivity, belligerence, and selfishness might have been excellent training for a boy growing up in war-torn 9th-century Scotland but it isn't clear that it's useful in our woven world, where communication skills are in more demand.

Parents who instill macho values, habits, and attitudes in a young boy today may be sentencing him to a life of failure, frustration, and irrelevance—to be one of the drudges, the grunts, the expendable bodies in a world that demands flexibility and receptivity. Such parents are burdened by:

> outmoded ideas about masculinity and what it takes for a boy to become a man. These models . . . simply have no relevance to today's world.

4 On Thinking: Becoming a Verb

Static visions depend on hiding the connections between
disparate aspects of life.
VIRGINIA POSTREL

She . . . told him how quantum mechanics would
feminize physics, all science, make it softer,
less arrogantly detached.
IAN MCEWAN

Beliefs are like glasses. If you don't change the prescription once in
a while you're probably not seeing the world very clearly. Part of the
reason life seems confusing today is because much of the time—
despite all the Integrative changes taking place in the world—we're
still looking at it through Controller lenses.

Psychologists once found, for example, that white North
Americans could see horizontal and vertical lines more easily than
diagonal ones, and thought this difference must be innately human.
But when they repeated the experiment with Native Americans
raised in wigwams the difference disappeared.

Integrative Culture provides new lenses that change how we see
the world, a change congruent with new scientific discoveries.

Integrative Culture and Modern Science

Science is supposed to be above cultural differences, but scientific theories and assumptions are deeply influenced by the times and cultures that gave them birth.

Science is a people-driven activity like all human endeavor, and just as subject to fashion and whim.

If there isn't a receptive mental climate, a new theory—no matter how correct—will be dismissed as a wild or irrelevant idea. No one will pursue it, and its author will become an historical footnote. As Robert Laughlin observes:

Scientific theories always have a subjective component that is as much a creation of the times as a codification of objective reality.

New ideas in physics stimulated the growth of Integrative Culture, and at the same time the growth of Integrative Culture provided a supportive climate for the emergence of those new ideas.

Bits and Pieces

Traditional science was fueled by the desire to control nature—to suppress its capriciousness, its unpredictability. In Newtonian physics:

Nature becomes an object, something to be observed, conquered, and used.

Ultimately, Control Culture scientists thought, they would make everything in the universe predictable, and hence, controllable. This fantasy was laid to rest by Chaos theory. The obsession with control over nature will probably continue to play a major part in applied sciences, but modern physics is more in tune with Native American thinking, as in this remark by Elizabet Sahtouris:

> A Tewa Indian . . . Dr. Greg Cajete . . . said to me: "The differ-
> ence between the way the red man does science and the way
> the white man does science is interesting. The white man
> isolates a piece of nature and takes it into the laboratory to
> study it because he wants to control it. The red man goes into
> nature because his purpose is to integrate with it."

It helps to imagine that you can control your world if you see it as fragmented, rather than as an indissoluble unity that incorporates yourself. Hence Controller science had a kind of Lego image of the universe—seeing it as little hunks of matter that could be put together and taken apart, like a machine. Newtonian physics envisioned the universe as a big clock—a mechanism with removable parts—much the way doctors viewed the human body.

Modern physics shattered this image.

> The new science gives us the vision of an entangled universe
> where everything is subtly connected to everything else.

The new physics, says David Bohm, compels us to look at the universe as an undivided whole: any seemingly individual element *actually contains enfolded within itself that whole*, and each event that occurs is influenced, not by a linear causal chain, but by the whole universe.

John Markoff points out that the breakthrough in the development of the personal computer and the Internet occurred when programmers began mimicking the cellular structures of living systems. In Integrative Culture not only is the machine passé as a metaphor for living things—biological metaphors are now used to describe what used to be viewed as mechanical. The Internet, says Kevin Kelly, is best described in biological terms—David Brooks compares it to a rainforest. William Knoke likens modern companies, with their fluid boundaries, to amoebas. Biomimicry is a rapidly growing trend in technology.

Unity Dissolves Mysteries

Have you ever watched a cat walk over a fallen branch lying in its path? With its eyes focused on something in the distance its front legs step over it, and then, without hesitation, the hind legs. How do those hind legs know where the object is, when and how high to step, and so forth, when most of the cat has already passed over it? It seems rather clever to us bipeds, who stumble over things we're not looking at even when they're right in front of us. But it would seem positively spooky if we didn't know that the eyes, brain, and hind legs of that cat were all part of the same unity.

Many events that seem mysterious to us are hard to understand only because of the illusion that we're disconnected from each other and from the rest of life. Freed from this illusion, the blurring of the material and the nonmaterial in modern physics is less disturbing. If we're all part of the same fabric, mysterious events become natural, ordinary. We don't find it supernatural that widely separated cells in our body behave in concert, or that our thoughts affect our health.

> The discoveries of science have begun to make sense of mystical experiences people have been describing for millennia.

Controller thinking—both scientific and everyday—was linear, dualistic, hierarchical, and static. Integrative thinking—both scientific and everyday—reverses these tendencies.

Controller Lense	Integrative Lens
Linear, Left brain Approach	Pattern, Right-brain Approach
Universe as Contending Opposites	Universe as Evolving Unity
Universe Hierarchical, Pyramidal	Universe Balanced, Circular
Universe as Static Structure	Universe as Process

I. From Linearity to Pattern

The neurotic billionaire Howard Hughes demanded that his staff only discuss subjects that he himself had brought up first, because he could only think about one thing at a time. This is left-brain thinking, and it has its uses in dealing with very simple, circumscribed, logical problems. In linear causality A causes B, B causes

C, C causes D, and so on. But this kind of thinking tends to break down in the face of real-life complexities. In quantum theory there are no linear pathways—everything in the universe is in a certain sense adjacent to, and a cause of, everything else.

The Need for Complex Thinking

The peculiar Controller belief in the virtue of right-handedness perhaps arose from the over-development of the left hemisphere (which controls the right hand) in Control Culture. The left hemisphere segments, analyzes, and orders—a most important function if you're preoccupied with control—while the right brain "thinks in images, sees wholes, detects patterns." As Daniel Pink says:

> The right hemisphere is the picture; the left hemisphere is the thousand words.

Before 1950, when studies of hemisphere differences began to be studied seriously, linear mechanical thought processes were the only ones valued. Scientists saw the right brain as a primitive relic. This was due in part to the fact that it was more developed in women. Barred from male pursuits, women found it easier to retain a balance between the brain's hemispheres. Hence women often seemed a little mysterious to men, and 'women's intuition' inspired both contempt and fear.

It's not that men of science never relied on their intuition—most scientific innovations began with right-brain flashes—but they had to be validated by strict, linear, left-brain processes before they became acceptable. Men were contemptuous of intuition, and had to rename it "gut feeling" to make it respectably butch.

> The left brain can organize new information into the existing scheme of things, but it cannot generate new ideas. The right brain sees context, and, therefore, meaning.

The right brain is also capable of holding two contradictory ideas at the same time. In Controller thinking one of those ideas must always triumph over the other.

In Newton's fixed space–time framework, there is only one way of looking at any situation. Newtonian truth is a truth of either/or. But either/or thinking can't cope with paradox and ambiguity.

The ascendancy of women in Integrative Culture has been accompanied by a new appreciation of right-brain functioning. The future clearly belongs to those able to embrace contradictions without panic, capable of keeping several mental balls in the air at once.

Daniel Pink, in his book *A Whole New Mind*, sees the future as right brain dominant, and the scientist Karl Pribram even suggests that:

children should learn about paradox in grade school, since the new scientific findings are always fraught with contradictions.

II. From Contending Opposites to Evolving Unity

We can't live without making distinctions, without contrasts, without saying *this* is different from *that*. That's what this book is doing: setting up polar ideal types to make it easier to understand what it is that's changing. The limitation of Control Culture was that it viewed the world *exclusively* through this either/or lens, and tended to make physical walls out of these mental conveniences.

Controllers have always been intolerant of symbols of unity, and when the Controller era began, Controller societies everywhere replaced the Goddess—symbolizing the oneness of life—with partisan male war gods who would aid them in battle against other societies with other male war gods.

This Controller conquest was expressed in myth by the slaying of a dragon. The dragon—a universal symbol associated with wisdom in many cultures—has been said to represent the "union of two opposed principles." No wonder Controllers felt they had to kill it.

The Great Divide

To make themselves feel more in control of their world Controllers were continually splitting it in two ("Divide and Conquer"). This strict dualism was reflected in traditional scientific thought, which maintained rigid walls between mind and body, material and spiritual, mass and energy, space and time, subject and object, 'man' and nature. Modern science has torn down these walls, one by one.

Einstein's work showed that concepts. . . which had previously seemed to be separate . . . are actually interwoven.

"Cleansing"

The most famous Controller duality of all, and the most lethal, was splitting the universe into good and evil segments. Once you've divided humanity into Good Guys and Bad Guys, life seems, on the surface, vastly simplified: it's just a matter of finding the Bad Guys and eliminating them.

In the 12th century, Godfroi de Bouillon murdered the entire population of Jerusalem, "children and mothers with infants, by way of a solemn sacrifice to Jesus." Jews were herded into synagogues and burned alive, Muslims were killed where they stood. A century later Pope Innocent III sent an army to slaughter the Cathars—man, woman, and child, for their heretical beliefs, wiping out Europe's most highly civilized community. Both acts were viewed by the perpetrators as ridding the world of evil.

This desire to cleanse the world of 'evil' has led to virtually all the great atrocities of history: the Holocaust, the Inquisition, the Crusades, the Killing Fields of Pol Pot, the Stalinist purges, the witch hunts of the Middle Ages, the Cultural Revolution in China, ethnic cleansing in Yugoslavia and Rwanda, and the slaughter and torture of radicals by dictators in Indonesia, Argentina, Chile, El Salvador, and Guatemala, to name a few. In each case the perpetrators were in pursuit of political, religious, or racial purity.

Human beings are perhaps never more frightening then when they are convinced beyond doubt that they are right.

And, of course, these attempts to get rid of 'bad guys', far from simplifying the world, just created more evil, more chaos, more misery.

The Controller model is also ineffective in dealing with social problems. Since the Controller sees the world split into good and evil, any misfortune must have been caused by an evil force. The Controller doesn't see misfortune simply as a problem to be solved. His first thought is to find out who's to blame, and once the enemy has been identified and punished, he often feels satisfied even if the conditions that produced the problem are unchanged.

The Dualistic Model in Medicine

During the 1980s a group of midwives in California pooled their resources to found a local birthing center. As they were holding a workshop with new mothers and their babies, a SWAT team with drawn guns and bulletproof vests burst in and arrested the midwives for practicing medicine without a license. At that time, giving birth was defined by the medical establishment as a disease—an example of the Controller fear of letting go.

Modern Western medicine was founded on the study of cadavers, which led doctors to view the body as a passive object to be manipulated by the physician. This tended to steer medical emphasis away from healing, toward control and power. Disease was an enemy that invaded this helpless body and had to be fought and killed by the knight-like doctor. Health was a matter of dominating and vanquishing enemy germs and cancer cells with biological and chemical weapons, 'magic bullets', and knives.

If no enemy germs or cells can be found, this military model tends to leave the physician helpless:

> The classical view [of immunology] with its military metaphors
> has been one of the main stumbling blocks in our under-
> standing of auto-immune diseases such as AIDS.

There are, of course, many genuine healers who enter the medical profession, pay attention to what their patients tell them, and attempt to treat the whole person. But the military model is not supportive to them. Traditionally, doctors are trained to see their role not as making a patient healthier but only as killing the 'bad guys' that are making him ill.

Integrative Influence in Medicine

The limitations of Controller medicine led to wholesale defections by patients during the seventies, eighties, and nineties. In 1996, for the first time, there were more visits by American patients to alternative practitioners than to traditional physicians.

Fortunately, there is more acceptance today of alternative forms of medicine by open-minded doctors. Until the sixties, acupuncture was completely unknown in the United States outside of Chinatown. When its successes were first reported in medical journals a prominent physician told a junior colleague he didn't want her talking about "that voodoo". Now its practitioners are on many hospital staffs. Chiropraxis, acupuncture, homeopathy, Ayurvedic medicine, and other healing techniques are increasingly accepted, and there's renewed interest in herbal techniques and spiritual healing—long stigmatized as quackery. Meanwhile Americans have begun taking charge of their own health. In the sixties health food stores started springing up all over the country, and magazines today are packed with articles on how people can take care of themselves through diet, exercise, herbs, meditation, and so on.

The fundamental difference between the Controller approach and the Integrative approach is a strategic one: by and large, the Controller is more likely to look for sickness and try to destroy it, while the Integrator is more likely to look for health and try to reinforce it.

The Integrative View of Conflict

Conflict is vital to growth. Without conflict, we would become stagnant, inert. The problem with Controller thinking is that it tends to reduce every conflict to an unproductive battle, rather than seeing it as an opportunity for development.

Resolving conflict doesn't mean someone has to win, nor does it require self-sacrifice. Many Integrators think the only alternative to a 'black-and-white' situation is 'shades of gray'—that is, some sort of wishy-washy compromise. They can't envision color—a creative redefinition of the problem—Mary Parker Follett's 'third way'.

Creativity, Follett insists, requires both self-assertion *and* flexibility; for it's the joining of differences, not their sacrifice, that creates new opportunities:

> Our 'opponents' are our co-creators, for they have something to give which we have not.

Redefining Conflicts

The "third way" demands that all parties redefine their needs—take them to a deeper and more long-range level. Few conflicts, after all, are just about the surface issue. If John opposes Pete's new project it may be because he feels it will marginalize him, while Pete may feel the project is his last chance to save his job. At this level several solutions emerge that weren't there when the conflict was defined simply as project vs. no project. Pete can make John project manager, for example, or John can come up with a better way to improve Pete's position.

Environmentalists and commercial fishermen often see each other as enemies—environmentalists wanting to protect the ocean at all costs, fishermen wanting to make a living at all costs. But it has begun to dawn on some that at a more basic level they both want the same things—a sea full of fish, and fish for dinner—and some agreements have been reached that not only protect the environment and prevent over-fishing, but also stem the continuing decline of small commercial fishing operations.

In the Integrative view, conflict is simply a tool for creating more complex unities. The uniting of opposites has always been a rich source of innovation.

III. From Pyramid to Sphere

Since the winners in any struggle write the history, in time they come to represent the Good, while the losers become Evil and their gods, devils. Conquered nations have to be convinced of their inferiority and their subjugation legitimized. So after conquerors have held their conquests for a while their ownership becomes the law. The descendants of the conqueror become 'noble-' or 'gentle-' men, while 'villain'—which originally meant peasant—comes to mean an evil person. Might makes right.

Looking High and Low

Since everything in Control Culture was defined vertically, 'higher' and 'lower' acquired moral overtones. The words 'superior' and 'inferior', which had simply meant above and below, came to mean 'better' and 'worse'. Our language today is so loaded with these habits of speech that it's almost impossible to communicate without using them. We speak of the 'moral high ground' and 'lofty' motives, for example, of 'lower' (rather than smaller) test scores, and 'lower' (rather than looser) standards.

To drive home their 'superiority', rulers were placed on elevated daises and thrones, and their social 'inferiors' were expected to demonstrate their unworthy status by physically lowering themselves—bowing, genuflecting, curtseying, or salaaming. Religion was also affected by this obsession. Deities were banished from the earth and elevated to mountaintops or the sky.

But while the key symbol of the Controller era was the pyramid, for the Integrative era it's the sphere.

People are fond of saying we're at the 'top' of the food chain. You could just as well say that maggots are on top of the food chain, since they, along with various bacteria, eat us. Control Culture tried to deny this by embalming people and putting them in boxes, but the reality is that, like all other forms of life, we both eat and are eaten. The food chain is just that, a chain, with no top, no bottom, just a circle of life.

Deborah Tannen tells how a scientist completely missed a biological discovery because he was looking for a "boss cell". One wonders how many other areas of science have been retarded by hierarchical notions of this kind.

In moving away from the pyramid thinking of the Controller era we are once again imitating nature:

> Whereas we spend a lot of energy building things from the top down—taking bulk materials and carving them into shape—nature does the opposite. It grows its materials from the ground up, not by building but by self-assembling.

The self-creating coherence that Follett speaks of as the essence of democracy is, in a sense, another form of biomimicry.

Vertical metaphors like the 'ladder' of success, 'making it to the top', the 'stairway' to paradise—Zeus on a mountain top and God on a cloud—arose from, and depended on, the belief that the earth was flat. But they persisted long after people knew better. After all, everyday experience didn't contradict them. This is why images of our blue planet taken from space had such a profound impact. It went beyond mere words and diagrams, which may lodge in the left hemisphere but have no real effect on our psyches. It was a stunning, revealing, defining image—one that could get under the skin, permeate the unconscious, re-frame concepts.

Seeing the planet from this distance, the hierarchies of Controller thinking seemed trivial, and it was easier to re-configure Earth as a complex, interdependent system in which everything played an equally important part. Today we really know that 'up' is just 'out'.

IV. From Structure to Process

The Big Clock of Newtonian physics, the chronic war between Good and Evil, the authoritarian organizations, the hierarchies of caste, the fixed pathways of linear causality—these were static institutions. They assumed a fundamentally unchanging universe and social system.

But Integrative Culture stresses process.

> A universe where nothing new or surprising ever happens is replaced by a self-organizing universe of constant invention.

Discoveries are both exciting and a little scary. To *dis*-cover something is to open it up, free it, let it loose. Every discovery is a potential loss of control. So each new discovery makes many people want to narrow their vision, constrict their world, blind themselves to its complexity. Integrative Culture facilitates dis-covery, for it is itself a kind of opening, a freeing, an uncovering, and produces a sensation akin to vertigo in those who depend too strongly on a static, compartmentalized vision of the world.

Einstein vividly described his response to the first challenges to Newtonian physics:

It was as if the ground had been pulled out from under one, with no firm foundation to be seen anywhere, upon which one could have built.

While Einstein rose to the challenge—opening the door to a new age—he was sentimentally attached to the old one, and was still trying to find such a foundation when he died. But the very notion of a theoretical 'foundation' is archaic in the space age.

The Marquis de Condorcet said in 1794 that universal laws were the "foundation for belief in the natural sciences", but Rupert Sheldrake advances the radical Integrative idea that nature is a process of evolving habits rather than subject to laws laid down by some godly authority. His notion of "formative causation" means everything that has form organizes itself—that atoms, molecules, crystals, animals are not put together by an external hand, like machines. They evolve spontaneously, in "morphic fields" that grow ever stronger with repetition. He points out that the whole idea of scientific 'laws' is totally mysterious—a notion closer to religion than to science.

Process-Thinking in Everyday Life

Controllers saw their environment as a static thing. With effort you could change this thing, making it into a new thing. But it was always a *thing*—something you shaped and molded. You were in control of it. Integrators see themselves as an interacting part of a moving, proactive environment—more like sailors or surfers than sculptors.

During the last half of the 20th century there was a boom in goal-less activities like meditation, where the process itself was the goal.

Some people, of course, justified this 'useless' pursuit by saying they were trying to become enlightened, or that achieving a more relaxed state was good for one's health. But there is no end point to a given meditation, when you can say, "I've achieved my goal, I've won, game over." It is 'pointless', a process.

During this same period there was a boom in athletic pursuits that were similarly goal-less and intrinsically non-competitive. Activities such as surfing, skateboarding, Frisbee, hang gliding, and windsurfing are engaged in for the sheer pleasure of the physical sensations they produce, and for the joy of exercising skills and extending oneself. Some of these activities have been co-opted for contests and competitive games, but the average person pursues them for their own sake—the process is everything.

Communication, too, though essential in achieving many extrinsic goals, is its own reward, as anyone knows who has struggled with a foreign language spoken by new friends. Most of our everyday communication—the social noises we make in greeting, the endless phone conversations and text-messaging of teenagers, the chats in and out of chat rooms—is goal-less. We communicate to 'stay in touch', that is, to communicate. It's a process, an end in itself. And communication is the core of Integrative Culture.

This emphasis on process resolves an ancient Controller dilemma. Since for Controllers everything was a means to some end, the question often arose: does the end justify the means? This was a favorite preoccupation of Controller ethics. But since Integrators see everything as process, the dilemma disappears. For if process is the goal then it has to be justifiable in itself—there's nothing to justify the means *with*, since the end *is* the means and vice versa.

Trapped in a Static Language

Among the world's peoples there are language systems that have no nouns. Their languages don't distinguish between short events and long events the way Western languages do. We say, for example, "it's raining" (short event), but "this is a table" (long event). But they say, "it's raining" and "it's tabling".

These languages view the world as a process, and in that sense are far more relevant to the Integrative world-view of modern physics. Imagine how much easier it would be for physicists today if our language were like this. To say, for example, "it particles and it waves, depending on how you approach it" doesn't present the same awkwardness as, "well, somehow it's both a wave and a particle." It also suits the thinking of modern physicists who see the universe not as a collection of separate units but as an indissoluble whole. The "it" in "it particles" is the entire universe.

The whole universe could be thought of as unfolding or expressing itself in its individual occurrences.

This is perhaps what Blake meant when he said:

If the doors of perception were cleansed every thing would appear to man as it is, infinite.

We'd also have an easier time living if we thought of ourselves as verbs rather than nouns—as events rather than as objects. If we thought, "the universe is John Smith-ing at the moment" (as well as Jane Brown-ing and Betty Green-ing and pelicaning and raccooning and daisying and pebbling). Maybe we wouldn't take ourselves so seriously or get so stuck in rigid and limiting self-concepts.

The Universe as Learning

We think of a whole as something complete, something finished. But the world around us is always evolving. In nature harmony is fleeting, with constant changes upsetting every achieved balance, and the same is true of cultures. George Soros, a global capitalist and philanthropist, understands this:

We yearn for perfection, permanence . . . but . . . each step forward has some flaw in it, which can be corrected only by taking another step forward.

At the subatomic level everything is moving—even rocks are in violent motion. There are no 'basic building blocks', only energy.

And this energy is always changing. Our new economy works the same way:

> The sustained vitality of a complex network requires that the net keep provoking itself out of balance. If the system settles into harmony and equilibrium, it will eventually stagnate and die. . . . the goal of a well-made network [is] to sustain a perpetual disequilibrium.

A favorite unifying image in many religions is the mandala—a richly filled, encompassing circle. In the infinite fractal variations of the Mandelbrot set there are many of them. But quite a few, on closer inspection, turn out to be spirals. These are the mandalas of the Integrative era. For Integrative culture is in its essence the fusing of a static but sustainable hunter-gatherer type of culture with the dynamism of our Western, linear, unsustainable one.

Participating in the evolving Integrative Culture means thinking of yourself as a process. It means thinking of everyone and everything around you as a process. It means becoming a verb.

5 | On Authority: Getting Out from Under

So long as men worship the Caesars and Napoleons,
Caesars and Napoleons will duly rise and
make them miserable.
ALDOUS HUXLEY

The strongest poison ever known
Came from Caesar's laurel crown.
WILLIAM BLAKE

In a multitude of systems from economics to biology,
events are driven not by any preexisting center
but by the interactions of equals.
DUNCAN J. WATTS

Democracy is basic to Integrative Culture. It's also part of our genetic heritage as human beings. We think of democracy as something invented by the Greeks, or 18th century theorists, but it's as old as humanity, and the basis of our survival as a species.

For most of the time humans have existed on earth they lived in small bands, gathering what food grew wild in nature, fishing, and hunting. They lived cooperatively of necessity—they knew they couldn't survive alone. Their lives were characterized by:

personal independence, general equality among group
members, including women, consensus-based decision-making

achieved through open and protracted discussion, and freedom of movement, particularly as a means of conflict resolution.

Europeans 10,000 years ago, and for 30,000 years before that, had:

an egalitarian social structure and highly mobile life styles.

Even when they became civilized, settled in towns, and worked the land, they remained democratic until the Controller age. In their art, artifacts, and ruins there are no symbols of power, no emblems of authority, no sign of chiefs. Even in the highly sophisticated civilization of Crete there was little variation in wealth and no indication of social classes.

Surviving hunter-gatherer cultures are also egalitarian:

There was a confusing, seductive informality about everything [the Pygmies] did . . . Everyone took part in everything . . . There were no chiefs, no formal councils. In each aspect of Pygmy life there might be one or two men or women who were more prominent than others, but usually for good practical reasons.

Among the Bushmen, too, there was neither sign nor memory of chiefs. Respect for those older and wiser was the closest they ever came. The Teduray of the Mindanao rainforest also had no chiefs or rankings. People were esteemed for special skills, but only in context.

This democratic lifestyle of hunter-gatherers simply echoed the world around them. Janine Benyus has this to say about ecological systems:

What makes a mature community run is not one universal message being broadcast from above, but numerous, even redundant, messages coming from the grass roots, dispersed throughout the community structure. A rich feedback system allows changes in one component of the community to reverberate through the whole, allowing for adaptation when the environment changes.

Democracy, in other words, is the most natural form of social organization, mimicking Nature.

The Ladder that War Made

Controllers replaced the informal leadership style of the hunter-gatherers with authoritarianism—fixed, permanent positions demanding obedience and deference. Obedience to those 'above' you and domination over those 'below' you became virtues. Unified action was achieved through the giving and taking of orders. 'Cooperation' was merely a euphemism for obedience, as it still is in authoritarian settings.

As Control Culture swept over the globe, hunter-gatherer societies were mostly wiped out or converted to Controller ways. This happened well before Europeans took over that mission. Most cultures we call 'primitive' today are Control Cultures. They make war, have chiefs and nobles, and share many of the values of 'civilized' Control Cultures.

Formal leadership—what we call authority—was a Controller invention arising out of the special needs created when war became part of life. Controllers were faced with two problems that made formal leadership necessary.

First, the conquerors had to control their conquered slaves and peasants. Although they had the advantage of owning weapons, and although they were stronger and better fed (nobles were often as much as six inches taller), a peasant or slave might still have leadership skills, or be a talented fighter despite all these disadvantages. A line had to be drawn that couldn't be crossed.

Second, men were being trained to be competitive and belligerent. How could order be kept among such men? Who could such men accept as a leader? Would he have to fight constantly to maintain his position? And if so, how would the group ever have the energy or manpower to fight anyone else?

This was the origin of formal hierarchy, or the abolishing of equal opportunity. People now held fixed status positions in society. Formal rankings and levels of authority created order and consistency. Those at the top of the pyramid conferred titles, positions, and benefits on those below. They established tests and trials and criteria for moving from one rank to a higher one, and rules and demerits and penalties for demoting someone to a lower one. You could improve your position only by gaining the approval of those above you.

Over time legitimacy was established through birth, with fathers passing their status down to their sons. The entire known world became redefined as a pyramid, with kings and nobles at the top and slaves and peasants at the bottom.

Scapegoating

Hierarchical institutions are unnatural for human beings and arouse frustration and anger. Robert O'Connell observes that authoritarian systems were:

> fundamentally dissonant to human nature as it had evolved during the millions of years we spent as wanderers, hunters, and collectors.

In the Controller system the frustration aroused by hierarchy is discharged by scapegoating—that is, blaming a powerless outsider or low-status person for abuses by powerful insiders and high-status persons. People in the middle of a hierarchy can take out their frustrations on those further down the ladder, but those at the bottom are forced to look abroad.

In armies it isn't hard to deflect hostility—the anger that soldiers feel toward their officers can be displaced onto an enemy. Heads of government regularly whip up hatred of foreigners or minorities to maintain their popularity. Hitler used the Jews, Stalin used the bourgeoisie, American Cold Warriors used the "red menace", Saddam Hussein used the Kurds, Milosevich used Muslims and Croats, and so on. It's the easiest way on earth for a leader to retain despotic power. He need only hint that some group is dangerous or unworthy and those members of the populace who tend to grovel before authority will feel emboldened to attack and often kill.

For everyday frustrations the preferred scapegoats were women.

The Return of the Suppressed

Many years ago a sociologist named William Stephens did a cross-cultural study of family patterns. He discovered two things.

First, he found—not surprisingly—that authoritarian societies were composed of authoritarian families. Wherever he found centralized authority, armies, a hereditary king or chief, and at least two social classes, he also found a high degree of son-to-father deference and wife-to-husband deference.

Second, Stephens found that authoritarian societies were at an intermediate level of cultural development—both the simplest and the most highly developed societies tended to be democratic.

We question Controller values today partly because of our increasing awareness of this earlier way of life. Robert O'Connell sees documents like the Bill of Rights and the Declaration of the Rights of Man as "virtual hunter-gatherer manifestos."

It was contact with living pre-Controller societies in the 15th and 16th centuries that brought about the first meaningful challenge to the Controller ethos. When European ships first began to circle the globe most of the cultures they encountered shared the Control Culture: the Incas and Aztecs, the Zulu, Ashanti, Dahomey, and Masai, the kingdoms of India and the Far East, the nations of Islam—all were Controller systems.

But in a few remote areas they found pre-Controller survivors. People with no chiefs, no armies, no classes. Here the germ of a shatteringly new idea was planted—the realization that Control Culture was just one way of living, not 'human nature'. It was an idea that resonated with some very old instincts.

The most important of these encounters occurred on the shores of North America, when explorers from England and France found Native Americans who exposed the invaders to a new way of life:

The most consistent theme in the descriptions penned about the New World was amazement at the Indians' personal liberty, in particular their freedom from rulers and social classes based on ownership of property. For the first time the French and the British became aware of the possibility of living in social harmony and prosperity without the rule of a king.

These reports fascinated Europeans, and were a major influence on men like Thomas More and Jean Jacques Rousseau. Although Americans tend to trace their democratic roots to French and English political thinkers, the ideas of these thinkers were themselves shaped by reports of how Native Americans lived. The US Constitution and many of our democratic political practices are heavily indebted to Native American customs.

Bureaucracy

But long after political democracy had begun to take hold, Controller customs still predominated in formal organizations. Hierarchies were the norm for all institutions, even those—like schools, universities, corporations, and churches—that had nothing to do with fighting. The system worked fairly well for centuries but contained two flaws that have ultimately proved crippling.

The first flaw was the poor fit between status and ability. Authority means you get to exercise leadership whether you're any good at it or not.

In informal groups leaders emerge spontaneously. They may be the best liked, the wisest, the most fun, or the ones with the best ideas. Often leadership will circulate, depending on the group's activity. But leaders that emerge spontaneously tend to share certain traits. Successful leaders, say Warren Bennis and Burt Nanus in their classic work on leadership, have a clear vision of where they want to go, an ability to communicate this to others, and a realistic and positive sense of self. They're trustworthy, pay attention to people, and induce self-esteem in others, often by challenging them. These are qualities possessed by emergent leaders that may or may not be possessed by formal ones.

In bureaucracies leaders are often appointed to their positions as a reward for past services. Employees ascend the pyramid until, as Laurence J. Peter says, they reach their "level of incompetence", where they remain indefinitely. I once heard middle managers of a large multinational corporation sharing stories about alcoholic or otherwise incompetent managers they routinely ignored and circumvented—walling them off like alien bacteria in an organism.

The second flaw in authoritarian systems is their inability to adapt quickly to change. And change today is chronic. A study of over 200 successful companies found that fewer than half could maintain their success for more than two years.

'Procedure'

During World War II a time-motion expert was called in to increase the firing speed of artillery crews. Puzzled by the fact that two men always stopped all activity and stood at attention for several seconds before and during each firing, he asked everyone what it meant. No one seemed to know. It was just "the way it was done." Finally he asked an old cavalry officer. "Ah, I have it," said the old man, after some thought, "they are holding the horses." There were no longer any horses to be frightened by the noise, but the procedure lived on.

Authoritarianism can survive in places where nothing much changes for decades at a time but falters under conditions of rapid change.

For a system to respond well to unforeseen situations it must be able to utilize all its resources, which in turn requires rapid communication among all parts of that system. But hierarchies require that all communication be routed through managers at the top.

Watts tells the story of what happened when a disaster threatened to shut down Toyota production for months—an event that would have had massive international economic repercussions.

Toyota cars are actually manufactured by over 200 separate companies, all of which exchange personnel, assistance, and intellectual property—in other words, a network. In 1997 a plant that was the exclusive manufacturer of a crucial brake valve burned to the ground, leaving Toyota with only a two days supply of the valves and no way to make any more until the plant was rebuilt. Car production ground to a halt. Yet within three days 62 of the other companies—none of whom had any previous experience with the valves—had become emergency valve producers, with 150 other companies indirectly involved as suppliers. Two weeks after the disaster struck car production was back to normal levels.

The Toyota experience exemplifies what Benyus says early in this chapter about mature ecological systems: grass-roots communication throughout the system ensures that changes in one part of the community will quickly travel everywhere, enabling rapid adaptation when environmental change occurs.

Toyota's amazing recovery would not have been possible without decentralization—without a rich tradition of lateral communication at the ground level and cooperative daily problem solving. This flexibility is what makes networks so successful in an age of chronic change. And what makes it so easy for groups like Al-Qaida to evade conventional military bureaucracies.

Hierarchies, says Duncan Watts, "respond poorly to ambiguity", and ambiguity is the essence of the age we live in. When change is chronic, "intense communication becomes an ongoing necessity". James Surowiecki, in *The Wisdom of Crowds*, points out that the hierarchical, top-down nature of NASA caused the *Columbia* disaster, since the information that would have prevented it was available at lower levels of the Agency. And the authoritarian bureaucracies of the American auto industry were a major factor in its rapid decline.

Washington has been slow to learn this lesson, however. Despite all the evidence, the Bush administration has responded to every national crisis by creating or enlarging unwieldy, secretive, over-centralized, and deeply authoritarian bureaucracies (see Chapter 9).

The Decline of Authoritarianism

When Warren Bennis and I predicted, in 1964, the demise of the Soviet Union and other autocracies, our prediction had nothing to do with the Cold War or idealistic values. We argued that global democracy was inevitable in our modern world because it was more efficient. Right-wingers credited Ronald Reagan with the USSR collapse, Osama bin Laden claimed he himself was responsible, while the Russians themselves blamed exposure to rock and roll. But in fact, Russian authoritarianism made it inevitable.

Authoritarian systems are too cumbersome and inflexible to survive long under the conditions of chronic change that prevail today. Bennis and I were saying that Communist and other authoritarian governments could not survive as they were *whether we did anything about them or not*. Unlike government policy makers at the time we believed both in the value of democracy and in its inevitability. Time has proven us right, although Republican policy makers in Washington still complain that democracy 'handicaps' them, still believe that America enjoys a 'weak' political system sustainable only by brute force and by circumventing it as much as possible.

Bahrain used to be typical of the autocratic and repressive regimes of the Middle East, with a particularly brutal security force. It was a breeding ground of Al-Qaida extremists and deemed unsafe for Western firms. Then the old Emir died and his son, Emir Sheikh Hamad al Khalifa, decided to embrace democracy. He freed over a thousand political prisoners, abolished the laws that allowed police to hold prisoners without charge, and held free elections in 2002, giving every single Bahraini—male or female—the right to vote. While protests occurred when the U.S. invaded Afghanistan and Iraq, they were peaceful. In the past, as one Bahraini observed:

> U.S. soldiers would have been afraid to step outside the bases
> . . . Today, if we disagree, we can protest, write editorials,
> campaign. But in Saudi, what can they do? Only use bombs.

Authoritarianism is on the decline everywhere. Dictators may survive for a time in Third World countries where multinational corporations are looking for cheap labor, but they cannot survive long when consumer markets are sought in those same countries.

Why Democracy Prevails

Malcolm Gladwell tells of Paul Van Riper, who commanded the Red Team (enemy) in 'Millennium Challenge'—the war games in 2000 that served as a rehearsal for the Iraq invasion. The Blue Team had at its disposal the most modern equipment, computing system, and analytic tools the world had ever known. But in the games they were utterly routed by the Red Team, who were using archaic equipment and communication methods. The secret of Van Riper's success was no secret at all: a completely decentralized, democratic, management structure, in which subordinates were told the overall intent but "were to use their own initiative and be innovative". As Gladwell says, it's a 'messy' system, but "allowing people to operate without having to explain themselves constantly . . . enables rapid cognition."

Most government leaders and media commentators share a misconception: that democracy is an idealistic luxury that handicaps us. Military dictators installed by, or supported by, the United States are referred to wistfully as "strongman Suharto" or "strongman Pinochet". Democracy is so poorly understood in Washington (as opposed to the private sector) that the government's first response to any crisis is to create a bureaucracy and appoint a 'czar' to run it—the precise opposite of the successful Toyota response to disaster, or Van Riper's success in the Millennium Challenge.

Mere idealism would not have allowed democracy to sweep the globe. As Jeffrey Sachs points out, the reason the British were the first to enter the industrial age and able to establish global economic supremacy was that their society was the most open and democratic at that time.

In a laboratory at M.I.T. several decades ago, two types of groups were compared on their ability to solve problems. One type had a centralized leader through whom all communication had to be funneled. The other was completely egalitarian.

Given simple tasks and unchanging rules the autocratic groups were more efficient, but when the experimenters gave the groups tasks that were more complex, and introduced changes in the middle of the experiment, the autocratic groups unraveled. The democratic groups solved the complex problems more quickly and made fewer errors. They were more adaptable, corrected their mistakes more quickly, and were more open to new ideas.

One reason for the failure of the autocratic groups was that the 'bosses' were too busy to pay attention to crucial new information. This is compounded in real-life autocracies by the tendency of dictatorial leaders to be protected by their subordinates from information they don't want to hear. The messenger who brings the bad news that the boss needs to change his policy is seen as disloyal, and is ignored, fired, or shot. But the leader who manages to eliminate all opposition usually finds that far from solving his problems, he's amputated the solution to them.

The First Casualty

Mao Zedong was at the top of his gigantic pyramid only a few years before the rigidity of his system began to destroy what he was trying to build. He refused to believe that the Great Leap Forward was a failure, and his unwillingness to face facts was nourished by his subordinates, who were afraid to report any news that would challenge his optimistic view of the matter. The only one who told him the truth, Liu Shaoki, was ever after considered an enemy.

Top-down corporations, says Surowiecki, "give people an incentive to hide information and dissemble." In top-down governments this incentive is magnified, since the lust for power is more intense, and the lag time between error and catastrophe far longer.

The results are familiar. Unchallenged generals following outdated military principles send their troops to be slaughtered by guerillas. The unchallenged ship captain plows confidently into an iceberg. Hitler exhausts his armies in Russia. Corporate heads, thriving on past successes, ignore the invention that puts them out of business.

The WMD (weapons of mass destruction) fiasco is a case in point, with the White House walling itself off from inconvenient data. Unwilling to rely on existing information sources, Bush Administration officials set up their own mini-agency inside the Pentagon whose 'loyal' personnel "'cherry-picked' the intelligence they passed on, selecting reports that supported the administration's pre-existing ideology and ignoring all the rest."

In the Bush administration personal loyalty and ideological commitment outweighed all other values.

> The President was caught in an echo chamber of his own
> making, cut off from everyone other than a circle around him
> that's tiny and getting smaller and in concert on everything—a
> circle that conceals him from public view and keeps him away
> from the one thing he needs most: honest, disinterested
> perspectives about what's real.

Carefully prepared reports by the CIA, the State Department, the Army War College, and non-governmental groups all agreed that the welcome of United States troops in Iraq would be short-lived, that a large and extended commitment of personnel and money would be necessary to rebuild Iraq; and warned of the inevitability of looting and the serious dangers that would be incurred if the Iraqi army was disbanded. But the inner circle of the administration regarded any consideration of what it might take to rebuild Iraq as disloyal and anti-war. Those who publicly made what turned out to be realistic and even overly conservative assessments of the cost of the war and reconstruction were fired (Chief White House economic adviser Lawrence Lindsay) or humiliated (Army Chief of Staff General Eric Shinseki). The inner White House circle had apparently convinced themselves that the Iraqis would greet our troops with open arms and quickly transform themselves into a unified Western style democracy. They didn't want anyone raining on their fantasy.

As a result of this triumph of ideology over truth, junior officers in Iraq found themselves totally unprepared to deal with what they encountered there. Much of their military training was useless, and with no knowledge of the language or culture they were entirely unprepared to cope with the complex problems they were facing every day. When retired Lieutenant Colonel Leonard Wong undertook to analyze Army training methods he found its most serious defect was that it stifled creative thinking.

Lateral Communication

But when the war actually came, democratic culture triumphed over military training. Junior officers came up with ingenious solutions to crises, and created unauthorized web sites where they could exchange what they were learning with other young officers, without going through channels.

> Gen X officers, often the product of single-parent homes, or homes in which both parents worked, are markedly more self-reliant and confident of their abilities than their baby-boomer superiors. . . . Instead of looking up to the Army for instructions they are teaching themselves how to fight the war.

In time the Army set up its own web site, CALL, but it was run on the usual top-down basis, and young officers found that

the information often seems stale or, having been processed in
the maw of Army doctrine, irrelevant. The war in Iraq is so
confusing and it changes so fast that there's often no time to
wait for carefully vetted and spoon-fed advice.

Just as we saw in the Toyota example, lateral communication of
this kind is essential for coping with rapidly changing situations.
Which is why authoritarian systems are on the decline throughout
the world.

Open Systems

Controller societies depend heavily on secrecy to control their
populations, and the speed of modern communication is making
secrecy harder to maintain. Nations have been forced to adopt
transparency in their financial reporting to avoid sudden panics.

The days when governments could totally isolate their people
from information about what life was like beyond their borders
. . . are over.

There's a direct correlation between a country's openness and its
standard of living. Nations are being forced to democratize or find
themselves lagging behind the rest of the world in economic development.

In the era of globalization the most open-minded, tolerant,
creative and diverse societies will have the easiest time . . .
while the most closed, rigid, uptight, self-absorbed and traditional companies and countries . . . will struggle. . . . The
countries that are adjusting best to globalization today . . . are
the most democratic ones.

Despite the great reluctance of its leaders to decentralize power,
and their repeated crackdowns on dissidents, even China is being
forced, inch by inch, toward democracy. A few years ago President
Jiang Zemin ordered a study of Western democracies and ways to
create a two-party system, and Hu Jintao began opening policy dis-

cussions to the public. But the Chinese dread of splintering like the Soviet Union will probably prevent full democracy for some time.

Collapsing Hierarchies, Decentralized Networks

A survey of a thousand major corporations found that 80% practice some form of participatory management, where decisions are made and implemented by teams of co-workers rather than handed down by the boss. Workers in the field can then make decisions on their own rather than referring them to higher authority. Things happen too fast today for that. One reason the FBI failed to anticipate the 9/11 attacks, despite ample warning, was the incredible number of levels its quaint hierarchy still maintains.

William Knoke talks of the headless 'amoeba-like' form of modern private organizations, in which teams form and dissolve, with informal, spontaneous leadership.

> In today's . . . globalization system, most of the information needed to answer most of the problems now rests in the hands of people on the outer edges of organizations, not at the center.

Eighty-five percent of the firms involved in Hollywood movies employ 10 people or less. Hollywood films today are no longer made by big studios but by "loose entrepreneurial networks of small firms" that "convene as one financial organization for the duration of the movie project" and then disperse.

Times of change demand creativity. Although large pyramidal corporations pour massive amounts of money into research and development, very small firms produce *twenty-four times* as many new inventions per dollar.

The threat to corporate behemoths from small entrepreneurs has never been more persistent. You don't need a huge capital investment to start a new company today—especially when the product is an idea, a system, or information, rather than a thing.

> Entrepreneurs without capital can . . . build businesses with just ideas. They no longer have to own the tools of production to have access to them . . . In the United States, a third of all new

capital equipment is acquired through leasing.

Decentralizing bureaucracies and creating ad hoc teams and networks is a trend throughout the economy, and in state and local government. In times of change mistakes are a necessary part of doing business, and:

> Centralizing power only makes mistakes more catastrophic.

Warren Bennis once said that bureaucracy was a prosthesis for trust. In more organic organizations, the prosthesis isn't needed, according to Charles Handy:

> Organizations which rely on trust as their principal means of control are more effective, more creative, more fun, and cheaper to operate.

The Internet

Markoff shows how the development of the computer and the Internet sprang from members of the 1960s and 1970s counterculture, who were anti-authoritarian, anti-war, and had taken LSD. Prior to their influence, computer research had been centralized, military, and secret. The idea of giving the average person access to computers was anathema to Controller men, who were busy computing how many mega-deaths would occur under varying nuclear war situations. The younger programmers were loose-knit networks of men and women who felt information should be free and accessible to all.

The Internet has been a powerful force in the evolution of Integrative Culture. It has created a generation of people accustomed to finding their own answers, creating their own systems, forming their own new communities. And this despite the constant efforts by governments and corporations to control and limit the Internet.

Charles Leadbeater's new book, *We-Think*, analyzes the seemingly anarchic process through which Web products like Linux and Wikipedia have evolved. There are leaders—as there are in any situation—but they are not 'bosses':

They lead by establishing values and norms. They do not need to hog the limelight, claim all the credit or have a big office. They lead by setting the context for many thousands of other people, at all levels of the community, to take decisions for themselves.

This kind of self-organizing process epitomizes Integrative Culture. Control Culture is certainly not absent from the Internet, but it finds itself in hostile territory there, confronted as it is by the numbers, the openness, and the creativity of Web users.

Leadbetter compares Microsoft—a holdover from Control Culture—with Linux. Microsoft's software is owned, its use has to be paid for, and it has a hidden source code that cannot be adapted by the user. Linux is free, and is continually being improved and adapted by tens of thousands of programmers. Yet these programmers are not paid, no authority tells them to do what they do, and they have no financial stake in what they produce.

The web's underlying culture of sharing, decentralisation and democracy, makes it an ideal platform for groups to self-organise, combining their ideas and know how, to create together games, encyclopaedias, software, social networks, video sharing sites or entire parallel universes. That culture of sharing also makes the web difficult for governments to control and hard for corporations to make money from.

Money, of course, will never cease to be one of the driving forces of the Internet. But it is no longer the only one. Much of what occurs on the Web is driven by non-monetary motives.

Clots

Our planet is a bio-system of constant mutual adaptation. Every unit in that system receives information and normally reacts to it adaptively and transmits its learning to its neighbors. But when power is concentrated those transmissions are often blocked by the felt necessity of exercising control. Information is not transmitted on its merits but in terms of the power position of the person transmitting. Therefore information necessary for successful adaptation to changing conditions is lost. Information coming from the periphery of the system—invariably the source of new information about changing conditions—is ignored precisely because it comes from the periphery, from a low-power position. This is why empires always collapse in time, why small firms out-invent big corporations, why networks outperform bureaucracies.

Since those who profit most from an old system will always be most resistant to the new, resistance to Integrative Culture can be found in all centers of heavily concentrated power, from Washington and Peking to any multinational boardroom. For while the corporate world often embraces Integrative values in its organizational methods, the concentrated power of corporate giants tends to inhibit democratic processes.

Over half of the world's largest economic entities are multinationals rather than nations, and they are able to block democratic processes with the economic power they wield. Through campaign contributions they can determine public policy. Through their ability to buy air time and column space they can determine what ideas and images appear, and don't appear, in the media. Through their ability to hire large, expensive legal teams they can determine the outcome of trials. Yet they have all the legal protections and rights of private individuals. With the power of presidents, they have the privileges and freedom from responsibility of an affluent teenager.

All forms of concentrated power, public or private, block lateral communication and interfere with the organic fluidity of the Integrative process. Concentration of power equals abuse of power, for the only way not to abuse power is to share it.

Such concentrations are blood clots in the circulatory system of society. When an artery becomes clogged, blood doesn't get to the brain or the heart and people have strokes and heart attacks. Concentrations of power and wealth have a similar effect on the body politic. The circulation of wealth, resources, and, especially, ideas, is blocked. In a healthy system, information flows are unimpeded by clots of power or the sclerosis of hierarchy.

Democracy and Children

In traditional authoritarian thinking, children are not seen as the hope of the future, but merely as keepers of unchanging rules and traditions. Hence they are more likely to be considered expendable. Deuteronomy xxi, 18–21 says parents should bring stubborn children to be stoned to death. God regularly orders Israelite generals to slaughter Canaanite babies, which they are quite willing to do. (In Numbers xxxi, 17–18 only the male babies are killed, while the female babies become sex slaves.) Abraham is equally willing to murder his child on orders from above, and in Christian dogma, God sacrifices his son to be tortured and killed. A Controller father wouldn't dream of sacrificing himself for his child. Culturally, in Controller thinking, children were of little importance.

This doesn't mean, of course, that fathers in Biblical times didn't love their children. But they felt little *guilt* about sacrificing them if a male authority demanded it. Children were at the bottom of the Controller hierarchy, along with women.

Even in Victorian times, children had little standing in the world.

No matter how much they may have loved their own children, Controllers were always a little uneasy about the spontaneity of small humans. The energy, creativity, and curiosity of children were seen as a sign of Original Sin, and children were regularly beaten to rid them of "the old Adam." Children had to be tamed. Jesus may have said children possessed the Kingdom of Heaven, but fundamentalists even today view them with deep suspicion, and are in the forefront of advocates for corporal punishment, and even the death penalty.

When male doctors began giving women advice on childrearing during the 17th and 18th centuries they were almost unanimous in urging them to be more repressive of the child's needs and desires, more callous and less affectionate. Touching, cuddling, and soothing were frowned upon as making the child too dependent and weak-willed, and all spontaneous impulses were viewed as dangerous.

This attempt by men to take over what had always been the realm of women—trying to eliminate a contradiction to Controller values—is another example of purity leading to decay. Triggered, perhaps, by the early threat of democratic ideas, it began when the 'divine right of kings' was coming into vogue.

This medical push toward toughness in child-rearing steadily increased before collapsing in the mid-20th century, when the books of Benjamin Spock became so popular—books that were more in line with the spontaneous impulses of mothers.

Democracy and Learning

We learn in two ways—observation and experimentation (i.e., trial and error). Observation is quicker but more superficial: what we learn cramming for an exam is often forgotten the moment the exam ends. Experimental learning bypasses the ego and embeds itself in the tissues of the body. We don't forget how to walk, swim, or ride a bike.

For Controllers, knowledge is power, and it's important to them that only the right people get access to that power. If you want to control people you need to restrict their access to information and block their ability to communicate with each other. This is what a hierarchical structure does by its very nature—lower level sales personnel don't know what assembly-line workers are doing and they in turn don't know what clerical workers are doing. The only communication is at the top, and information is hoarded there. On the political front, keeping secrets helps authoritarian rulers hold their positions no matter how incompetent or corrupt, and the more incompetent and corrupt they are, the more of their actions become 'classified'.

Obedience was always the first thing that had to be learned in Control Culture education. A craftsman's apprentice was for years assigned only menial tasks until his willingness to take orders was established. And school children had to learn to sit still and follow orders before any knowledge was imparted.

Education, in Controller thinking, means indoctrination. It's as much about withholding information as sharing it. Knowledge is carefully compartmentalized, with impenetrable walls between disciplines; and educators are gatekeepers, allowing only 'appropriate' information to get to students.

Rote learning was the preferred technique in the Controller system, since it prevented children from exploring on their own, or grasping principles that would enable them to think for themselves. Rote learning fosters obedience, discourages curiosity, and teaches children that education is boring.

Spelling is ideal for this, since it's arbitrary. There's little logic to the way words are spelled in English, and a small child who grasps a language principle and says things like "swimmed" and "thinked" is made fun of, even though it's a sign of intelligence. But in the Controller system, no distinction was made between intelligence—the ability to grasp and use concepts, and knowledge—having stuff stored in your memory. Intelligence wasn't valued by Controllers because it was uncontrollable, while knowledge could be doled out or withheld by the proper authorities. Author Elizabeth Taylor describes the process aptly:

> Hour after hour they were made to learn lessons by heart . . .
> until their heads were so tightly crammed with facts that
> thoughts had no room to move in them.

Most schools in America today are still dominated by Controller thinking. There seems to be considerable agreement in America that children should be force-fed a standardized set of facts, to be memorized and regurgitated on a set of nationally standardized multiple-choice tests. This is the thrust of the 'No Child Left Behind' Act of the Bush administration. Such an approach, as Frances Moore Lappé points out, deprives children of precisely those qualities most needed in our changing world.

Marilyn Ferguson even suggests that *"the greatest learning disability of all may be pattern blindness*—the inability to see relationships or detect meaning," and believes that this defect may be caused by our schools.

The Radical Right has been waging a well-funded war against learning for the past twenty years. Wherever they have been able to exert influence, textbooks have been bowdlerized, literary classics banned, public schools deliberately under-funded, and any form of student participation in the learning process severely squelched.

If we look at the books the Radical Right has sought to ban, the message is clear: Integrative culture is the demon they're trying to exorcize. Ibsen's *A Doll's House* (1879), for example, is said to advocate "radical feminism"; *The Diary of Anne Frank* calls for tolerance of all religions; *The Wizard of Oz* contains the subversive idea that "traits such as courage, intelligence, and compassion are personally developed rather than God-given". Other books have been attacked as undermining parental authority, questioning traditional gender roles, or implying that racial injustice occurred in the United States or South Africa. As Jerold Starr points out, textbook publishers have to a very large degree caved in to this pressure, expurgating social and political controversy from American history texts and leaving students ignorant of the issues that concern them most directly.

The Right's assault has meant fewer electives, longer hours, more rote learning, less student participation, and multiple-choice tests that require no thinking but only the regurgitation of information. Courses that require students to think for themselves have been stigmatized as 'frills'. The 1978 Hatch Amendment actually required students to obtain parental consent before they could be asked to express an idea on any subject.

Integrative Education

Controllers felt it important to teach competitiveness, and most conventional schools today still perform that function. This is very poor preparation for the emerging Integrative world.

Corporations spend millions of dollars on workshops that teach teamwork and tolerance for diversity.

And they do this for the bottom line. Yet most schools are still operating on authoritarian models. In the traditional classroom, for example, all the seats are anchored to face permanently toward the central authority.

A model more relevant to today's world is what social psychologist Elliot Aronson calls the Jigsaw Classroom. A class is divided into groups of six students, each of whom is responsible for part of the assignment, and reports his or her individual piece to the other group members.

The only access any member has to the other five assignments is by listening intently to the report of the person reciting.

After doing his or her research, the student meets with students from other groups who have the same assignment. In this group they compare notes, exchange ideas, and hone their presentations. Then they go back to their original group and teach what they've learned. At the end everyone is tested on the entire subject.

This method has been very successful. Poorer students improve dramatically in just a few weeks time, and all students show more confidence, higher self-esteem, and more empathy. Not only do the students enjoy school more, they exhibit less prejudice and negative stereotyping.

In the old industrial economy workers were expected to be as robotic as possible, and rote training in school prepared them to function well on assembly lines. But in today's economy the emphasis is on information, services, invention—demanding imagination, creativity, and social skills—diametrically opposite requirements. Adaptation to the future means retooling our schools to make them relevant to the world we live in.

6 | On Our Psyches: The Illusion of Control

The ego is paranoia institutionalized.
TERENCE McKENNA

Lost my shape, trying to act casual.
DAVID BYRNE

I knew I would have to give up control if I hoped to
get real power, which is the power to adapt.
MICHAEL CONRAD

We like to think of our own organism as a monolithic unity, but each
of us is actually made up of other beings. Ten percent of our dry
body weight consists of bacteria—a few of which have simply taken
up residence, but many of which are essential to our survival.
Bacteria can genetically alter cells, correct defects, and transfer
mutations to other bacteria. Every cell in our body is a complex little
factory, in which millions of bacteria work collectively to maintain
life. They create the energy our bodies need to keep going, and the
wherewithal to repair them. Without them:

> we could not lift a finger . . . it is these swarms of bacteria . . .
> that keep us alive.

Bacteria are the stewards of our bodies. We might not like to dwell on the 100 trillion little creatures that bustle around inside us, working night and day to keep us going, but they're there all the same.

We're also home to a flock of contradictory impulses—thoughts and dreams over which we have no control, body parts that rebel and produce symptoms we don't understand.

Sociologists used to get in a tizzy when anyone compared society to an organism, because they thought it implied some kind of monolithic unity. Today we know how little unity there is in the human organism: how much inner conflict, how much 'class warfare' between the mind and the lowly body; how many rebellions and uprisings; how poor the communication between body and mind at times.

Every human organism is an astonishing enterprise. When you consider the millions of living entities that operate it, and the amount of information it processes, it's a miracle of coordination. The most ordinary organism makes billions of subtle adaptations to its physical environment each day, receiving and organizing billions of bits of data, acquiring, ingesting, and processing several different types of fuel for itself—oxygen, water, food—and healing itself when injured.

Who's The Boss Around Here?

We like to think our minds are in charge of all this, but in fact most of an organism's functions are performed quite well before it can be said to have much of a mind. With regard to 99.99% of what goes on in the human organism the mind doesn't have a clue.

I notice one day that I have a sore on my tongue, for example. I have no idea how I got it. It looks like someone took a chunk out of it and it's hard to ignore, but I try, and finally, in sleep, succeed. The next day I remember it and take a look. It's gone. How was this done? I don't remember giving the order.

And many of the orders I do give seem to be ignored. I play tennis regularly with an aging group of doubles enthusiasts—none of them famous for 100-mile-an-hour serves. Our second serves, in fact, are viewed by the recipients much as a cat views a bird with a broken wing. Yet we win quite a few points off those weak serves. There's too much time to think about all the things you can do to it—opportunity knocks so loudly your return ends up in the net, which is what comes of letting the boss get too involved in day-to-day operations. I've come to accept the fact that my eyes and my arm are better tennis strategists than the 'rational' part of my brain.

Yet we all try to micromanage our bodies.

Up to the age of three a child tends to eat the same amount of food no matter how much you put before her. But by five, a child will eat whatever's there—if it's something she likes—regardless of the size of the portion. This pattern—well established in adults—is a major cause of obesity in our society. Our minds have taken over the job of deciding how much is enough.

Biologist Cindy Engel gives countless examples of how wild animals, suffering from illness, parasites, or vitamin deficiency, will search out plants, animals, insects, soil, or even bones that remedy the problem. Often this remedy is a substance normally avoided as highly toxic, but which is medicinal in small doses. Yet many humans are so out of touch with their bodies they require a machine to tell them what they're feeling and a pharmaceutical company to tell them what to do about it.

When we get the message that we're tired we ignore it and have a cup of coffee. When we get jittery we have a martini. We push and prod, ignore messages we don't want to deal with, try to control our internal functioning with drugs, until our bodies get rebellious and have a sickout in protest.

"No pain, no gain" is the mantra of athletes, runners, dancers, body-builders, and people trying to lose weight. Their bodies are treated like enslaved enemies. In the "gain" part of this equation they fail to factor in long-term damage to the body that results from ignoring pain messages. The "gain" for many athletes is having eighty-year-old bodies at fifty.

The Simpleton

Controller men wanted to make sure they wouldn't be overcome by 'soft' or 'weak' emotions. But what does it mean to 'control yourself' in this way? What part of you is doing the controlling? What part of you is being controlled? Who is it that's micromanaging your body and ignoring pain messages? If I am not my body or my feelings or my desires, who am I? Who is it that's treating body, feelings, and desires as *other*?

Clearly there's a lot of coordination going on below the level of human consciousness or we'd die every time we took a nap. Maybe this unconscious coordinating function is our true 'self'. But when we think or speak about 'self' we're usually referring to a conscious entity—to mind, or what is generally called the ego.

From a DNA viewpoint the individual's only function is to reproduce ("a hen is just the egg's way of making another egg"). As individuals, of course, we take a different view of the matter—seeing our personal survival as an end in itself. When someone doesn't, we think there's something very wrong with him.

To address this issue each of us has a department head that deals with threats to our personal survival. This bit of ourselves we call the ego, and most of us identify with it entirely. When I say, "I told myself" something or other, it's my ego doing the telling and the rest of me getting the lecture.

As the principal instrument of control over oneself and one's environment, Control Culture valued the ego above all other parts of the psyche. And in keeping with the Controller sense of hierarchy, anyone successful—a political leader, a captain of industry, a famous general, scientist, scholar, artist, musician, or writer—was expected to have a 'big ego'. They were seen as having earned the right to be self-absorbed, obsessed with status, desperate for praise, competitive, self-aggrandizing, pompous, and touchy. Of course there have always been successful people who were none of these things, but they tended to be viewed as anomalies ("He acted just like a regular person!").

Some authoritarian cultures actually demanded that those with superior status display their inflated egos—to strut, to bully, to be arrogant, to show contempt. As democracy spread into more and more corners of the globe, however, this expectation tended to decline. People in democracies more often find the strutting of military dictators a source of comedy.

All by Myself

Part of having a 'big ego' is maintaining an illusion of self-suffi-
ciency. Many successful men are gifted amnesiacs when it comes to
remembering those who helped them get there. They often redefine
this assistance not as a gift but as booty—"they didn't help me, I
used them."

The truth is, no mammalian organism is self-sufficient. In their
book *A General Theory of Love*, Lewis, Amini, and Lannon point out
that monkeys and humans raised in isolation cannot function as
adults. Babies learn how to cope emotionally through resonance
with the mother. A toddler who falls, for example, will look to his
mother to find out how serious the fall is—whether to cry or laugh.
The human organism, in other words, is an open loop—its nervous
system develops in relation to others. This means that

In some important ways, people cannot be stable on their own
. . . The mammalian nervous system cannot self-assemble.

Although Zen Buddhism exhorts us to perform every act 'mind-
fully,' most of us are on automatic a good deal of the time. While
the ego is making plans, a healthy organism may get out of bed, turn
off the alarm, go to the bathroom, go jogging, wash, get dressed,
prepare and eat breakfast, drive to work through crowded city
streets, listen to the car radio—constantly making the most complex
adaptations without any help at all from the ego, which may be
entirely absorbed in security issues—that is, thinking about getting
rich, powerful, famous, or loved.

Unlike the rest of the organism the ego is a very simple mechanism. All its intricate thinking and planning is just an elaboration on
one binary distinction—threat vs. no-threat. Computers, which are
also binary, are modeled on the ego.

To say the ego is simple may sound strange. What could be more
complicated than the productions of logical thought? But the fact
that the ego *makes* things complicated doesn't mean the ego *itself* is
complicated, but just the reverse. This is what we mean when we
say a picture's worth a thousand words (an understatement if you've
ever seen a picture digitalized on a computer). The words make

things complicated for us because they're too simple for the task of conveying what the picture shows. The picture *is* complicated, and therefore makes things easy for us to grasp.

Yet most of us are ruled, with varying degrees of tyranny, by our egos. How did this come about? How did such a simpleton gain so much control over something so subtle and complex?

The Commissar of Internal Security

The answer is that in times of danger that binary simplicity is just what the doctor ordered. When a truck's bearing down on us the big picture no longer seems important. We want simple binary answers to questions like run/don't run, left/right, forward/back. And the ego's good at this. In times of stress we give the ego dictatorial powers.

But who defines 'times of stress'? The ego is not so good at deciding how severe a threat is. This, after all, isn't a binary question.

The Roman dictator Cincinnatus was famous because when the crisis he was called in to deal with had passed, he gave up power and went back to his farm. In this he was unique. When the time comes for most emergency leaders to go back to the farm they start to hem and haw and find excuses. Martial law becomes a way of life.

After all, there's always something to be nervous about if you're inclined that way, and how could you *not* be inclined that way if it was your job? How could you justify your existence otherwise? If the threat is gone you'd better find another one, like the Pentagon did when the Soviet Union collapsed.

The ego has the same concern for job security. It says things like: "I know we have a hundred million dollars, but what if we lost it all? We need to make some more!" Or, "I know the bully who beat us up in the third grade is a bank teller in Akron now, but what if he comes back? Better add to our gun collection!" Or, "I know I've slept with three different women this week, but what if tomorrow I'm all alone and unloved, or I become impotent or it turns out I'm gay? Let's find somebody new!" None of this is conscious, of course, for the ego, like all despots, keeps its policy decisions in the dark.

A Permanent State of Siege

The ego maintains excellent records of life-threatening situations. Unfortunately, its filing system makes no distinction between situations that are truly life-threatening today and those that merely felt life-threatening in infancy.

Alienating a parent feels life-threatening for a toddler, and whatever strategy the child stumbled on to avoid losing a parent's love may continue to get the nod from the ego long after the child reaches adulthood. The strategy may be overachieving, underachieving, being meek, being aggressive, being tidy, being a slob—whatever made the child feel safe.

We learn by making mistakes and incorporating that experience. Such learning is deeper and more permanent than any warning, advice, or instruction can ever be. Pediatricians say that a toddler with no bumps and bruises is overprotected—bruises are the way we learn to make our way in the world. An organism that takes risks can learn on its own—it doesn't need to send every little piece of information through Central Processing before acting.

But the ego doesn't like this. It loathes risk of any kind. Its job is to anticipate threats. It's not interested in learning, creating, exploring, adventuring—only in avoiding mistakes.

Internal Memos

When egos become despotic they censor information—a process psychologists call denial, or repression. Only 'relevant' data gets past the censors—information that justifies the ego's control. Like other despots, the ego hates negative feedback, because it always includes the message that it's arrogating too much power to itself.

It doesn't want to hear, for example, that it's driving the body too hard, or subjecting it to too much stress, or harming it with addictions. It doesn't want to hear messages from the unconscious, in the form of dreams or unbidden thoughts, that it's propelling the organism on a life course that will cause untold misery.

It doesn't even want to hear intuitive messages that the organism is entering a dangerous situation. Many people who have been beaten, shot, or raped, for example, report that just before entering a life-threatening situation they had a feeling of foreboding that they ignored or dismissed. In other words, the scouts did their job and the message was delivered to the despot but the despot ignored it.

This is the ultimate irony: that the ego, whose main function is to protect the organism from danger, sometimes—in its obsession with control—fails to do even that. How could this be?

First, the ego is often forced to choose between two dangers—an old chronic one and a new acute one. The old danger is losing parental love. It provokes thoughts like "don't be a wuss, guy", or "be a nice, sweet girl and do what the man tells you". And this old, chronic danger often gets the nod, because it's familiar and the ego knows how to deal with it.

Second, the ego, like all despots, makes no distinction between threats to the organism as a whole and threats to itself. Responding to intuition feels like a challenge to the ego's position, so intuitive reports may be routinely ignored.

What's Good for Me is Good for the Country

To stay in power despots try to create a chronic feeling of crisis—incessantly warning of potential dangers: "The enemies of our nation are everywhere! We must be eternally vigilant!" The ego uses the same strategy. "Don't trust anyone!" it says. "They're all just out for themselves!" It manufactures threats, and claims that if it were weakened the organism would be plunged into chaos. At the same time it tries to centralize control to the point where this claim becomes true.

The ego's fear of losing its grip on the organism is called anxiety. It feels the same as fear of an external danger but no real danger is present. We feel we ought to be doing something to protect ourselves, but we don't know what it is we should be guarding against. This is the function of anxiety: to encourage us to give more power to the ego. Just as a dictator will drum up an enemy threat to shore up his position.

When things reach this pass the ego is no longer a capable leader for the organism—acting against many of the organism's best interests. It has become blind and rigid to the point where not only is the organism in constant stress and misery, but also in increasing danger. The ego's rigidity makes it unable to adapt to changing conditions and its narrowness makes it unable to absorb necessary information. As is so often the case in life, the protector becomes the most serious threat.

Some egos are even unwilling to allow the organism to sleep. Normally an organism will pull the plug on the ego for a third of each day, so that the populace can get its work done without constant government interference. But some tyrannical egos are willing to sacrifice the health of the organism to their own obsession with control.

Many people find themselves in this condition today. At some point early in life they called in the Marines and now can't get rid of them. They're kept in a state of chronic mobilization by being continually reminded of obsolete dangers. The ego may claim that safety lies in being uptight, punctual, and reliable, or that it lies in being slovenly, disorganized, and helpless. What reveals the despot is the consistency—the use of the same strategy in all situations, protecting us from dangers that have long since vanished.

Democratization

As Integrative Culture grows in strength, interest in reducing the relative power of the ego in the human organism grows with it. This is at the center of many spiritual disciplines and the thrust of much 'New Age' literature and practice, as well as an increasingly popular topic in magazines and talk shows. The modern preoccupation with 'expanding your creativity' also demands reducing the ego's power, for the ego can't create—it can only organize what's created.

Some people, in pursuit of enlightenment, approach their egos with revolutionary fervor—attempting a kind of self-decapitation. This usually results in the ego becoming more tyrannical than ever. You can't get rid of your ego—you need it to survive. Democratization of the ego depends not only on nourishing and strengthening the rest of the organism but also on reassuring and relaxing the ego itself.

The ego is quite capable of becoming less rigid and more democratic. Therapists often help people do just that. Give the organism a less centralized, more fluid and flexible structure. Encourage the ego to listen—to the body, to intuition, to feelings. This sometimes happens spontaneously—people mellow as they get older—a sign that the ego is relinquishing a certain amount of control. Unfortunately the opposite may also happen—as the ego encounters the assaults of the aging process it may become more rigid than ever.

But why is it so difficult? The ego, after all, is outnumbered. It may be busy and active two-thirds of every day, but the rest of the organism is at work all the time, keeping the engines going, maintaining, enhancing, repairing. These other components go about their daily business with only occasional interest in what the ego considers important, just as most Americans pay little attention to what's going on in Washington. So why isn't it easier to bring the ego into line?

The Ego-Mafia

Unfortunately, despotic egos don't exist in a vacuum. Each day they encounter other egos, with whom they cooperate to create a world in which ego-despotism will thrive. This unconscious collaboration I call the Ego-Mafia.

The Ego-Mafia is our egos' effort to create a world that reflects themselves more and their organisms less. A simple, binary world that contains as little as possible of the organic messiness that reminds the ego of its dependence on a body. It is the world inhabited by economists and game theorists and people who like to call themselves 'realists'.

It's the Ego-Mafia that replaces the curving, irregular shapes of the organic world with straight lines and right angles and geometric structures—that constructs rectangular buildings and rectangular plots and grid-like cities. If a man lives his life in a box it's a lot easier to believe that his whole being is coextensive with his ego.

> Schools and factories, malls and supermarkets, prisons and hospitals are so often set out as massive concrete lumps in the middle of sea-of-asphalt parking lots, apart from everything, relating to nothing.

We can see the Ego-Mafia at work when gardeners attack

nature with their arsenal of machines. Exuberant hedges are carved into boxes. Grass is caged in rectangular plots, and edgers make certain that no errant tendril of green violates the linearity of the ego's cold universe. Leaf blowers and herbicides eliminate any stray bits of life that venture rudely into forbidden areas. The result is a plastic-looking world, and if the ego had its druthers all this messy growth would be replaced by plastic flowers, plastic hedges, and Astroturf.

Reducing life, spreading death, is the general impact of man-made environments. For the ego dreams of a world without bodies, without emotion, without uncontrolled movement. No animals, plants, clouds, oceans, insects—no "blooming, buzzing confusion", no mystery. It wants a controllable world—a homogeneous world, a world of uniforms and monoculture. It wants a world of simple, mechanical processes—a world in which egos can sort out threat from non-threat without being distracted by the squirmings of living things.

The man-made world we live in today was created by the efforts of the Ego-Mafia to achieve such 'perfection'. Our egos like it, but the other parts of our being aren't too happy with it, for it frustrates our needs for wholeness, balance, adventure, play, passion, and connection. And it's ugly. Man-made environments not only reduce life, they reduce beauty. They seem to have an inherent trend toward drabness, monotony, and clutter. Our craving to 'get away from it all' and 'back to nature' is a recognition of the suffocating and soul-destroying environment created by the unending fears and obsessive control needs of our egos. Dissatisfaction with this environment is one of the springs of Integrative Culture.

Walls

Control Culture created a sympathetic milieu for the Ego-Mafia, and under its sway human energy has been largely expended in fighting against nature—especially our own—as if it were an enemy. Controllers sought control over their feelings by splitting themselves into Mind and Body. They sought control over others by splitting them into Good Guys and Bad Guys. They sought control over the environment by splitting it into Mine and Yours.

The problem is that none of these splits work: Body leaks into Mind, and Mind into Body; Good guys act bad, Bad Guys act good; your river, air, leaves, gophers, noise, water table, etc. are also mine. No matter how many boundary lines we draw and fences we put up, we always share far more than we can divide. Rivers, aquifers, and ecosystems pay no attention to man-made boundaries, and this interconnectedness of life is a headache for anyone trying to control the environment

The mad billionaire Howard Hughes probably achieved as much control over his life and environment as anyone ever has. He was one of the richest men in the world, lived in a state whose political system he virtually owned, and was surrounded by toadies who obeyed his every whim. Yet he spent his days in a dark room that he hardly ever left, watching the same movie, *Ice-Station Zebra* over and over again. He was in miserable physical condition—partly because he was terrified of germs and couldn't stand to be touched—and died of ailments caused by his own obsessions.

Hughes was deeply disturbed by the fact that underground oil and water disregarded property lines. The idea that something of his might be shared with others horrified him. Hughes wanted control, but control can only be achieved through self-limitation, self-constriction, walls.

The wall was a central metaphor for Control Culture. A wall separates, limits, protects, insulates. But unfortunately there's no way to insulate yourself from the bad things around you that doesn't at the same time insulate you from the good things around you. A wall protects but it also imprisons. Every fortress is also a jail.

A Tropical Suburbia

Many years ago I did some consulting for a mining company in South America. Traveling by boat up a winding river through miles of jungle I came upon a mid-sized city built around a bauxite processing plant. On one side of the plant was a suburban community of rolling hills and trees that except for the tropical vegetation could have been in Connecticut. The managers lived here. On the other side of the plant, built largely on flat, open land was a much larger community of small, slightly shabby houses where the workers lived. The only link between the two towns was a bridge across one end of a tailings pond.

Driving through the workers' community on a warm tropical night the streets were filled with groups of people, talking, laughing, dancing, and occasionally providing a Greek chorus for domestic disputes.

Surrounded by a fence, the gate guarded by armed men with dogs, the managers' community was a stark contrast. Driving through it on the same night it seemed deserted. An occasional light could be seen, but not a single person. All were isolated within their homes.

During the heyday of the Controller era every city and town had a wall around it to keep out enemies. Enemies came anyway, and sat outside the walls until the inhabitants were starved into submission. Gated communities—a growing phenomenon in America—are starved in a different way, walled off from the enrichment that comes from being around people who aren't clones of oneself. Homogeneity is stagnation. Evolution depends on the juxtaposition of differences.

Control is achieved primarily by reducing the amount of life in the environment—the amount of variety, complexity, mutability. The impulse to control is hostile to life, and therefore leads regularly to death and destruction; and hence, even greater loss of control, and greater desire for it. Control is an addictive drug, eternally unsatisfying.

Letting Go

In the film *Pushing Tin*, an Air Traffic Controller, driven nearly mad by his job and his obsessive need to control his world, is cured by lying in the wake of a passing jet and being hurled off the runway by the air stream—a reminder of his true place in the larger scheme of things.

Before the 1960s people thought being in control an entirely positive thing. People who were good at 'getting things under control' were admired, if not always enjoyed. New products were advertised as 'giving you control'. Doctors stopped making house calls so they could have more control over the conditions of treatment. Scientists wanted to get as much of the world into their labs as possible so they could do 'controlled' studies. Indeed, control over nature was "almost synonymous with the scientific method". The idea was to isolate variables so their separate impacts could be measured. Life, of course, fails to copy this mechanistic model—nothing ever happens one variable at a time. But it was only in the sixties that the term 'control freak' came into vogue.

In the 1950s advertisers used the slogan "Better living through chemistry" and no one laughed. DDT was eradicating the pesky mosquito, and chemical fertilizers were increasing farm production. Ecology was a term only a few scientists used. There was talk of 'conservation', but this was a Controller concept—whether we saved or exhausted the world's resources, they were ours. We owned them.

Today 'ecology' has become part of everyday speech. It acknowledges that we ourselves are part of nature, not the absentee landlords of it. And Chaos Theory has demoted prediction—once the sacred cow of science—to a merely secular bovine.

Loosening Control in Art

In 1998 two potters, George Dymesich and Danny Farber, built a traditional Japanese kiln in California. They went to a great deal of trouble to create a kiln that they knew was inefficient, unpredictable, and extremely labor-intensive. Why did they do this?

They did it *because* the kiln was unpredictable. They were willing to put up with its inconveniences because they knew that the unknowns in the process were capable of creating works of unparalleled beauty. They sacrificed ego-control to creativity. They were willing to share with Nature the credit for their products.

They're not alone. Allowing chance into the creative process is a concept that has inspired many in the arts. John Cage in music, for example, and in the visual arts Nam June Paik, Yoko Ono and many others. Joseph Bueys created art with a coyote, and Andy Goldsworthy's creations are often interactive with nature.

Improvisation in theatre is, like jazz, a process of collaborative creation, and has become increasingly popular. The golden rules of

Improv are (1) accept any initiation another actor makes toward you, (2) try to make the other actors look good, and (3) since failure is an inevitable part of the process, be good-natured about it.

Giving up control makes available the creativity of others. Inexperienced playwrights sometimes want to direct their own plays so they can be sure everything conforms to their vision. The result is often sterile. Directors, actors, and designers will see creative ways of enhancing the playwright's vision that the playwright never dreamed of. Inexperienced playwrights also write stage directions telling an actor how to do or say something. These are usually ignored by directors because they encourage phony gestures. Good actors will have ways of realizing the playwright's vision that are more natural, and that more powerfully express that vision.

Loosening Control in Farming

On his farm in Japan Masanobu Fukuoka hasn't plowed or turned the earth for 30 years and uses no pesticides or fertilizer or even compost, since "microorganisms and small animals act as nature's tillers." Yet he gets much higher yields than his neighbors who plow and fertilize and spray and irrigate. He doesn't worry about pests because he leaves weeds as a habitat for their insect enemies, and "a natural balance asserts itself." His method of 'do-nothing' farming has spread throughout Japan and is beginning to take hold in China, because of its extremely high yields, the elimination of the need for fertilizer, the preservation of the soil, and the low amount of labor required. This technique is based on a concept diametrically opposed to that of the last six millennia: cooperating with the soil rather than bullying it.

Dominique Browning, an avid gardener, found herself in the grip of a severe depression for years after her husband left her. When she finally ventured into her garden after recovering five years later she was shocked to find it flourishing, and realized that the severe control she'd exercised over it in the past had little to do with the garden's health.

Modern American agriculture has been increasingly subject to corporate control, to the point where the average farmer's largest expenses are those paid to chemical companies. But this dependence, as Michael Pollan points out, is itself a result of the desire to exert control over nature by mass-producing single crops (the approach that created the Irish potato famine). Crop monotony is a magnet for pests, which require pesticides, and the need to control weeds requires herbicides, which deplete the soil, requiring chemical fertilizers, and so on. The mania for control is ultimately self-defeating.

The domestication of animals provides a similar example: the more animals are penned in and controlled, the less ability they have to fight disease and parasites—they can't, for example, forage for the medicinal plants that they would normally seek out in the wild— and have to be continually and heavily medicated as a result.

A movement called 'grass farming'—that is, letting cows out to graze rather than cutting the hay and schlepping it to their stalls— is currently spreading in the Midwest. Cows treated this way are healthier, produce and distribute more manure, and the farmers save money on machines and fuel. It seems absurdly obvious, and illustrates the way in which our desire for control can blind us and subject us to needless labor. Grass farming has also created a sense of community, as farmers get together to share their experiences. This is in sharp contrast to their bottom-of-the-pyramid relation to chemical companies and the Department of Agriculture.

Evolutionary success depends on variety, adaptability, versatility. The attempt to reduce nature to some simple, monolithic, geometric pattern is ultimately suicidal.

> The gardener knows . . . that his garden fence and path and cherished geometries hold in their precarious embrace. . . a great teeming effulgence of wildness—of plants and animals and microbes leading their multifarious lives . . . of everything affecting everything else.

The more we try to control something the more we limit its options, its possibilities. As Janine Benyus points out, digital computers can never equal the brain because they're based on the wrong principle: linear control. They have to "freeze out all side effects".

> The power to be unpredictable and to try new approaches is

what gives life the right stuff. Our computers, by comparison, are in shackles. Computers can't brook too much change . . . No self-organizing allowed.

A Grandiose Fantasy

As recently as 1990 theorists were worrying rather pompously about our ability to 'destroy' nature. But the conditions for life on this planet were created and are maintained by bacteria—which constitute the overwhelming majority of all living matter on the planet—and they will continue to support life in some form, with or without us. As Andrew Knoll points out, "we have evolved to fit into a bacterial world, and not the reverse". Planetary life will balance itself—our choice is merely whether that balancing will entail our participation or our demise.

We "overestimate our own agency in nature" says Michael Pollan in his best-selling book, *The Botany of Desire*. When we talk about domesticating species or 'inventing' agriculture it "leaves the erroneous impression that we're in charge" when we're also being manipulated.

All these plants, which I'd always regarded as the objects of my desire, were also, I realized, subjects, acting on me, getting me to do things for them they couldn't do for themselves.

He sees domestication as a "clever evolutionary strategy" of plants and animals—similar to the ways plants seduce bees, birds, humans, and other animals into spreading their seeds around.

Loosening Control in Business

When Apple tried to make its operating systems a scarce resource it fell on hard times. And when Citibank tried to maintain a closed network of ATM machines, several smaller banks banded together to form an open ATM network, which Citibank was ultimately forced to join because it was larger.

Success in today's economic world often comes from relinquishing control rather than exerting it. With an economy based more and more on communication, it's no longer profitable to hang on to things and restrict their use. You want to make them accessible to as many people as possible.

The new economy, says Kevin Kelly, rewards open systems.

> The more networks a thing touches, the more valuable it becomes.

The significance of this change is huge. It reverses the whole thrust of economic behavior. The old industrial economy rewarded those who were controlling, tight-fisted, and domineering. The network economy rewards egalitarianism, openness, and an experimental attitude.

> The new organizations are, in fact, always tending to be slightly out of control, their structures flexing, their people innovating. Nonlinear systems . . . tend to feed back on themselves, creating unforeseen results.

One reason we try to control our environment is to avoid mistakes. But mistakes are the most important way we learn. Successful Internet executives say that to be successful in the new network economy you need to screw up, to experience failure. People who consistently avoid this aren't respected.

Adam Kahane, talking of the new South Africa, observed that:

> People seemed to be much more effective when they gave up the illusion of being in control, and instead tried to work things through with others. When they held onto the need to deal only with what was under their control, they weren't very effective.

'Letting go' doesn't mean becoming passive. It means putting the energy that's usually tied up in wall-maintenance into give-and-take. As Mary Parker Follett stresses, true cooperation demands honest self-assertion as well as openness to the needs and ideas of others. 'Letting go' means letting out along with letting in. It means communicating what you really want, not just what you say you want.

Integrative Culture is a process of substituting open-ended cooperative communication for coercive limitation—of substituting "self-creating coherence" for socially imposed or self-imposed bondage.

7 | On Warfare: The Decaying Glory

> "It means the rage went on when the war ended,
> does it?"
> "Yes. Of course the rage went on. We're not just in
> a war we don't understand. We're in a *life*
> we don't understand."
> ROSE TREMAIN

> Life did not take over the globe by combat,
> but by networking.
> MARGULIS AND SAGAN

Anyone who had said in the 1930s and 1940s—when the world was filled with dictators—that democracy was going to sweep the globe, would have been laughed out of the room, yet from this distance we can see that the age of European dictators was just a momentary setback in the steady spread of democratic systems throughout the industrial world. And the fact that war is so much in the news today doesn't change the fact that, from a long-range perspective, war is on the way out. Irrelevant to a woven world and useless against terrorism (as Russia, Israel, and the United States have all been learning the hard way), war has become obsolete.

On March 3rd, 2003, speaking in San Francisco on the eve of the U.S. invasion of Iraq, Dr. Robert Muller, former Assistant Secretary General of the UN, stunned his audience of peace activists and anti-war protesters by his optimism:

> Never before in the history of the world has there been a
> global, visible, public, viable, open dialogue and conversation
> about the very legitimacy of war.

To Muller, who had witnessed the UN's founding, the change in global attitudes toward war was more significant than the fact that an anachronistic militarist in the world's most heavily-armed nation could ignore the overwhelming majority of world opinion and the most massive peace demonstrations in history and invade a small weak Mid-East country. In the past a nation going to war was no one else's business.

There are three reasons why war has declined in acceptance today: (1) the growth of the global economy, (2) the loss of glamour, and (3) the ever-increasing involvement of civilians.

1. We Have Met the Enemy . . .

When NATO planes bombed Belgrade in the spring of 1999, the managing director of McDonald's in Yugoslavia redesigned the company logo by putting a Serbian cap and Serbian flag on it. McDonald's employees handed out free cheeseburgers at anti-American rallies, set up a bomb shelter in a restaurant basement, and donated part of the restaurant's profits to bombing victims. Although McDonald's is entirely American-owned, the Serbian managing director was praised by his American superiors for his ingenuity in staying open and making a profit.

We might trace the earliest seeds of Integrative Culture back to the very beginning of trade, which linked alien cultures together, created a diffusion of ideas, increased understanding, and demanded a higher level of trust between partners than the shifting alliances of Controller warlords. But Integrative Culture couldn't really take hold until international corporations had become commonplace.

International trade has mushroomed during the last thirty years. Today there are more than 40,000 multinational corporations.

> Boundaries of every sort are coming down. Political, economic,
> and ideological borders among nations continue to erode.

The whole concept of 'imports' and 'exports' is dated: Companies today are constantly importing from and exporting to themselves. Almost anywhere we attack today we're attacking our own companies, our own products, our own creations, our own citizens.

War is no Longer Good for Business

In the spring of 2002 India and Pakistan were threatening to go to war with each other, and the rhetoric coming from India was particularly belligerent. Then the rhetoric was abruptly toned down and the tension de-escalated:

India's huge software and information technology industry . . . essentially told the Nationalist Indian government to cool it.

A similar situation arose in 2004 between Taiwan and mainland China. Campaign rhetoric in Taiwan about independence—a concept that has Beijing reaching for its warheads—became muted as Taiwanese businessmen pointed out Taiwan's increasing economic dependence on the Chinese market.

For thousands of years war was profitable. Nations enlarged themselves through war. Land could be acquired, cities and seaports captured, valuables looted. Individuals could become wealthy—acquiring grants of land through valor in battle.

But modern war has become unprofitable for all but a handful of war-related industries; and for a nation the advantages of winning have all but vanished. The losers in the two World Wars emerged stronger than many of the winners. No nation, however powerful, can conquer and hold another nation today, as Russia found out in Afghanistan and the United States discovered in Vietnam, and is having to learn all over again in Iraq. Changing economic conditions have made warfare between major industrial nations an antiquated concept. The global economy:

increases the incentives for not making war and increases the costs of going to war in more ways than in any previous era in modern history.

The five highest per-capita income nations today—Norway, Denmark, Switzerland, Ireland, and Luxemburg—are not even military powers. War no longer advances a nation, but holds it back. The World Bank, the World Trade Organization, regional trade organizations, multinational corporations—all are seeking ways to minimize violent conflicts, for obvious reasons of self-interest.

War today is a symptom of backwardness. While nations mired in poverty and fanaticism are busy making macho gestures and killing one another, Western Europe—once a luxuriant breeding ground of mutual slaughter—has a common market and currency.

The United States is the only exception to this trend—primarily because for decades it's been able to wage wars on small, weak Third-World nations with little fear of retaliation. But the attacks of 9/11 made it clear that retaliation can come in non-military forms.

2. Fading Glamour

In World War I soldiers were sent off to fight with brass bands and cheering crowds as if they were a football team heading off to a championship game. For while there have always been those who decried the horrors of war, before the 20th century it had considerable glamour. Soldiers fought hand-to-hand and their deeds were celebrated in epic poems and ballads. Inspirational books for young boys were written about their exploits, and in popular novels, plays, and operettas written before 1914 the cavalry officer was the preferred choice for the blushing ingénue.

History itself was largely a record of battles. Like the sports page of a modern newspaper, it was all about who won, who lost, what individual heroes stood out, what their feats were.

But the great epic heroes carried swords, not guns. How could you be a swashbuckler with a gun? After all, the most devout sissy can do as much damage with an automatic weapon as Rambo. Hollywood Westerns tried to make gun-fighting heroic, but it never had the inspirational power of hand-to-hand combat. In *Star Wars* the antagonists were reduced to having sword fights with fluorescent bulbs.

Martial Arts and Samurai films have moved in to fill the gap, and even futuristic space dramas often have to fall back on old-fashioned fistfights during their climactic battles. Both hero and villain always seem to have an attack of butterfingers at the crucial moment: their guns, phasers, or whatever, go flying, and they have to duke it out.

The Purification of Homicide

As a killing system, hand-to-hand combat was 'corrupted', in Mumford's sense, by elements of skill that were carryovers from hunter-gatherer days—skills used in gathering, fishing, hunting, and avoiding large predators. Hunting in its original form—before modern weapons reduced it to the equivalent of shooting fish in a barrel—required characteristics almost the opposite of those needed for battle: flexibility, sensitivity, empathy, subtlety, and a profound knowledge of, and appreciation for, nature.

But as technology made killing more efficient—more 'purified'— abilities like quickness, agility, good peripheral vision, good hand-eye coordination, and so on, became less and less important:

Swiftness, skill, cunning, and bravery were rendered largely irrelevant.

All the skill in the world won't prevent you being killed by a land mine or a bomb or a shell. The development of better and better means of killing people has taken the glamour out of war. Today machines do the killing, and tanks and bombers can never achieve the appeal of the sword-wielding hero on horseback. And it would be hard to imagine anything less courageous than dropping bombs upon, or firing missiles into, a community where children are the most frequent victims—a form of aggression in which the perpe-trator is protected even from seeing the results of the carnage he has inflicted on his unsuspecting targets.

3. Enter Civilians

Beginning with World War II and the widespread use of aerial bombing, all wars have been wars against civilians. Today the macho threats that nations hurl at each other can be translated as: "if you kill my women and children I'll kill your women and children", which doesn't quite have the heroic ring of ancient battle challenges.

Atrocities are no longer merely an occasional result of war, but are intrinsic. It isn't possible to wage war today without slaughtering large numbers of children. Even during peacetime children all over the world are being killed and maimed by leftover land mines. Guns are so powerful today that a bullet fired at an Iraqi insurgent can go right through him and kill a child playing half a block away. All modern wars are atrocities.

Any bombing kills children. We call it 'acceptable collateral damage' since it isn't our children. We feel innocent of crimes against humanity because our military leaders clearly state our intent not to target civilians, but this is disingenuous, for in the same breath we're told that collateral damage is inevitable and must be expected. Most drunk drivers are also innocent of the intent to kill, but we jail them anyway, for operating a lethal weapon they can't control. The simple truth is that any declaration of war by anyone today is a statement of intent to commit crimes against humanity.

One reason the United States lags so far behind other industrial nations in committing ourselves to international peace programs is that American civilians in the 20th century never had to face the kind of large-scale civilian slaughter and destruction that war can bring—the violence and misery most European and Asian nations have suffered through being invaded and/or bombed. Eighty to ninety percent of Europeans polled opposed the war on Iraq, while a majority of Americans supported it. This difference is probably due to the fact that Americans have never had to experience 'acceptable collateral damage'.

The global trend away from war has expressed itself in two ways:

(1) directly, through the growth of international institutions and international law;

(2) indirectly, in the global cultural trend toward dissolving old boundaries and tearing down traditional walls.

International Peace-Seeking

During most of the 20th century peace was a little like the weather—
everyone talked about it but no one did anything about it. Everyone
said they were all for peace, but kept fighting—insisting it was the
other guy that made war necessary. In parts of the world this is still
true.

During the 1990s, with the end of the Cold War, it seemed as if
people were taking peace more seriously. Even in places like
Northern Ireland and Korea, where for decades war seemed like the
normal state of affairs, people began to act as if it needed to end.
The Wall Street Journal in March 2000 claimed—oxymoronically
and quite prematurely—that peace was "on the march."

> Wars between nations are becoming more rare . . . even civil
> wars . . . are being settled more quickly.

During the 2000 rapprochement between the two Koreas,
stores were selling out stocks of the sunglasses and worker's uni-
form Kim Jong Il had worn in his television talk to the South
Korean public, and couldn't keep up with the demand for books
on North Korea and its leader—so eager were the Koreans for an
end to the conflict. And at the 2000 Summer Olympics the two
Koreas marched together holding a single flag. They continued to
cooperate in trade expansion and the clearing of land mines even
as Washington and North Korea engaged in an extended period of
trash-talking.

When wars broke out in Third World nations, international
forces were intervening to snuff them out. Regional conflicts that
had once been nourished and funded by the Cold War superpowers,
were being 'ghettoized' and their participants discouraged by the
withdrawal of investments.

This is one reason why opposition to the Bush administration's
invasion of Iraq was so widespread around the world. Peace was
spreading, and although terrorist attacks by individuals of every race
and persuasion were occurring in all parts of the globe, the world
seemed to be settling down. An unprovoked attack on another

country was seen as archaic—something only backward, undemocratic countries did.

Robert O'Connell observes that war evolved in an economic context that was almost exclusively agrarian, and sees its decline as a result of the waning of this context. But the cultural context has also changed. As women gain more power in the world, their prevailing opposition to war is making itself felt, and as democracy covers the globe, people are having more and more say over whether they want to be killed or not. For the most part, war only persists in parts of the globe where women are still oppressed and authoritarian governments prevail. The United States—the only major nation that has consistently attacked other nations during the last three decades—is a glaring exception to this rule, but as noted before, its civilian population has never been at risk from the bombers and tanks of other nations.

Today most people in the world view war the way we view crime. They don't think it's going to disappear, any more than we think crime will disappear, but when fighting breaks out people expect someone to do something about it. The world has begun to expect peace, and to regard war as unacceptable, rather than simply a part of life. So strong is this new attitude that it's even beginning to chip away at the hoary concept of national sovereignty.

New Concepts in International Law

In 1999 Augustus Pinochet, the notorious dictator of Chile from 1973 to 1990, was arrested in England at the request of a Spanish judge, Baltasar Garzon, who has also sought the arrest of high-ranking Argentine military officers and a former president. These men—even when they've been given amnesty in their own countries—can no longer travel freely in countries that are part of Interpol, who would be obliged to arrest them. Legal scholars say even carrying diplomatic passports will not protect the guilty.

[The arrest] shows the growing significance of international human rights law, suggesting that officials accused of atrocities have fewer places to hide these days.

Before World War II the concept of war crimes would have been inconceivable. And conflicts between a state and its citizens were considered nobody else's business. Today there's a

mounting belief in much of Europe and North America that human rights matter more than national sovereignty—that no leaders, whether democratically chosen or self-appointed, have the right to slaughter their citizens.

The International Covenant on Civil and Political Rights, which became law in 1976, has influenced new national constitutions in Africa, Asia, Latin America and Eastern Europe, and the International Tribunal is gaining momentum and prestige as it prosecutes high-level Balkan and African war criminals.

Today's routine discourse of human rights could not have been imagined fifty years ago.

But these slender gains may in the long run be less important than a more indirect attitudinal change taking place around the world.

Disappearing Walls

Back in the 1960s John Gardner wrote a book called *Grendel*, about the monster slain by Beowulf. What was different about the book is that it was told from the monster's point of view. By the end of the century this practice of telling old stories from the point of view of someone other than the traditional hero had become commonplace. Tom Stoppard's *Rosencrantz and Guildenstern Are Dead*, Marion Zimmer Bradley's *The Mists of Avalon*, Jean Rhys's *Wide Sargasso Sea*, Jane Smiley's *A Thousand Acres*, Gregory Maguire's *Wicked*, and *Confessions of an Ugly Stepsister*, Paula Vogel's *Desdemona: The Story of a Handkerchief*, Anita Diamant's *The Red Tent*, Rebecca Reisert's *The Third Witch*, Sena Jeter Naslund's *Ahab's Wife*, and Alice Randall's *The Wind Done Gone*, are just a few.

This trend may seem trivial, but it's symptomatic of a conceptual change—a mental broadening—that has taken other, more dramatic forms.

The sixties saw the emergence of a series of liberation movements that expanded rights and opportunities for previously
stereotyped, marginalized, and suppressed segments of the population—beginning with the Civil Rights Movement and spreading to
other ethnic minorities, then to women, the disabled, and gays and
lesbians. This was another series of walls coming down—part of the
process of reintegrating as equals people who had been excluded or
placed in a stigmatized 'lower' category. Hate crimes became a legal
concept.

During the same period people became more curious about how
other cultures work, particularly those most different from our own,
looking perhaps to rediscover benefits our own culture lacks. Books
about Pygmies, Bushmen, Australian aborigines, and indigenous
American tribes were bestsellers.

Kipling said "East is East and West is West, and never the
twain shall meet"—a characteristic Controller pronouncement—
but time has proven once again what a risky word 'never' is. A
religious rapprochement between East and West began in the sixties with Thomas Merton—a popularizing Catholic monastic, who
became interested in Buddhism and Yoga—and continued with
Matthew Fox, Alan Watts, Joseph Campbell, and many others
who have stressed the underlying commonalities of differing spiritual traditions.

What these phenomena have in common is an expansion of
consciousness—of commonality, of the boundaries of "we". Since
war demands that we define some group of people as 'other', not
like us, preferably evil and/or not quite human, Control Culture
creates rigid boundaries, the better to avoid seeing the humanity of
others—to avoid recognizing them as kindred in any way. One of
the most profound trends of the past fifty years has been the dissolving of such boundaries. Control Culture fueled itself on
exclusions, but Integrative Culture gains its momentum from
*in*clusions.

Sorry About That

There seemed to be a passion in the 1990s for public apologies
by governments and institutions guilty of old atrocities. The

Japanese apologized for Pearl Harbor. The United States apologized for putting Japanese-Americans in concentration camps. The Germans apologized for the Holocaust. The Catholic Church in Brazil apologized for oppressing minorities there. The Pope apologized for the Inquisition. A group of Christians from Texas even went to Lebanon for a 'Reconciliation Walk' to apologize for the Crusades.

All this apologizing might have seemed ridiculous, but it revealed a very modern impulse. All these atrocities shared a denial of the humanity of some group of people. The craze for apology was a way of reconnecting with designated non-persons.

In 1999 Veterans from the United States, Britain, France, Germany, Japan, and Vietnam dedicated a village near Hanoi to house Vietnamese children suffering from birth defects caused by Agent Orange, and other returning Americans have been warmly welcomed. In 1997 an American woman—ignoring warnings that she would be raped or killed—hitchhiked safely from one end of that nation to the other, with many friendly encounters.

Even with Other Species

Right after World War II interest in animal studies burst academic boundaries with the popular books of Konrad Lorenz, and in the sixties this developed into an enthusiasm for making connections with other species. Field workers began living in the wild with chimps, gorillas, orangutans, wolves, grizzly bears, elephants—not only to learn how they live and communicate, but to make personal contact and share that experience with the general public. Jane Goodall and Dian Fossey became familiar names as they learned the ways of primates and used this knowledge to establish their own relationships with them. Others learned to communicate with apes through sign language.

Separation from the rest of the animal kingdom—indeed from the rest of nature—lay at the heart of Control Culture. While hunter-gatherers throughout the world identified deeply with animal species, reminders of our animal nature were a constant source of embarrassment for humans once Control Culture had taken hold. The names of animals—especially domesticated ones—

are still used to express contempt for others. Although we are obviously fauna, Controllers were determined to deny our membership in that category. It was vital to the whole edifice of Control Culture to claim that humans were somehow qualitatively different from animals, and an array of conceptual walls was erected to serve this end.

But during the 20th century the many Berlin Walls erected to distinguish ourselves from other members of the animal kingdom—the boundary of language, the boundary of tool-making, the boundary of symbol-making, the boundary of logic and reasoning, the boundary of culture-creation—have crumbled one by one. Chimps use tools and sign language, sea lions use logic, and cultural differences between groups in the same species have been found even among rats, birds, and fish. The breakdown of elephant societies through poaching and human encroachment has been found to produce violent adolescent gangs and PTSD symptoms, just as with humans. Biologists have been humbled to discover that our genetic makeup—which they expected to be ten times as complex as that of the roundworm—was less than twice as complex. Our closeness to other forms of life is getting harder and harder to deny.

This expansion of our ability to identify with other forms of life—the willingness to put ourselves in the role of the other—is a key index of the growth of Integrative Culture, and a vitally important one. For as we put up more and more walls between ourselves and the rest of life we become less and less alive. To be completely disconnected from animals, plants, and insects is to be completely dead.

Learning from Neighbors

For thousands of years humanity's relationship to the horse was one of domination. Horses had to be 'broken' before they could be ridden. You had to 'show them who's boss', and they were tethered, trussed up, hobbled with weighted sacks, and whipped repeatedly to achieve this goal, which usually took weeks. Monty Roberts, a horse whisperer, revolutionized this process. Roberts observed wild horses and learned how they used their bodies to communicate. By imitating the signals with which mares manage young rebellious mustangs, he got a wild horse to accept saddle, bridle, and rider in 30 minutes. But even when he became world-famous, and his techniques widely copied, his abusive father—a particularly brutal 'broncobuster', was unconvinced. "Keep doing it that way and they'll get you", he said—illustrating the degree to which dominating behavior is rooted in fear. Despite many publications and demonstrations, Roberts' technique was rejected and scoffed at everywhere until his technique was endorsed by Queen Elizabeth after demonstrations with her stable. Not surprisingly, women were much more open to his approach than men.

We often expect new connections will complicate our lives, but as this example illustrates, the reverse is often true. A lot of wasted energy is required to sustain artificial barriers.

Furthermore, holding ourselves apart from other species requires us to be perpetually reinventing the wheel. In recent years, for example, pharmacologists have been paying more attention to the way animals in the wild maintain a balanced diet and heal themselves when ailing—recognizing that animals, who have lived for countless millennia in their habitats, know better than we do which foods are healthy, which are poisonous, and which are medicinal. In this way pharmacologists are merely copying the habits of hunter-gatherers:

> For 99 percent of the time that humans have been on Earth, we watched the ways of animals to ensure our own survival.

The Big Mix

On February 14, 2001, public radio carried two stories back to back. One reported that right-wing nationalists in India were mounting violent protests against the increasingly popular observance of Valentine's Day by young Indians. The second featured the German director Werner Herzog raving about a new Korean film to an American audience.

People used to worry that the world was getting Americanized, with McDonalds and Coke in every corner of the globe. They didn't anticipate that Chinese, Japanese, Italian, French, Thai,

Vietnamese, Indian, Moroccan, and a dozen other foreign cuisines would be covering the United States at the same time. African-Americans in large numbers have become Muslims, while Muslims in Jordan are celebrating Ramadan with crescent-shaped Christmas-type lights, greeting cards, parties, and gifts. In Dubai women wear thongs under traditional black robes. Movies have become increasingly international, as has music, with unpredictable blends, like Afro-Celtic and Russian Bluegrass. The number of international phone calls more than sextupled in a decade and contact through the Internet is growing even faster. We're living today in a world in which every individual is bound by subtle but increasingly visible ties to everyone else on the planet.

The Control Culture Strikes Back

The Controller must have an enemy. It's the only way he can make sense out of his world. That's why dualistic religions and belligerent patriotism have always had such appeal. U.S. Cold Warriors and the Politburo supported and reinforced each other, as do Arab and Israeli hard-liners. One side can always be counted on to commit some violent outrage whenever the other side seems ready to make peace. It takes very little time for enemies at war to begin to resemble one another, no matter how much they try to differentiate themselves.

Resistance to the spread of Integrative Culture with regard to war and combat takes three forms: the persistence of Controller fantasies, the persistence of Controller language, the persistence of Controller behavior.

Not all of these holdovers should be viewed with alarm by Integrative enthusiasts. Integrative Culture will only thrive if there are Controller residues within it. This is particularly true of fantasy, which is often a great help in easing transitions in times of change.

I. Persistence in Fantasy

Since there's less and less place for them in today's civilized world, men saturated in the Controller tradition often take refuge in violent cinematic fantasies—fantasies about the brutal dark ages of the past, or the equally brutal dark ages of an imagined post-apocalyptic future, where civilization has broken down and militaristic values once again make sense. Many look longingly into space for the threats that would reinstate the value of killing.

This dream of a world once again engaged in perpetual combat reflects the irrelevance of the Controller ethic to the main currents of modern life. Fantasies of this kind serve to ward off the feeling of obsolescence. Christian fundamentalists repress the reality of the Integrative future with fantasies of Armageddon, and dream of a 'holy war' with Islam.

One of the appeals of Control Culture was the simplicity of its worldview. Although I was a child at the time, I remember my reaction when the Japanese attacked Pearl Harbor and the United States entered World War II. Life, which had been complex and often confusing before, was transformed into a thing of comforting simplicity. Everything was subordinated to winning the war—all complications instantly dissolved. (The same singleness of purpose is one of the appeals of drug addiction.) Though life became richer when the war ended, I've always understood the simplistic appeal of Controller dualism.

II. Persistence in Language

Controllers tend to envision life as an unending, stagnant battle between hostile forces, and this vision is preserved by our archaic linguistic habits. Democratic politics are still defined in military terms—an attempt to garner votes is a 'campaign', and the language used to describe it ("so-and-so took Nevada", "a bitter battle for Iowa", "a veteran of many congressional battles") could easily be mistaken for a military report.

In the business world the verbal carnage continues, with corporate 'raiders' and 'empires' and price 'wars' and advertising 'campaigns'. Sales 'forces' 'invade' each other's 'territories'. Even charities have fund 'drives'. We have no way to talk to each other without using military language. A major success is called a 'blockbuster' after a World War II bomb, and a major failure is a 'dud', a bomb that fails to detonate. We even 'fight' tooth decay and static cling.

Most of this is harmless, and it would be ridiculous to try to expunge Controller metaphors from our language (coerciveness of that kind is in itself a symptom of the Controller mentality). These metaphors enrich our language and the contradictions they present help anchor Integrative Culture. At the same time we need to be aware how they influence our thinking. We've seen the limiting effect military language has on medicine, and Deborah Tannen shows how military metaphors frame American media—who tend to stigmatize as wishy-washy any signs of statesmanlike behavior by public figures.

David Riesman used to say that debating contests were foolish because they assumed there were only two sides to a question, and this is what handicaps the Controller in a complex and changing world. Collapsing the world into two dimensions makes depth perception impossible, and making everything an either/or issue squeezes out all opportunities for solution.

Prisoners of Language

There are 'wars' on poverty, drugs, and crime—language that may have something to do with why these programs always fail. The 'war' on terrorism is cast in the same mold. Israel has been conducting a war on terrorism for decades, and if war were the best strategy for dealing with terrorism, Israel would be the safest place in the world to live.

The use of military metaphors tends to block creativity and limit our imagination when we approach the world's problems. You can't shoot your way out of ignorance, poverty, ill health, or environmental destruction.

The Vietnam War, costing thousands of American lives and millions of Vietnamese lives, might have ended before it began were it not for Lyndon Johnson's fear of appearing 'weak'. Before he escalated the war Johnson confided to those closest to him that he knew it was un-winnable, that it would prevent him from achieving his domestic policy goals, and would destroy him politically. But he felt he couldn't back down. He was fatally susceptible to the taunting comments of hawks, especially Joe Alsop's statement that he "lacked Kennedy's guts." Although he knew the war was hopeless Johnson was trapped by his own machismo.

The irony is that Kennedy—far from playing chicken with Krushchev during the Cuban missile crisis—had actually made a statesmanlike concession to him: agreeing to remove American missiles in Turkey that had been aimed at the Soviet Union. This concession was of course kept secret at the time, so that the public could still view the event in macho terms. But the cold warriors of the Pentagon and CIA were aware of the concessions and continued to view Kennedy as a traitor for refusing to launch the preemptive strike on the Soviet Union they were demanding.

Politicians and the media have a strong bias in favor of behavioral rigidity—to the point of seeing blind persistence in bankrupt policies as a virtue. In the 2004 presidential campaign the Bush administration continually attacked Kerry for having changed his mind about the Iraq war. Bush touted 'staying the course' as if it were superior to the ability to listen to warnings, adapt to change, or learn from one's mistakes. The captain of the *Titanic* stayed the course, and if staying the course were seen as a virtue in the private sector medals would be given to executives who refused to adopt new technologies and went bankrupt. 'Sticking to your guns' is just another way of being stuck.

We need to begin using metaphors that are relevant to the interdependent world we inhabit. Instead of newspaper headlines saying that someone was 'firm' in a negotiation, perhaps we need to use more appropriate words like 'rigid', 'close-minded', 'mulish' and 'pig-headed'.

III. Persistence in Behavior

There's an old Controller saying: "my enemy's enemy is my friend." This notion was central to Cold War thinking and has led to costly foreign policy mistakes, such as building up Saddam Hussein's military capability to fight Iran, or building up Osama bin Laden's terrorist organization to harass the Soviets in Afghanistan.

Dubious Friends

Only a few years after the elder Bush administration gave Saddam Hussein the wherewithal to manufacture weapons of mass destruction we were at war with him, and only a few years after the CIA set up a terrorist training camp for Osama bin Laden in Afghanistan (then described as a 'freedom fighter' against the Communist evil) we were bombing that same camp in retaliation for his attacks on our embassies in Kenya and Tanzania; and a few years after that we were trying to track him down for the 9/11 massacre. American taxpayers paid billions to prop up these 'enemy's enemies' and then has had to pay many billions more trying to destroy them.

The converse motto, "my enemy's friend is my enemy," was also popular during the Cold War—often creating enemies where none existed. These two mottoes formed the concept of 'linkage' developed by Nixon and Kissinger. 'Linkage' meant simply that no issue could be decided on its merits, but only on the degree to which it made trouble for the Soviet Union.

Nations have always made alliances, but the purpose of these alliances varies widely. Controller alliances are formed for one purpose only—to increase one's advantage in war. Integrative alliances, on the other hand, are usually made to increase trade. These purposes often overlap, of course, but it's important to understand the distinction. Integrative alliances tend to be self-perpetuating—that is, they bring nations closer together by increasing their economic interdependence. Controller alliances, on the other hand, tend to be short-lived and constantly shifting, like those of Afghan or Somali warlords. Today's allies are tomorrow's enemies and vice versa. In a shrinking world, the Controller approach has come to seem like an expensive luxury.

Those who talk lovingly of 'the American Empire' are operating with a model of the planet that is 50—perhaps even 100—years out of date. A model in which the interests of one national entity could conceivably be considered separately from all the others.

"Solving the Wrong Problem Precisely"

In the years before World War II, France built what it considered to be an impregnable line of defense on its border with Germany—the Maginot Line. Designed for the trench warfare of World War I, it didn't even slow the Germans down.

In the American Civil War, Army manuals taught Napoleonic tactics . . . even though they were suicidal against rifled muskets. . . . In Iraq, the Army's marquee high-tech weapons are often sidelined while the enemy kills and maims Americans with bombs wired to garage-door openers or doorbells.

Generals are famous for preparing for the last war, and the Pentagon today is no exception. Our military expertise is largely devoted to what Ian Mitroff calls "solving the wrong problem precisely".

The only serious threat to the United States today is from international terrorism, against which our trillion-dollar war-making machine is useless. Tanks, planes, ships, artillery—not to mention the expensive and unworkable missile defense system—can't stop a terrorist from sending anthrax through the mail, or contaminating a water supply, or booby-trapping a building. Using an army to combat terrorism exemplifies a common failing of authoritarian bureaucracies: they tend to do what they know how to do rather than what needs to be done.

An old Sufi tale tells of a man who is discovered by a friend scrabbling around in the dirt outside his house. When the friend asks him what he's doing he says, "I dropped my key in my house and I can't find it." "But if you dropped it in your house, why are you looking out here?" the friend asks. "The light's better out here," is the reply.

Defining terrorism as United States vs. Enemy Nation rather than World vs. Criminals is a good example of "the light's better out here."

John Arquilla, professor of analysis at the Naval Postgraduate School in Monterey, California, argues that the founding of the Department of Homeland Security compounds this error—that a huge bureaucratic hierarchy is

a clumsy tool to use against a nimble network: it takes networks to fight networks.

Current administration policy, he says, is organized around two erroneous Controller assumptions, both of which have led to actions that are fatally counter-productive:

First, the focus on attacking nations has caused us to be distracted from the prime mission of ripping apart terror networks . . . A resistance network has the power to prevail against an enemy whose strategy is based on territorial conquest. The second problem . . . is that as networks become targets, we concentrate far too much on going after their leaders . . . We must see that networks are about individual initiative and creativity rather than about "great man" leader- ship. This has already been proved true in cutting-edge business networks over the past decade. Now we know that it is true of terrorist organizations as well.

A number of terrorist leaders—in Israel, Indonesia, and Iraq— have been captured or killed, without any noticeable impact on terrorist activities. The concept of fighting terrorism by killing its leaders derives from an antiquated Controller concept of a world made up of pyramid-type organizations. Networks are an Integrative phenomenon and cannot be countered with Controller techniques. In a conflict between a network and a bureaucracy, a network will always prevail.

Another flaw in the war approach to terrorism is that it dignifies the terrorists by giving them a kind of political legitimacy as enemy combatants. Both Bush and Putin have fallen into this trap. Terrorists are criminals, not soldiers. They do not represent any nation as a whole. The 9/11 terrorists were mostly Saudis, but they did not represent Saudi Arabia. The terrorists who murdered schoolchildren in Beslan were Chechens, but they did not represent Chechnya, nor even the cause of Chechen independence. Timothy McVeigh did not represent America when he perpetrated the Oklahoma City massacre. When we lump terrorists with the cause they claim to represent we not only give them a legitimacy they don't deserve, we cripple ourselves, in that we're prevented from seeking peaceful solutions with those who more truly represent that cause— a cause which may have validity. If, on the other hand, we treat

terrorists simply as criminals—as an international police problem—
we can both pursue the perpetrators and treat their alleged issue on
its merits.

The ideology and the actions of terrorist groups are an extreme
expression of Controller values. But the *form* of these networks is an
Integrative phenomenon. This is one reason they're so difficult to
combat—so extremely archaic and yet so modern at the same time.

Survival of the Fittest

The soldier ethos, which involves cutting communication to
others ('enemies'), oneself ('soft' emotions), and the environment,
is getting in the way of our adaptation as a species. Survival on a
small planet requires *heightened* communication of all three kinds.
The blind rigidity that results from successful indoctrination in the
Boy Code and the military 'virtues' is the greatest single stumbling
block to human evolution.

8 | On Religions: Back to Nature

Everything that lives is Holy.
WILLIAM BLAKE

I have put duality away
and see the two worlds as one.
RUMI

Men never do evil so completely and
cheerfully as when they do it from
religious conviction.
PASCAL

Every religious system is—like science—locked into the cultural customs, habits, beliefs, and attitudes prevailing in the era in which it began. And those that have their beliefs written down in sacred texts become resistant—often impervious—to the advances of human evolution. Sacred writings are among the most powerful armaments of the caterpillar's immune system in its battle against the proliferating imaginal cells.

All of today's major world religions had their origins in the Controller era. All these religions are steeped in warlike attitudes and images, in hierarchy, in misogyny. This in spite of the fact that most of their founders—Buddha, Jesus, Muhammad, for example—were ardent Integrators in their teachings.

Leonard Shlain shows how once priests established their

authority in Christianity and Buddhism, the original message of the religion became wildly distorted. Controller attitudes crept back into the teachings, often reversing them entirely. Political support heightened this effect, for a ruler's endorsement of any religion inevitably corrupts it. Christianity was able to hold onto much of its egalitarianism until Constantine was converted.

Jesus was nonviolent, tolerant, democratic—a threat to the Controller traditions of his time. Christianity would probably never have survived without the distortions that Paul and other early Orthodox patriarchs brought to it—re-introducing authoritarianism, sexual repressiveness, hierarchy, misogyny, militarism. Controller priests made Jesus into another one of the dying and reviving gods popular in that era, so they could ignore what he had to say.

Muhammad

Based on the actions and attitudes of fundamentalists like the Taliban, Al-Qaida, and the Iranian Mullahs, most Westerners would consider Islam the ultimate Controller religion. As if the two billion Christians in the world should be judged by the actions and attitudes of Jerry Falwell or John Ashcroft.

'Fundamentalism' is really a misnomer here, as it is in Christianity, since in both cases the extremists don't hark back to the fundamental teachings of their founders, but rather to the agrarian values dominant in the time they lived—the very values, in fact, that Jesus and Muhammad were attempting to reform. It's ironic that Islamic and Christian fundamentalists should be so invested in fighting each other, since they both want exactly the same thing—a return to the authoritarian, patriarchal, misogynistic, and bellicose values of the Controller era.

When fundamentalist reactionaries were in control of our government, for example, the United States joined with Iran in supporting a United Nations clause allowing violence against women when custom or religion permitted it. They also tried to edit out references to sex education and birth control in the UN Declaration on the Rights of Children, and were the only countries to want the death penalty for minors.

Muhammad was strongly egalitarian, felt wealth should be distributed fairly, and that all people should be involved in community decisions. He believed in the emancipation of women and shared in domestic chores in his own household. He was deeply opposed to violence and once led a thousand unarmed followers safely into Mecca past a host of armed enemies waiting to kill him. He exhibited a tolerance toward other religions that is almost unique in religious history.

Constantly the Qur'an points out that Muhammad had not come to cancel the older religions, to contradict their prophets or to start a new faith.

He argued that Jews and Christians had already had their revelations and didn't need to be converted. Anti-Semitism was virtually unknown in the Arab world until the founding of Israel, when its forms were borrowed from Christians. Jews and Muslims in Jerusalem had lived together in peace for four centuries before the crusaders slaughtered them. And when the Moors conquered Spain, Muslims and Jews lived peacefully side by side with Christians until the Inquisition.

Muhammad's goal was a just, all-embracing community on earth:

The aim was . . . the integration of the whole of life in a unified community, which would give Muslims intimations of the Unity which is God.

But over the centuries these goals were swallowed up by the traditional values that dominated the Muslim world. Warlords and monarchs maintained their power in the usual way—by attacking outsiders, and *Jihad* lost its original meaning of a struggle to become more like God, and came to mean 'Holy War'. At the height of Islamic power and influence in the 14th century, when Islam was the most civilized part of the Western world, Sunni Muslims declared that henceforth scholars could no longer apply their own reasoning to religious questions, but must rely on the authority of Islamic religious leaders, who alone were capable of interpreting the

Qur'an. This triumph of Controller thinking helped bring about the decline of Islamic influence.

Authoritarian Religion

Fundamentalists are fond of talking of 'God's plan', as if God were some sort of communist dictator, committed to centralized government planning. The authoritarian personality always needs an absolute, rigid, fixed despot he can submit to, and sacred texts—no matter how barbaric, foolish, and obsolete—provide this. That they are forever locked in a particular moment in time and unable to evolve and grow is pleasing to those frightened by the fact that the world around them is forever changing.

But many deeply spiritual people today find it difficult to take the Bible seriously as a religious document, let alone as the 'Word of God'. It seems almost blasphemous to assume that God or Allah would write flawed, mediocre books that read like they were written by a hung jury. Books whose heroes are mass murderers, and whose Deity orders those heroes to slaughter babies and pregnant women. The Bible is so deeply primitive that fully one-third of the book of Leviticus—the moral basis for many fundamentalist pronounce-ments—is devoted to the proper method of making burnt offerings of various animals.

Fundamentalists have never felt comfortable with democracy. The authoritarian personality depends on a boss for its peace of mind—hence the need for a micromanaging Creator who person-ally manufactures every single living thing in the universe. The idea that intelligence could emerge spontaneously from the integrative interaction of living things is as incomprehensible to the authori-tarian personality as the idea that political order could derive from the collective interaction of an electorate. For the Controller mentality, all order must derive from centralized authority. Even evil has to have a boss. This is why Controllers cling so desperately to Creationism. There's nothing in the theory of evolution, after all, that's incompatible with the idea of a Deity—one who could create the DNA and let it evolve. But without an ongoing spiritual dictator the Controller feels lost.

A religious system that creates unity and a sense of oneness with others is a positive influence on humanity. But one that teaches its participants to disparage and look down on those who don't share its particular beliefs is a profound source of evil in the world. Faith may not move mountains, but it has always had the power to move men to slaughter large numbers of their fellow beings.

This has occurred even *within* the same faith: among Christians, Catholics and Protestants have ruthlessly murdered each other, as have Sunnis and Shiites among Muslims. In his book *The End of Faith*, Sam Harris shows that the evil done in the name of faith is a *direct result* of faith—that you cannot be moderate and believe that the Bible or Qur'an is the word of God, because both books justify and promote homicide and genocide.

Pre-Controller Religion

Prior to the Controller era religion had a very different face—a face that reflected a different way of living and a different way of envisioning the world.

> Wherever [the Bushman] went he belonged, feeling kinship
> with every one and every thing he met on the way from birth
> to death.

Hunter-gatherers have always lived close to the land. They didn't worship invisible gods in the sky; they worshipped everything around them—nature was miracle enough, with "little altars everywhere". A Pygmy says:

> The forest is a father and mother to us . . . [it] gives us every-
> thing we need— food, clothing, shelter, warmth . . . and
> affection . . . So when something big goes wrong . . . it must be
> because the forest is sleeping and not looking after its children.
> So what do we do? We wake it up by singing to it, because we
> want it to wake up happy . . . [and] when our world is going
> well then also we sing to the forest because we want it to share
> our happiness.

But the Controller's need for an enemy limits his sense of

belonging. He cannot see himself as an intrinsic part of all nature. His idea of Divinity must always leave out something—something to be opposed.

The 'Golden Age'

Most of the world's cultures share a tradition of an ancient Golden Age when life was peaceful and easy. The Greek writer Hesiod, for example, describes a 'golden race' who lived "free from toil and grief":

> They had all good things; for the fruitful earth *unforced* bore them fruit abundantly and without stint. They dwelt in ease and peace . . .

'Golden' is romanticizing it a bit. We wouldn't want to live as hunter-gatherers lived and eat what they ate. Yet in many ways they enjoyed what Marshall Sahlins calls "the original affluent society". Sahlins found that the productive members of surviving hunter-gatherer societies worked only about three hours each day and yet still managed to support over a third of their members who didn't work at all. And they were healthier. Archeological evidence indicates that hunter-gatherers were:

> robust, strong, and lean, with no sign of osteoporosis or arthritis— even at older ages.

They lived unhurriedly, with plenty of time for pleasure, and their view of life was one of abundance—they neither stored food nor worried about the future. Laurens van der Post felt humiliated on parting with his Bushmen friends because he realized no present he could give them would make their lives easier.

Between 7000 and 3500 BC people in Europe and the Middle East began to cultivate crops. Before they were attacked by waves of warlike invaders they had created a rich, peaceful, and egalitarian civilization.

> [They] had towns with a considerable concentration of population, temples several stories high, a sacred script, spacious

houses of four or five rooms, professional ceramicists, weavers, copper and gold metallurgists, and other artisans producing a range of sophisticated goods.

There are no battles in their art, nor do we find weapons of war among their artifacts or buried in their graves. There are no forts or signs of battle. Communities built in unprotected open plains and valleys, survived for over *fifteen centuries* with no sign of war.

In a passage that has always been considered mere fancy, but with our growing archeological knowledge has taken on historical significance, Ovid speaks of a benign time before war came to humanity:

> Golden was that first age, which, with no one to compel,
> without a law, of its own will, kept faith and did the right.
> There was no fear of punishment, no threatening words were
> to be read on brazen tablets . . . Not yet were cities begirt with
> steep moats . . . There was no need at all of armed men, for
> nations, secure from war's alarms, passed the years in gentle
> ease. The earth herself, without compulsion, untouched by hoe
> or plowshare, of herself gave all things needful.

The Fall

There's also a myth of some sort of 'Fall' in most cultures around the world. This 'Fall'—this disconnection from nature—leads to suffering and unremitting toil, and seems to correspond with the development of agriculture and the coming of Control Culture. Benyus similarly talks of our eight millennial approach to agriculture as a process of "decoupling ourselves from nature".

Hesiod's gold and silver races are followed by a bronze race, who:

> loved the lamentable works of Ares and deeds of violence; they
> . . . were hard of heart . . .

Then by an iron race, who "never rest from labour and sorrow."

The story of Adam and Eve recounts a similar loss. What Eve gave Adam was fruit she had grown herself. In a sense, Eve is correctly blamed for the 'Fall', for it was women in pre-Controller times who were the main food-gatherers. It must have occurred to more than one of them—observing that plants grow from seeds—that you could plant your own food and save yourself a few steps. The knowledge Adam and Eve gain by eating the fruit is the awareness that they can exercise control over their food supply. But by giving up the life of gatherers and hunters their descendants are forced to toil endlessly all their lives.

When we were gathering, hunting, and fishing, we lived much like other species. We knew we were part of Nature, and were intimate with other forms of life. We grazed together like deer and hunted together like wolves. We knew we were part of a much larger organic complex, and that if other species didn't survive, we wouldn't either. Like the 'lilies of the field', we took what nature provided and didn't try to improve on it.

But with agriculture and animal husbandry we began to set ourselves apart, psychologically, from the rest of Nature. In taking this very natural step we embarked on a course from which there was no turning back: the attempt to ensure our personal security by exercising control over other parts of Nature. This created civilization with all its wonders, but it also created great misery, for security is an illusion, and the more steps you take to achieve it, the less secure you tend to feel—as witnessed by our own fear-obsessed nation.

Rejecting Creation

In Control culture, religion rapidly changed from a celebration of Nature to an attack on it. Much of primitive religion involved gratitude toward Nature. Hunter-gatherers believed in the Mother-Goddess because nature *gave* to them. But when Controllers began trying to subjugate and control nature, gods began to be seen as angry, spiteful, and vindictive beings who had to be propitiated with offerings and sacrifices. As humans increasingly set themselves apart from the rest of life, religious concepts became narcissistic—deities were seen as interested only in the activities of humans, especially in their wars. Religion ceased to be a celebration of the wonders of creation, and became a self-serving preoccupation with one's own personal spiritual destiny. Life came to be regarded as merely a sort of exam, and real life was seen as coming only in death. The disconnection from Nature was complete.

In keeping with the Controller passion for hierarchy, all deities were removed from the earth and elevated to the sky. For Controllers, the Deity had to be at the top of some hierarchical pyramid. Sacredness was not something accessible to everyone—it was set apart, set above—the province of specialists, authorities. Love was replaced by submission, gratitude and celebration by genuflection. Instead of a Goddess who was everywhere, Controllers introduced Gods who were elsewhere.

When Controllers conquered their pre-Controller neighbors they tended either to reduce their earth-mother goddesses to minor characters in their pantheon, or—in the case of monotheistic religions—tried to stamp them out altogether. The Catholic Church compromised by sweeping them all up into the cult of the Virgin Mary.

But in all cases, the earth, fecundity, sexuality—which had been sacred in the old religion—were stripped of their sanctity. Whereas at one time everything in nature had been holy, now nothing was. As Rupert Sheldrake says, it was the world's 'disenchantment'.

The Protestant Reformation was particularly fanatical in this respect. Protestants were obsessed with:

eradicating the traditional idea that spiritual power pervades the natural world . . . All traces of magic, holiness, and spiritual power were to be removed from the realm of nature.

Often this obsessive rejection of earthly things was extended to art. Once having gained control of Afghanistan Taliban despots began destroying huge, centuries-old Buddhist statues wherever they found them, in accordance with an Islamic (and Biblical) prohibition against idols.

Profaning Sexuality

In *The Thousand And One Nights* women married to rich Sultans capriciously betray their husbands with slaves. A woman, captured by a Djinn and kept locked in a nested series of seven trunks, boasts that she has nevertheless managed to cuckold him over five hundred times. "What woman willeth, that she fulfilleth, however man nilleth," is a constantly repeated theme in the Nights. Which is why the Shah decides to marry a virgin every night and kill her the next day—a fate that Sheherazade escapes with her many unfinished tales, most of which echo these same anxieties. Keeping women's sexuality shackled was a Controller obsession.

As Riane Eisler shows in her definitive study of sexuality and religion, what was an open and joyous activity deeply enmeshed in the spiritual life of pre-Controllers became, in the Controller Age, a secret, forbidden, and even evil thing. In keeping with their dualistic habits Controllers split sexuality apart from spirituality, and what had once been whole turned into two violently opposed halves—the sacred and the profane.

Integrative Spirituality

A single bacterium, working away in your gut to digest your food or keep a cell in order, is acting independently yet is part of a larger organism—you—of which it is unaware. We're in a similar relation to our planet, but our capacity for awareness is presumably greater.

Spirituality in Integrative Culture is based on this awareness that we're part of something larger than ourselves. This something doesn't stand apart from us, or over us. We participate in it—we belong to it. Integrative spirituality is an appreciation of our oneness with all life, with all spirit.

A tacit assumption of Integrative Culture is that every apparent separation—between people, ideas, systems, species—is an illusion; that all are interdependent parts of an organic whole; that this whole is eternally changing, evolving, complicating itself. Ecology is a recognition that every living thing is dependent on every other living thing:

> Every creature is involved in maintaining the entire system . . .
> Ants . . . loosen and aerate the soil around plant roots, helping
> to make it permeable to water. Trees transpire and purify
> water, make oxygen, and help cool the planet's surface. Each

species' industry has not only . . . local implications but global ones as well.

Re-Sacralizing Nature

As we find ourselves increasingly living in man-made environments—breathing our own exhalings—the sacredness of Nature seems especially compelling. This is why there is so much interest today in Native American and other nature-oriented spiritual traditions.

A friend of mine in the sixties, taking LSD in a rural part of Mexico, experienced this oneness vividly. He felt an ecstatic sense of belonging and devoted the rest of his life to spiritual disciplines like meditation that would enable him to sustain that feeling without drugs.

Unitive experiences of this kind triggered many such spiritual quests in the sixties. Some looked to pre-Controller religions like Wicca for a spirituality uncontaminated by Control Culture—a difficult path since these traditions, having been stamped out by more belligerent religions, often lack any clear record of ritual or practice. Others sought it in existing religions—Buddhism, Christianity, and Islam. Most religious traditions have Integrative themes buried under the mass of repressive attitudes that Controller priesthoods have built up around them. Matthew Fox argues that what he calls "creation-centered spirituality" is a Judeo-Christian tradition far older than the doctrine of Original Sin spawned by Augustine.

The Quest for an Uncorrupted Spirituality

Spiritual experiences, says Sam Harris, can be gained without abandoning rationality, and this has been a persistent goal for Integrative seekers. Perhaps one reason the Dalai Lama has achieved such popularity in the West is that he accepts this goal. When told that science contradicted parts of the sacred Tibetan texts, he simply said that the texts would have to be corrected. By contrast, many fundamentalist Christians still swear that every word in the flat-earth, children-stoning, animal-sacrificing, genocide-promoting Bible is true and the Word of God.

Another goal of Integrative seekers has been finding more benign and less childish concepts of Deity. This is more difficult. When the Pacific Lumber Company was trying to knock Julia Butterfly Hill out of 'Luna', her redwood tree, she prayed to the 'Universal Spirit'.

> Living in a tree this size, I felt balanced right at the center of Creation . . . I learned firsthand how everything that we can— or cannot—see is interconnected like strands in this web of life, from the microorganisms in the soil helping feed nutrients to Luna, to the stars that are billions of light-years away . . .

She had a concrete expression of that Spirit in Luna, which gave her an emotional connection to it. But for most people, being part of an all-inclusive spiritual entity is an idea they might embrace intellectually but can't experience at an emotional level. It's a cold, abstract concept whose vastness tends to undermine our feeling for it, and makes us want to personalize it in the form of a humanoid Deity.

But while that solves one problem, it creates another: what works for the feelings often insults the intelligence. The problem with personal deities is that they tend to acquire human traits—the God of the Old Testament is jealous, spiteful, vain, petty, boastful, vindictive, murderous, genocidal, dictatorial, and capricious, which makes for an unappealing Deity to those who neither share nor value those characteristics. The image of God the Godfather, constantly ordering his followers to whack someone, seems increasingly irrelevant to our modern interdependent world. As theologian Sallie McFague points out, 'God the Father' belongs to an authoritarian era. It's harder for people today to relate to it in a spiritual way.

Early religions most often pictured their Deity as a Goddess, a symbol that has resonance for many people who have had unitive experiences today. No one except a Siamese twin has ever been part of another male body, but everyone has been part of a mother's body.

> The Goddess in all her manifestations was a symbol of the unity of all life.

But our world is still lacking the new religious images, symbols, rituals, and stories that would be congruent with science and with the more tolerant, egalitarian, and inclusive society toward which we're gradually and fitfully moving.

Ethics

When Jesus of Nazareth argued that the multitude of rules and commandments issued by the micromanaging Old Testament God could be condensed into "love God and love your neighbor" he was challenging Controller authoritarianism, with all its do's and don'ts and dozens of 'abominations'. For the Integrator, of course, the two loves are one and the same, since Deity is in everything.

Controller ethics had a negative emphasis—they were focused primarily on what was *not* to be done, and these prohibitions tended to be spelled out in great detail. There was no trust in the ability of the individual to apply a general intent to a specific situation. Jesus' condensation was a radical transformation of Controller ethics into Integrative ones, but it was short-lived. Once the Christian Church was established the Controller approach quickly reasserted itself and soon most of the old specific prohibitions were reinstated.

Integrators today approach ethics from the positive end—how to lead a more positive life, be more loving, more giving, more forgiving. This has the advantage of eliminating the sadism and mean-spiritedness that so often accompanies Controller attempts to combat 'evil'.

Toward a Science-Based Faith

Right-wing fundamentalists advocate a 'faith-based science', which is a little like asking for a 'meat-based vegetarianism'. Science cannot and should not for a moment relinquish its demand for open-minded empiricism. 'Faith-based science' is Galileo being forced by the Vatican to recant his statement that the earth orbits the sun rather than vice versa.

What our world seems to be moving toward today is a science-based faith—a religion that finds its spiritual center in the true wonder of the universe, rather than in archaic fantasies of a cantankerous white-bearded old man living in the clouds. There is certainly far more true spirituality to be found among physicists and biologists than in sex-obsessed, bible-thumping fundamentalists interested only in hellfire and damnation.

Consider, for example, this statement by a contemporary scientist:

> Rather than having a universe filled with things, we are
> enveloped by a universe that is a single energetic event, a
> whole, a unified, multiform, and glorious outpouring of being.

No one who has deeply considered the wonders of modern physics and biology—the miracle of the DNA that unites all living things into one pattern, for example—is likely to be awed by accounts of cheap magic tricks: the tawdry miracles with which the lives of all great religious figures have been garnished to impress and convert the ignorant and credulous.

Far more miraculous is the reality that

> everything that exists in the universe came from a common
> origin . . . Our ancestry stretches back through the life forms
> and into the stars, back to the beginnings of the primeval fire-
> ball. This universe is a single multiform unfolding of matter,
> mind, intelligence, and life.

Most of the world's major religions evolved among people who believed the earth was flat—people who lived in feudalistic societies and felt little control over their existence. Dimly aware that their lives were determined by larger forces, they couldn't conceive of these forces as a constantly evolving entity of which they were a part, but interpreted them in accordance with the societies they lived in. So their deity was a kind of micromanaging slave owner, and they imagined this deity as living in the clouds, because they'd never been in the clouds.

Now that we know that the earth is round, surrounded by space, that life is constantly evolving, that the universe is indivisible, that we are all stardust, composed of the stuff of the primeval fireball, we are evolving toward religious ideas that reflect this grander and more complex vision.

We know now that it isn't necessary to posit a führer-god in order to understand creation. Life has steadily and spontaneously evolved by means of 'self-creating coherence'. Congruently we are slowly moving toward religious ideas that are compatible with scientific knowledge and reflect the grandeur of its visions.

PART III

WHERE WE'RE HEADING

The United States has, for two centuries, provided the densest concentration of cultural imaginal cells on the planet. So it is perhaps not altogether surprising that today it has also become a rich source of cultural antibodies.

Once the world's greatest democracy, the United States today seems to be in full flight from its democratic institutions, increasingly mimicking the structure of 20th century Latin American military dictatorships, where the legislatures have little power, the head of state defines himself as above the law and shrouds his acts in secrecy, and individuals can be arrested, imprisoned, and tortured without being charged of any crime. As Europe and Asia move into the Integrative world of the future will our great nation, once an Integrative leader, become a has-been? Will it be left behind because of a last-minute failure of imagination and nerve—an inability to see beyond its missile shield? Chapter 9 looks at the American position in the global metamorphosis.

As individuals we will always find ourselves acting, variously, both as cultural imaginal cells and as cultural antibodies. This is true whether we want change or resist change. Indeed, change itself is equally likely to be governed by Controller or Integrative concepts. Chapter 10 looks at the different ways the two cultural systems approach change.

9 | Is America's Decline Irreversible?

> Most of those [cities] which were great once
> are small today . . . in this world nobody
> remains prosperous for long.
> HERODOTUS

> If the fool would persist in his folly
> he would become wise.
> WILLIAM BLAKE

In 2004 the United States sent two "dream teams" to compete abroad—a group of basketball stars certain to win at the Olympics, and a group of golfing stars certain to bring the Ryder Cup back to America. Both teams suffered humiliating defeats at the hands of relative unknowns.

The reason, according to sports analysts, was the superior teamwork of the European athletes. Stardom is highly valued in America, cooperation and teamwork—though given lip service—are not. Teams win, but stars get the credit, and the individualist myth is preserved.

Something similar happens in science. Popular histories of science preserve the star myth by focusing on individual discoverers and inventors, although, as Surowiecki points out, modern science is inherently collaborative, especially at the top. He notes that Nobel prize winners collaborate more than other scientists, and more internationally, and that discovery of the quark was credited to 450 different physicists. The cause of SARS was detected by an international network of labs, with no top-down direction. Each lab "had the freedom to focus on what it believed to be the most promising lines of investigation."

The same star myth occurs in the corporate world. Corporate superstars draw astronomical salaries, giving the United States a CEO-to-worker salary ratio thirty to fifty times that of Europe and Japan, and handing us the uncontested title of Land of Inequality. Yet these superstars produce little of value. Corporate profit margins don't increase, 80% of their new products bomb within a year, and two-thirds of their mergers reduce shareholder value.

Individualism is a sacred cow in America, and it certainly brings us benefits—the freedom to choose our own spouses (not that we do that well at it, judging by the divorce rate), and the freedom to set our own goals and plan our own lives. But when carried to the point where our cooperative muscles atrophy, it begins to look like pathology. When Alexis de Tocqueville wrote about American society in the 19th century, he was impressed not only by our individual freedom but also by our amazing capacity for working together to achieve common goals. What happened?

The Roots of Democracy

During the 1970s and 1980s Robert D. Putnam carried out a study of democracy in Italy. It was based on an ambitious Italian experiment in decentralization—the formation of regional councils to take over some of the functions heretofore carried out by an over-centralized national bureaucracy. This decentralization program was very successful in the North but far less so in the South, and the reasons were revealing.

Historically, southern Italy (including Sicily and Sardinia) has been subject to constant authoritarian rule and dominated by landed aristocracies, while the North has had long periods of communal government, and this difference has persisted to this day:

In the North the crucial social, political, and even religious allegiances and alignments were horizontal, while those in the South were vertical.

Since the South is less industrialized than the North, Putnam and his colleagues thought maybe the North's greater success was due to economic development. But the strongest predictor of success was a 'civic community index', comprised of voting behavior, newspaper readership, and the density of private organizations devoted to sports and cultural activities.

The northern regions were high on this index, the southern ones low. And the index was not only a far better predictor of the councils' success, it was also *a strong historical predictor of economic development.*

> Economics does not predict civics, but civics does predict economics, better indeed than economics itself.

As former UN Secretary General Kofi Annan once said, in a speech at Harvard University: "democracy is a condition for development, not its reward."

Northern Italians belonged to groups of all kinds, while Southern Italians were isolated within their families, except for the patronage of mafia-like authority figures. Northerners were more egalitarian and felt more empowered as individuals. They were happier, more trusting, less cynical, saw the world as more honest, less corrupt than Southerners. And it was the individualistic Southerners who wanted stricter law enforcement.

Cultural norms are often reinforced by proverbs. In Southern Italy people reinforced each other's cynicism with warnings:

> 'Damned is he who trusts another'. 'Don't do good, for it will turn out bad for you'. 'When you see the house of your neighbor   on fire, carry water to your own'.

Is This Where We're Headed?

Southern Italy, compared to its Northern counterpart, is backward, undemocratic, and dominated by Control Culture. Yet in many ways, it's a cultural pattern toward which America seems to be moving. We, too, have our cynicism-inducing proverbs: "Nice guys finish last", "Look out for number one", "No good deed goes unpunished," etc. We, too, support stricter law enforcement, even at the expense of our constitutional freedoms. And fewer and fewer of us get our news from print media, preferring the sound-bite superficiality of TV.

In his later book on civic behavior in America, *Bowling Alone*, Putnam showed that all his indices had in fact declined in the United States during the previous two decades—not only voting and other forms of political engagement, but newspaper readership and membership in egalitarian organizations of every kind. Putnam calls these measures of civic involvement 'social capital', and comparing Americans born in the 1920s and those born in the 1960s, finds it has been in sharp decline.

Is it coincidence that as Americans have become more atomized, as we've moved further and further from the egalitarian, politically engaged, optimistic zeitgeist of the past to the cynical, suspicious, litigious, uninvolved mood of the present we've become increasingly fascinated with the culture of the Mafia—from *The Godfather* and its countless imitations to *The Sopranos*?

One of the factors in this loss of 'social capital' was television, which not only produced a decline in all forms of community activity and political involvement, but an increase in aggression, cynicism, and ignorance, as well as a decrease in academic achievement. This is hardly surprising. While Europe is dissolving borders and creating a peaceful international community our media seem peculiarly invested in portraying a world that affirms the proverbs of Southern Italy.

Deborah Tannen points out, for example, that television and radio are relentless in trying to frame everything as a combat. No idea can be put forward without first dredging up an opponent "from the margins of science or the fringes of lunacy." Unless your news item promises a debate of some kind, she says, the media tend to ignore it. "No fight, no news." There's no interest in ideas, only in seeing fur fly and trying to decide who 'won'.

Lethargy

Viewing humanity as hopelessly corrupt also saps the courage and motivation for change. Network cynicism, its obsession with violence, its fanning of fear and paranoia, seem designed to create apathy in the public.

> 71% of network news time was devoted to stories that showed their central characters as having little or no control over their fate.

TV news-magazines are especially fond of stories about people being victimized by trusted family, friends, and neighbors. The formula is to present a bland-looking house in a bland-looking neighborhood with some ordinary-looking people leading an everyday sort of life, and then to introduce some 'little-did-they-know' hints leading inevitably to the climactic cliché: "And then s/he realized that something was *terribly* wrong!"

The consequences of selling cynicism are severe. The United States today has the lowest voter turnout of any major democracy in the world. In the latter half of the 19th century, 70% to 80% of eligible voters were able to walk to the polls, but today less than 50% manage to drive there. The current fad for a "none of the above" option on ballots suggests a populace that likes to rant on talk radio but hasn't even the energy to write in alternatives.

Non-voters justify their inertia with statements like "none of the candidates interested me", or "I just didn't like either of them". They see politics as another kind of consumerism: "I don't care for your product, don't you have anything else for me?" Democracy is not a spectator sport. It cannot long survive this kind of passivity.

Deborah Tannen observes that while other nations are learning democracy:

> we seem to be unlearning how democracy can work.

We've drifted so far from democracy, in fact, that reporters routinely distinguish between "what the public wants" (as indicated by polls) and "what the government wants" without seeming to feel there's anything strange about this discrepancy.

Paradigm Paralysis

All great empires—both political and corporate—have shared the same flaw: persisting in the behavior that made them successful after that behavior had become obsolete. Success sows the seeds of its own decay by weakening the motivation to adapt to changing conditions. Joel Arthur Barker calls this 'paradigm paralysis'—clinging to an old paradigm when a new one comes along. Our government seems to be in the grip of such paralysis.

When the Japanese attacked Pearl Harbor the United States was forced onto the international stage by a war from which it emerged as the world's dominant power. This position was maintained, some believe, by military force. But in fact our influence in the world—both before and after World War II—has been primarily a function of our dynamic economy, our democracy, and the vitality and innovativeness of our culture.

To prioritize military strength in today's interdependent world is clinging to an obsolete paradigm—one more appropriate for a world in which economies, populations, and interpersonal communication were all pretty much contained within national borders. That world no longer exists.

Going Backwards

Much has been made of the triumphs of the Radical Right in American politics. Through brilliant organization, billions of dollars, and successful manipulation of the media, it is said, they have persuaded the poor in America to vote against their own self-interests, with the result that in 2000 the Radical Right captured Congress, the Presidency, and, in a short time, the Courts.

But although the violent backlash of the past 25 years was undoubtedly a reaction to the rapid expansion of Integrative culture, to what extent has the Radical Right succeeded in reversing that trend?

The answer is, not at all. As Michelle Cottle pointed out in a TIME article, the Radical Right may have won the electoral battle, but the cultural changes that provoked their effort cannot be stopped. As noted in Chapter 1, none of the movements that were so disturbing to the Controllers of the Radical Right have been reversed, or even slowed, at a global level. What little impact it's had has been national. It may reinstate back alley abortions in the United States, but cannot slow the steady rise in the rights and power of women over the globe. It may increase environmental pollution and degradation in the United States, but cannot stop the growth of ecological awareness planet-wide. It may curb democracy in the United States, but won't stop its global expansion. It may stop the teaching of evolution and eviscerate our once proud public school system, but won't slow the growth of education in the rest of the world. It may curb our freedoms and slow the progress of human rights in the United States, but cannot stop their expansion abroad. It may invade and bomb other countries at will, but cannot stop the growth of global pacifism. It may close our borders, opt out of all international agreements, and create 'Fortress America' but cannot stop globalization—economic, cultural, or political.

In other words, all that the 'patriots' of the Radical Right have achieved is to sabotage our nation's future. For the reviving of Controller values and habits—authoritarianism, militarism, misogyny, proliferating walls, mental constriction, and rigid dualism—will make the United States increasingly marginal, increasingly isolated, increasingly obsolete, increasingly irrelevant to the woven world of the 21st century.

This is the "success" of the Radical Right.

The Radical Right Agenda

Consider the Third World Countries we consider 'backward':

1. They have authoritarian governments that withhold information from the public. In 2003 the federal government spent a record 6.5 billion dollars keeping information away from its people. Government control over the media—with scripted press conferences and punishment for reporters who ask difficult questions or report news unfavorable to the government—is at an all-time high. Some news sources are barely more than propaganda outlets for the administration.

2. They over-invest in the military. The Pentagon's budget is higher than those of the 25 next highest nations combined. A hundred nations have military budgets smaller than what the Pentagon spends in a day. Fifty have budgets smaller than what the Pentagon spends in two hours. What government hawks have long said about other governments (usually our military victims) seems to have become true of our own: "the only thing they understand is force".

3. They educate only the rich. The outdated techniques of our conventional schools, together with the puny salaries we pay our teachers, would help explain why the American educational system ranks at the bottom of industrialized societies. This at a time when money spent on teacher salaries is the single best index of a nation's future economic health.

4. They violate civil liberties. Since 9/11 and the passage of the ill-named Patriot Act, hundreds of individuals—including U.S. citizens—have been imprisoned for years without charge, without a trial, without access to a lawyer. Habeas corpus has been revoked. At least 44 prisoners have been tortured to death.

5. They have a huge gap between rich and poor. For thirty years after the end of World War II, economic equality actually increased in the United States, but since 1979 the gap between rich and poor has ballooned. GINI coefficients—the most effective measure of economic inequality—are growing at an accelerating rate. Every year the gap increases, and every year, when the figures are released, there's a brief bit of clucking over it, and then it's back to business as usual.

This last trend is the most disturbing from a survival viewpoint. Many of the defunct societies Jared Diamond studied destroyed themselves when wealthy minorities further enriched themselves at the expense of both the poorer majority and the society as a whole.

Decaying institutions are characterized by short-term thinking. They sacrifice future assets to maintain present dominance. The United States is increasingly handicapped by its enormous investment in military superiority at a time when military might is becoming less and less relevant to a nation's strength. Subordinating education and economic health to war is suicidal in today's world. Washington's militarism and its reluctance to join other nations in tackling international problems—these are signs of the mental scle-rosis that has always marked the decline of great nations.

The Great Retreat

In internationalism the United States was once a trendsetter. The Integrative motto of our nation—*e pluribus unum*—celebrates the expanding vision of our Founding Fathers. And it was with this same vision that Woodrow Wilson worked to create the League of Nations and Franklin Roosevelt led the creation of the UN—carrying the vision a step further in keeping with modern realities.

Today our government is leading the resistance to internation-alism. The nation that once astonished the world by establishing the Marshall Plan to rebuild Europe after World War II now lags far behind other Western countries in foreign aid.

The share of the U.S. GNP devoted to helping the poor [of the world] has declined for decades, and is a tiny fraction of what the United States has repeatedly promised, and failed, to give.

The nation that helped the UN work for years to establish a permanent International Criminal Court, in order to try cases of genocide and other crimes against humanity, began vigorously to oppose it when it started to become a reality. And once it was estab-lished the Bush administration refused to ratify it without obtaining immunity for United States troops. U.S. soldiers, in other words, were to be the only ones allowed to commit atrocities.

The United States was virtually alone among the 191 member nations of the UN in opposing the creation of the Human Rights Council. The United States is one of very few nations refusing to sign the treaty banning land mines, despite universal popular support for it. The United States and Somalia are the only non-signers of the Rights of Children agreement. The United States also refuses to sign the Kyoto accord on global warming. The United States long opposed the World Health Organization's treaty to prevent the spread of tobacco deaths, signed by 171 nations. And the Bush administration was even reluctant to have the Senate ratify the 22-year-old Women's Rights Treaty—already accepted by 170 nations around the world. The United States is becoming a minority of one—the 'nyet' nation of the 21st century.

The result of this isolationistic stance by the Bush administration has been a 30% drop in American prestige in Europe and an even larger drop elsewhere. Even many long-term allies have begun to avoid too close an association with the United States, ignoring our attempts to influence their policies.

Controller politicians are fond of talking about the American 'Empire'. But the Military Empire paradigm belongs to the 19th century and we're living in the 21st. The future is brains, not guns; money, not bullets; communication, not bombs. Failure to invest in this future means decay. Our poverty rate has risen for five years in a row, according to census reports, and median income is at its lowest point in eight years, despite the fact that we are working longer hours than people in any other industrialized country. We have higher rates of infant mortality, disease, and illiteracy than most industrialized nations. We're putting less and less money and energy into feeding and educating our children, and more and more into military hardware that in a few years will be junk, much of it polluting. The 'American Empire' is a joke.

The Rush Toward Ignorance

Nothing is a better index of a nation's future strength than its educational system, and the United States once had a public school system second to none. But that system has been under consistent and systematic attack from the Radical Right for the past 25 years. Fundamentalists have openly stated their desire to destroy this system and replace it with private religious schools.

Anti-tax movements in America have already decimated school budgets, and students in American schools today lack many of the resources that European and Asian students take for granted. American students lack scientific knowledge that students around the world possess because fundamentalists ban the teaching of evolution; they lack knowledge of social issues because their text-books have been drained of all reference to them; and they lack knowledge of literary classics because so many have been found offensive to fundamentalists. We are raising a generation of public school students condemned to the rote learning of archaic material. American students do especially poorly in comparison with other countries when asked to *apply* their math knowledge to real-life situations. This is the worst failure of all: we are no longer teaching our children to think.

Dumbing Down

Twenty years ago the U.S. ranked first in the world in the percentage of its people who held a college degree, and also in the percentage who held at least a high school degree. Today it ranks seventh in the first category and ninth in the second. In 1970 more than half of the world's science and engineering doctorates came from U.S. universities. By 2001 the European Union granted 40% more than the United States. Federal research money is spent on killing devices, while less and less goes to basic scientific research. As Thomas Friedman notes, teachers' salaries are so low that nearly half of all new teachers leave the profession within five years.

China used to generate one-sixth as many engineers as the United States, but now has four times as many. The United States is 14th in science graduates, partly because fundamentalism has made the American South abysmally ignorant in geology, biology, and astronomy. There has been a 50% drop in foreign student applications to study in the U.S., with the UK and Germany picking up the slack. We are far behind Asians in math literacy. Our share of scientific publications has fallen behind Europe and will soon fall behind Asia. And our technological standing in the world has suffered as a result of this educational failure. In 2000 the United States was number one in broadband Internet access, but has now fallen to 16th. In 2000 the United States produced 40% of the world's telecom equipment, now only 21%. Once the world's educational and technological leader, we're becoming an also-ran.

Charles Handy points out that free-market politicians never view government as a body concerned with the good of society as a whole. Governments have to run on a cash-flow basis:

Education, therefore, is always a cost and never an investment.

Yet education is the best long-run investment any society can make—especially in today's economy, where the only real assets are human ones. In another generation the United States, with the most gigantic and expensive defense establishment in the world, may find itself with nothing left to defend.

Cosmopolitan People, Provincial Rulers

Washington is not America. A series of polls conducted at the end of the millennium by the *Washington Post*, CNN, the Chicago Council for Foreign Relations, the University of Maryland, the Times Mirror Center, and the Center for International and Security Studies, found that the American people were far more internationally minded than our government. From two-thirds to four-fifths of Americans polled in these studies:

♦ Wanted the United States to pay its dues to the UN;
♦ Wanted the United States to take part in, and contribute money to, peacekeeping missions;
♦ Wanted to strengthen the UN, felt it was a good investment, felt it should stock military equipment, felt it should levy nations for its own peacekeeping force, felt strengthening the UN should be a political priority, felt the United States should spend more money on the UN and less on defense, and in fact had a more favorable view of the UN than of the United States Congress or the Supreme Court;
♦ Felt the United States should *not* act unilaterally to reduce international crises, but should share leadership with other nations;
♦ Felt the United States should end its embargo of Cuba.

These polls were taken before 9/11, when a desire for revenge made the populace highly susceptible to jingoistic sound bites, but they indicate a baseline Integrative attitude almost diametrically opposed to the Controller stance of Congress at the time. Washington politicos have been scornful of institutions like the UN, which are:

critical for stabilizing an international system from which

America benefits more than any other country . . . The "big enemy" is still the organizing principle for American internationalism, not the "big opportunity", let alone the "big responsibility".

In the new introduction to *Jihad Vs. McWorld*, political scientist Benjamin Barber noted that no democratic legislature in the civilized world has as many members without passports as ours, no other democratic nation pays a smaller percentage of its GNP for foreign aid, and no other democratic nation is so illiterate in foreign languages, so astonishingly ignorant of other cultures.

The United States is today inexperienced in the hard work of creative interdependence and international partnership.

This outdated insularity keeps us from enjoying the benefits of cooperative enterprise and foreign expertise. When then-President Clinton visited South Africa he spoke of the difficulty in persuading Americans to adopt programs that had worked elsewhere:

It drives me crazy . . . I consider it to be the major failure of my public life that every problem in our society today is being solved by somebody somewhere, and I can't get it to be replicated.

Multinational corporations don't have this problem—an idea developed in one country is immediately adopted in all other countries involved in that corporate empire.

Democracy Stops Here

One reason war persists when it achieves nothing, not even security, and is a spectacular waste of money, resources, energy, time, and lives, is that it's a boon for unscrupulous and anti-democratic leaders. When a head of state declares war, democracy goes out the window. Even in the United States he can rule as a virtual dictator. War and authoritarianism are Siamese twins.

In drafting our Constitution our Founding Fathers made one

serious mistake. Most democracies make a distinction between a nation's executive leader and its symbolic leader. Some, like England, have a monarch to play that ceremonial role. Others have both a president—a position largely honorary and symbolic—and a premier who actually gets his hands dirty running the country. The Founding Fathers neglected to take into account this need for a symbolic leader, and as a result our President must play both roles.

This means any politician can be transformed into a symbol of American unity by the simple act of attacking some foreign nation, and our democratic right to disagree with him is redefined as unpatriotic. Foreign policy adventures should be the most challengeable acts of a government rather than the least, since they are likely to have the most severe impact on the people. This is why Congress was given the exclusive power to declare war—a restriction that has proven all too easy to circumvent in the last 50 years—with disastrous consequences.

Compounding this defect, rigid bureaucracies have sprung up to deal with foreign relations and military matters (and for many Washingtonians these are indistinguishable)—bureaucracies that are shrouded in secrecy and little affected by changing administrations or public opinion. Foreign and military policy are considered the province of experts—not appropriate for public scrutiny, nor subject to democratic constraints.

When you permit secrecy in government, corruption and incompetence inevitably follow. In democratic organizations mistakes are more easily exposed, making it easier for those organizations to correct them and become more efficient. And a range of viewpoints gives them the flexibility to adapt to change. Authoritarian bureaucracies lack this trait, which is why they often seem incapable of learning from experience. Foolish policies go unchallenged, and mistakes covered up mushroom into disasters, as witnessed recently with the Iraq war. Classified material is released only when it's too late to recover from the follies it reveals.

Government by expert has been enormously costly to America. Overthrowing democratically elected leaders and installing military dictators—as we have done on four continents during the past century—has created a host of calamities for which we are still paying. The splitting of Vietnam and the Vietnam War, for example, were an attempt to prevent an election in which Ho Chi Minh (the Vietnamese hero who had defeated both the Japanese and French armies, and was the Vietnamese equivalent of George Washington) would have received, by conservative CIA estimates, 80% of the vote. Had we left them to choose their own leader, things would be pretty much as they are now in Vietnam, minus millions of deaths and a poisoned landscape; and fifty thousand American lives would have been saved.

The idea that the public, when not deliberately misled or kept in ignorance, will make better judgments than experts, is supported by evidence. Surowiecki, in *The Wisdom of Crowds*, cites several studies showing that groups make better decisions *than even the smartest individuals within them.*

> A large group of diverse individuals will . . . make more intelligent decisions than even the most skilled 'decision maker'.

"It's as if," he says, "we'd been programmed to be collectively smart." But this wisdom depends on three conditions—*that the people be diverse, independent of one another, and decentralized.* Individual intelligence is not a factor. Better decisions are made, Surowiecki found, when the naive, ignorant point of view is present.

> The organization with the smartest people may not be the best organization.

Many Americans like the idea of a decisive, individualistic leader taking 'strong, forthright' actions to deal with a problem. They chafe at the messiness of democracy. The media, who have never really liked or understood democracy, continually sneer at the bickering of legislative bodies, and cartoonists mock politicians and the seemingly endless time it takes to make decisions. They seem to prefer the speediness of rash dictatorial moves, even though these lead to follies like Napoleon and Hitler invading Russia, Tojo attacking Pearl Harbor, the Bay of Pigs fiasco, and the Iraq invasion. Large decisions lead to complex consequences that are difficult to see ahead of time—especially by those invested in a particular course.

Therefore they *should* take time, and be exposed to the greatest possible variety of viewpoints and predictions—i.e. 'political bickering'. As Surowiecki points out, "sometimes the messiest approach is the wisest."

'Experts' often claim that their policies are more 'realistic' than those of the public. 'Realism' is a Washington euphemism for inertia, for the unwillingness to change archaic habits ('the way we do things here') no matter how great the need.

No one would argue that the American public should be involved in the day-to-day conduct of foreign and military policy. But there's no reason why they should be excluded from a consideration of the general outlines of such policy, since they bear the burden of its costs and the repercussions of its failures.

Most American cities have a General Plan—publicly derived— against which specific development proposals can be measured. The United States needs such a General Plan for foreign policy— one that more accurately reflects the will of the people and could act as a restraint on the myopic and puerile adventurism that has characterized the 'expert' policies of the last fifty years. For while 'experts' are engaging in childish talk of 'empire', the United States is falling behind the rest of the world in every respect except military power—much like a muscle-bound teenager pumping iron while he flunks out of school. But there are no athletic scholarships in the global village. In the 21st century success goes not to the most powerful individual but to the largest network.

Narrowing

Success in the future requires a constant expansion of our concept of 'we'. Washington apparently doesn't understand this, but the corporate world understands it very well. When the Bush administration attacked affirmative action before the Supreme Court, labor unions and civil rights groups opposing the government's position were shocked to discover that among their allies were lawyers from over 40 of America's largest corporations. Companies like General Motors, Microsoft, Proctor & Gamble, Eastman Kodak, Intel, American Airlines, and PepsiCo had two reasons for joining in the struggle, neither of them ideological.

First, as global companies, they wanted to have a diverse staff of employees, and they wanted that staff college-educated.

Second, they wanted even their white employees to have spent time in classes with people from diverse backgrounds.

They wanted, in other words, people who had, or understood, traditions and experiences different from their own.

This is another instance of our government operating with an antiquated paradigm. Diversity is vital to economic survival today, and mandatory in the global economy. A study of business firms found those with higher percentages of women and minorities were more profitable. The boards and top executive positions of major corporations are increasingly being filled with individuals from several different countries.

Multiplying Resources

Half of our graduates in math, engineering, and computer science are foreign-born, and a much higher percentage of immigrants than native-born Americans are in the professions. These are vital assets:

> [Immigrants] produce more than they consume, pay more taxes than they take in social benefits, and are less prone to crime. It is the entrepreneurial, hard-working, forward-looking, even courageous person who seeks to immigrate; the others stay home.

One reason the United States has long been at the forefront of innovation is the constant revitalizing of our culture through the addition of foreign immigrants to our national mix.

Friedman points out that we're losing our competitive edge in technology, because of our closed doors, our weakness in education, and the weak government investment in basic research. U.S. firms are moving serious research and development to India and China.

> The Department of Homeland Security is making it so hard for legitimate foreigners to get visas to study or work in America that many . . . are opting to study in England, Western Europe,

and even China . . . In a decade we will feel that loss in
America's standing around the world.

Academic conferences and scientific meetings are less and less
often held within the United States, because of the bureaucratic
hassles over visas, and we're closing ourselves off from vital knowledge.

Every time a foreign scientist can't attend a U.S. technology
conference, our security suffers. Every time we turn away a
qualified technology graduate student, our security suffers.

In our terror of terrorism we have begun to starve ourselves of
human resources. Restricting immigration is like cloning—it limits
evolutionary options and produces cultural sclerosis. Just as we
preserve wild species to keep our genetic options open, we need to
enourage immigration and foreign visitors to keep our cultural
options open.

Diversity not only expands the range of possible solutions to a
problem, says Surowiecki, it also prevents 'Groupthink', in which a
small clique of homogeneous, like-minded individuals with an
'assumed consensus', insulated from outside perspectives, and
deeply submissive to authority, become overconfident to the point
of feeling invulnerable. Their shared fantasies become 'facts',
leading to fiascos like the Bay of Pigs, the Vietnam War, and the
invasion of Iraq.

Extending Horizons

Our uniqueness, strength, and staying power as a nation lie in
our willingness to engage in a continual process of self-creation.
This means maintaining an open-loop system. We cannot keep
developing if we cut ourselves off from the rest of the world. While
the Controller seeks to create a monolithic uniformity within walls,
the Integrator seeks a unity that embraces greater and greater
variety.

The world outside the United States is slowly but inexorably
achieving this unity. Hence the rapidly accelerating rate of interna-

tional Internet use. Google processes over 200 million searches a day, twice as many as three years ago, and two-thirds of them are in 88 foreign languages.

> While we may be emotionally distancing ourselves from the world, the world is getting more integrated.

Washington seems oblivious to the way the world is changing. Estonians and Indians have more up-to-date computers than the FBI, and administration officials talk about the world as if it were 1890.

> Europe . . . is much more in tune than the US with the thinking of the rest of the world . . . and its social legislation and economic practice are more congenial to foreigners and more readily exportable than the American variants. US policy and politics . . . are poorly adapted to the complexity of today's world.

For years now, the United States has been sacrificing its political assets, its social assets, its intellectual assets, its cultural assets, its human assets, and its moral assets, for the sole purpose of expanding its already overwhelming military superiority. In the process it has fallen behind Europe and parts of Asia in almost every measure of civilization. In a few decades, unless this policy is reversed, the United States will find itself on the ash heap of decayed societies—isolated, bankrupt, an angry bully continually offering to beat up the much younger kids that are now in the class he's still repeating.

Can the decline be reversed? Are there sufficient imaginal cells in our population to keep our nation from relapsing back into caterpillar soup? Enough to continue the cultural metamorphosis our nation once led?

As apathetic, timid, submissive, and politically inert as the American public seems to have become in recent years, it would be a mistake to underestimate its potential. The imaginal cells of our society are still proliferating.

But social change is complex, difficult, and chock full of unintended consequences. Even the desire for change itself often comes clothed in self-defeating Control Culture armor. This is the topic of the next chapter.

10 Changing How We Change

I was fascinated with the question of how such organized
collective behavior could go along with the almost
complete freedom of movement of the individual
electrons. I saw in this an analogy
to what society could be.
DAVID BOHM

It's not the strongest of species that survive, nor the most
intelligent, but the ones most responsive to change.
CHARLES DARWIN

A butterfly is not merely a caterpillar with wings. It has a completely
different metabolism, feeding on, and processing, nectar instead of
leaves, flying large distances instead of crawling from leaf to leaf. By
the same token, Integrative Culture represents not merely a change
in itself. It also represents a change in the way change is sought.

Most change today is ego-driven or tech-driven, not human-
driven. In this sense Integrative Culture is conservative. For the true
conservative resists any change that is not human-driven—that
doesn't preserve human connections, human values, human civili-
ties.

Seeking change is not necessarily Integrative. Many on the left,
for example, see themselves as godlike architects who stand outside a static world and try to mold it. They construct a mental

blueprint of change and attack all who fail to meet its specifications. This is a Controller approach to change. Integrators see themselves as participants exerting influence on a changing entity that includes them.

Controller-induced change is monolithic, coercive, and top-down. Integrative-induced change is heterogeneous, spontaneous, and grassroots.

Monolothic vs. Heterogeneous

A. A. Milne once wrote a poem for children about an old sailor marooned on a desert island who can't decide among all the many things he needs to do—like obtaining food, clothing, and shelter—which of them to do first, and in the end does nothing at all until rescued.

This has frequently been the plight of Controllers on the Left, squandering their energies fighting among themselves about the 'correct' way to achieve change—undermining each others' efforts and exhausting themselves in ideological dispute. This tendency was brilliantly satirized in the Monty Python film, *The Life of Brian*, in which a radical group—formed to fight against Roman rule—spends most of its energy battling a rival rebel group with an absurdly similar name.

The Controller wants everyone 'on the same page' before the 'battle' for change begins. Only after everyone has accepted the party line can any change take place. This is why so many radical efforts splinter into factions and never get off the ground.

Catch-23

Social systems are held in place by contradictions, and social change can take place only by asserting other contradictions. In Control Culture, for example, women were told, "You're not a real woman if you have the kind of career a man has, even though having a career is superior to traditionally 'feminine' activities." To which the only effective response was, "A real woman should be able to have a career even though traditionally 'feminine' activities are superior to a career." This meant that in order to stop being second-class citizens women had to *both* engage in 'male' activities *and* assert the superior value of 'female' ones.

Since it was unlikely that the same women would do these things simultaneously, women could achieve their aims only if different groups of women went in what seemed to be opposite directions at the same time. That they've been able to do this with only occasional bouts of ideological warfare is testimony to their right-brain capabilities.

The notion that there's only one best way to achieve change reflects the distrust of process, the love of combat, the need for control, the anxious belligerence that activates Controller ideologues of every stripe.

Coercive vs. Spontaneous

Social change is a difficult process. Controller ideologues want to do it all at once without regard to human needs. They tend to be product-oriented, and don't care what the side effects of their product may be. When successful they usually create despotic regimes that differ little from those they overthrow.

Attempts to achieve change coercively—like Mao's Cultural Revolution and Pol Pot's Agrarian Society—have led to colossal failure and terrible human suffering.

PC Soldiers

The Controller leftist tends to be past-oriented—more interested in punishing those who fail to live up to his ideals than helping people achieve changes.

He also tends to be dismissive of minor victories, and the grandiosity of his goals betrays the fact that ego-inflation has taken precedence over the desire for change. Controller radicalism often ends in violence, which is fundamentally masturbatory and invariably counterproductive.

It's difficult to achieve change by attacking Control Culture directly, since Control Culture feeds on combat. Requires it. Must have it to live. Combat awakens it. Nourishes it. Revitalizes it.

Creativity is what saps its energy.

Lasting change comes about through dialogue between people who currently disagree. This seems to be a chore many leftists find too exacting, and is often subordinated to the more enjoyable activity of impressing other ideologues on the left.

Collaboration

Collaboration is a bad word in wartime situations, and for Controllers, everything is a wartime situation. Leftist Controllers, like their right-wing counterparts, are uncomfortable with complexity—they want simple enemies like the Evil Capitalist. 'Collaborating with the enemy'—that is, any corporation—is horrifying to the Controller radical, who feels he will be forever tainted by the contact, no matter how beneficial to his cause.

William McDonough and Michael Braungart are currently working with Ford on a two billion dollar project to rebuild its River Rouge factory and make it environmentally sustainable. One of their solutions:

> cleans the water and the air, provides habitat, and enhances
> the beauty of the landscape while it saves the company a great
> deal of money—as much as $35 million by one estimation.

Controller radicals are appalled: "How can you work with *them*?" McDonough and Braungart are often asked. Their response is: "How can you *not* work with them?"

> Our questioners often believe that the interests of commerce
> and the environment are inherently in conflict, and that envi-
> ronmentalists who work with big business have sold out.

Yet as Frances Moore Lappé observes, efforts to get corporations to change have been a lot more successful than trying to get governments to force them to change, especially with right-wing Republicans dominating our courts.

On the left, unfortunately, demonstrating the loftiness of one's ideological sentiments often seems to take precedence over concrete achievements. But Jared Diamond warns:

> If environmentalists aren't willing to engage with big businesses, which are among the most powerful forces in the modern world, it won't be possible to solve the world's environmental problems.

He points out that environmentalists usually fail to praise companies for making positive, sustainable choices, but merely attack those that are doing harm. A company developing positive environmental policies is still trashed by eco-radicals if any single item on their exhaustive checklist of corporate sins is unchanged. They mimic the authoritarian parent who only comments on the worst grade in a child's school report. Needless to say, no one takes such critics seriously.

Corporations are the favorite bad guys in most leftist scenarios. Yet global capitalism—as brutal as many of its effects may be—is a powerful force for peace in the world today, since—aside from a few defense industries (who don't even have to compete in the market)—it depends on peace to exist.

Progressive activists waste a great deal of energy if they fail to make alliances with political 'enemies' and coordinate strategies to achieve common goals.

Process

For Controllers, life is a matter of successes and failures, of battles won or lost. For Integrators there are no failures, there is only learning—making mistakes and trying something else.

Controllers have little sense of process. Conservative Controllers tend to assume that a change, once begun, will continue at an accelerated pace until it reaches some terrifying extreme. A diet will lead to starvation. Affirmative action will force white males into poverty. Reducing our nuclear arsenal will lead to a Chinese invasion. Sharing housework will lead to male impotence. Giving a quarter to a beggar will make him move in with you. "Give them an inch and they'll take a mile" is their favorite slogan.

Radical Controllers tend to see humanity as a static, inert mass that can only be moved by militaristic organization, authoritarian rule, and brute force.

In other words, Controllers at both ends of the traditional political spectrum are firm believers in inertia—once stopped, can't start; once started, can't stop. Self-correcting processes don't exist for them.

Spontaneity

Often, when they've had a brush with death, people begin to examine their lives—to consider whether they've been spending them in a way that would allow them to say, if they suddenly came to an abrupt end, "I spent my time well, short though it was".

Radical politics has often been a gloomy, angry, guilt-motivated affair. For Control Culture placed the highest value on suppressing your own needs in the service of a distant goal. In Integrative Culture your own basic needs are a preliminary guess of what the world needs. Rather than thinking of them as a barrier to some distant goal, their satisfaction *becomes* the goal.

Only an egomaniac think it's a crime for him to have fun while a single child in the world is starving. Guilt-driven action is an energy drain on everyone involved. Consider how little energy is needed to learn about something that interests you and how much energy was needed to learn boring things you were forced to learn in school. Responding actively to something in your immediate world that you want to change takes no more energy than feeding yourself when hungry. The Controller radical who forces himself to squeeze energy into some issue that doesn't attract him personally, but which he decides is 'important', makes him part of the problem.

In Integrative Culture there's no pot of gold to recompense you for a long and miserable struggle. Kent M. Keith points out that if you're bent on doing good in the world there's no guarantee you'll be thanked for it, so you'd better be doing it for its own sake.

Top-Down vs. Grassroots

The biologist Lewis Thomas once said that feeling useful is one of the most powerful needs in human beings—innate, biological. Without it we would not have been so successful as a species. People are unhappy and uncomfortable when this need is unmet, though they rarely recognize the cause.

But when we look at the magnitude of the problems facing the world today it's hard not to get discouraged—hard not to get lost in wondering which of these monsters we should slay first, and then had not to get even more confused trying to figure out how to do it.

This is top-down, Controller thinking. It takes a highly inflated ego to think you're so gifted that (a) you have the ability to decide which problem is the most important one, and (b) it won't get solved without your help.

All the problems facing us today—climate change, inequality, environmental degradation, war, terrorism, energy shortages, over-population, etc., etc., are interconnected. This is the essential Integrative insight. We can think of them separately, approach them separately, but whichever problem we put energy into will affect all the others. So from an Integrative viewpoint the choice, as suggested above, can best be made by thinking not of which one I *should* be putting my energy into, but of which one do I have energy *for*—that is, what excites me the most? Every action we take causes change.

Priorities

The Controller wants to transform the world and right all its wrongs with one magic formula. And although the formulas vary from age to age, the strategy is always the same: "First I have to get power".

Our capacity for self-delusion usually prevents us from seeing it, but what we do first is invariably what we care most about. The word 'priority' derives, after all, from 'prior'. If we decide to seek power "in order to do some good in the world", the power is what's important to us, and doing good in the world a distant second.

There are, after all, a million ways to do good that don't involve power. Americans still cling naïvely to the fantasy of the 'good dictator' who will make everything right with a bold stroke. But people who are attracted to centers of power are the last ones capable of sharing it and the first ones likely to abuse it. Power attracts bullies. Our Founding Fathers understood this. Many Americans today seem to have forgotten it.

Since those at the centers of power are almost by definition those most invested in the status quo, innovative change is unlikely to come from that direction. What governments usually do (when they aren't preventing change) is certify in law or executive action changes already happening at the periphery.

The civil rights movement did not begin with government action. Nor did the women's movement. Nor did the environmental movement. We tend to overestimate the role of government in creating change because its certification is a media event, an announcement to the world that change has occurred. This is not to say governments can be ignored, only that their role in the change process tends to come later rather than earlier. Change begins at the periphery.

Grassroots Leaders

Our electronically connected world makes it easier for ordinary people to exert influence. The campaign against land mines began on the Internet, and it has played a critical role in the organizing of mass protests. Rosabeth Kanter gives several examples of Internet campaigns that have forced large corporations to change their policies, and governments have been impacted as well:

> In the April 2000 South Korean elections, as many as fifty of the leading candidates were defeated because of . . . publication of damning information about some candidates' records that did not appear in the traditional media.

Jim Kouzes and Barry Posner refute the popular notion that leadership is some magical trait possessed by only a gifted few:

> In nearly two decades of research we have been fortunate to

hear or read the stories of over 7,500 ordinary people who have led others to get extraordinary things done . . . Leadership is not the private reserve of a few charismatic men and women. It is a process ordinary people use when they are bringing forth the best from themselves and others.

When Dr. Charlie Mae Knight became the twelfth superintendent in ten years of the Ravenswood School District in East Palo Alto, California, fifty percent of the schools were closed and 98 percent of the children were performing in the lowest percentile in California. There were buckets in classrooms to catch the rain leaking through decrepit roofs. Gophers and rats had begun to take over the facilities. After assuming the post, she immediately enlisted support from Bay Area companies and community foundations to get badly needed resources. The first project she undertook was refurbishing the Garden Oaks School. Volunteer engineers from nearby Raychem Corporation repaired the electrical wiring and phone systems. A volunteer rat patrol used pellet guns to eliminate rodents. The community helped paint the building inside and out, and hardware stores donated supplies.

Parents began to demand more of a say. They provided volunteers and new leadership. Teachers noticed the change, and wanted to be part of it, too. In two years the children performed in the fifty-first percentile and East Palo Alto received the state's Distinguished School Award.

Knight didn't wait for grand strategic plans to be completed, new legislation to be passed, or consensus to be built. She knew she had to produce some early victories. To get people excited you have to show that something's happening—visible signs that change is taking place. This builds confidence and creates momentum.

In 1993, Yohanes Surya, an Indonesian doctoral student in physics at William and Mary, founded the Indonesian Physics Olympiad Team. With three other Indonesian doctoral students he recruited some promising Indonesian high school students and coached them to take part in the International Physics Olympiad in Williamsburg, soliciting funds through the Internet from Indonesian students studying abroad.

As soon as Surya got his degree he established a nation-wide network to scout gifted physics students from high schools all over Indonesia, and personally coached the more than 30 students from 26 provinces who made the final cut. Since 1993 Indonesian students have won several silver and bronze medals and one gold in international competition. Today hundreds of thousands of Indonesian high school students are eagerly learning physics, and hundreds of teachers are asking to be trained to help them.

> One young dedicated physicist and three friends have achieved what thousands of educational bureaucrats were not able to accomplish in decades after spending millions of dollars.

This is Integrative social action—people working cooperatively with others to bring about change in their immediate environment. Young organizers like Tara Church and Melissa Poe didn't sit around arguing about the 'right way' to change the world. They simply responded spontaneously to problems they saw right in front of them.

Starting Small

Controllers like to think big. But Kouzes and Posner point out that talking of big changes scares people who fear change, and discourages and exhausts those who want it. People who seek grandiose changes are usually more interested in personal fame than in achieving change. It's important, Kouzes and Posner suggest, to start with small, reachable goals that will build motivation and attract others. Small actions are self-reinforcing:

> Get things moving. Focus on small wins . . . .Little successive victories earn a lot of credit, and they inspire confidence.

Connecting

Individualistic heroes have always been a Hollywood favorite: alone and unaided they bravely battle gangs, the government, the Mafia, corporations, the police, small town conventionality, aliens, and foreign armies. Advertisers also love them: the Marlboro Man was a lone cowboy, but he herded millions of human sheep into the tobacco corral. Since individualistic revolt is ineffectual and harmless it's the approved form of rebellion in American society.

There's no one on this planet so bizarre that he or she can't find a kindred spirit somewhere. Especially with the Internet. If something isn't working for me, there are going to be other people for whom it isn't working either. I have several choices then: suffer in silence, complain in private, be a solitary heroic failure, or find allies and react together.

Cooperating with others is crucial to Integrative change. Modern business writers note that while the old rule was to hide your assets, knowledge, inventions, and plans from your competitors, today it slows you down and makes you less adaptable.

Here's the new rule: tell everybody everything.

This is an Integrative principle that applies even more strongly to social entrepreneurs.

Leapfrogging

Controllers see change as linear. There's one path, it goes in a straight line, and everyone has to follow it. This is the way the World Bank, for example, approaches development. Everyone has to follow the path the West did—mechanize, privatize, industrialize, and if you have lots of natural resources, like metals and oil, you'll have a head start. It should be a mammoth warning signal to the West that the most successful Arab country in the Middle East today has almost no oil. The absence of oil has in fact been its salvation.

In terms of resources, Dubai is the poorest of the seven United Arab Emirates. Fifty years ago it was just a bit of desert with a poor village by the sea. Today it is the economic hub of the Middle East. It boasts the world's tallest building, the world's largest man-made island, a banking center to rival New York and London, a thriving economy and booming real estate market, and several international news agencies, including Al Jazeera. Dubai, an entrepreneur's paradise, was created entirely by ambition, imagination, and energy.

Again and again projects labeled white elephants by skeptics have turned out to be enormously profitable.

These people never experienced an industrial revolution.
They've gone almost straight from a nomadic life on camels to the world of cell phones and faxes.

How did they do it? In part by embracing a few Integrative values. Dubai is completely open to foreigners, who constitute 80% of its population. They come from everywhere, are made up of all nationalities and all religions, living side by side without conflict, for religious and racial tolerance is the rule in Dubai, as is gender equality. Women have the same legal and educational rights as men, and hold positions of major economic power.

World countries don't have to follow the path we've taken. That isn't the way evolution works. New civilizations leapfrog into the future, bypassing the structures and patterns of the old.

A thousand years ago Europe was the 'Third World'—peopled by the backward tribes of the globe—while the civilized world was Muslim and Chinese. The United States was a backward nation only two centuries ago. The world hicks of today are the world leaders of tomorrow—this is the lesson of history.

The successful nations of the future will travel light. They won't need large industries or large armies, but only large brains. They won't need big plants but only big networks. They won't need oil because they have the sun. They're outsiders in the current cultural paradigm—ideally poised to catch the next wave.

In Estonia they're still plowing fields with horses and few people have ever used checkbooks, but almost all banking is done online. Estonia, in fact, ranks second in the world in Internet banking. In 1991 most Estonians didn't have even have telephones, but today 70% have mobile phones. And Estonia ranks third highest in the world in e-government. All inter-ministry government documents are sent electronically, except, of course, in the Controller strongholds of Defense and Intelligence. Cabinet meetings are held online and meetings that used to take four hours now take 10 minutes. Decisions are posted on the government website and citizens can register their ideas and reactions online.

There's no reason for Third World countries to develop a dependency on non-renewable energy resources like oil. What they need most isn't heavy industry but communication technology. Less dependent on transportation to survive, they can hook into the global grid and create sophisticated modern societies without destroying their local communities the way the West was forced to do. In India today, software engineers are leaving the cities and returning to their native villages for that very reason. You can work online anywhere.

Solar power can easily meet the energy needs of computers, and solar energy doesn't depend on a top-down distribution system— unlike oil, which tends to foster economic and social inequality and encourages corrupt dictatorial regimes.

The Third World, in other words, can leapfrog directly from the agricultural to the electronic age without bothering to undergo the brutalities of the industrial era. A big physical plant is unnecessary in a connected world, and the ability to prosper with a minimum of hardware and industrial pollution will make some of the least developed Third World countries increasingly attractive places to live and work

Beginnings

A tiny shop in a dusty town in rural India, without windows or air-conditioning, has three computers hooked up to a small plastic box that promises to have a revolutionary impact in the Third World. A dozen schoolchildren come there every day to surf the Web. The box is part of CorDECT, a simple wireless technology that is also being introduced in Mexico, Egypt, Madagascar, Fiji, Kenya, and Brazil.

In a poor rural village in Bangladesh a woman named Jamirunnesa sits outside her mud-walled hut with a cell phone, which she offers to her neighbors for a small fee. By the beginning of the new millennium GrameenPhone, a subsidiary of the micro-lending Grameen Bank, had set up phone service operators like Jamirunnesa in eleven hundred villages and planned to double this in another year.

Today the Grameen Bank has lent almost 6 billion dollars to

almost seven million individuals, 97% of them women—mostly poor rural women like Jamirunnesa with her cell phone, who ten years ago was barely able to feed her family and had, in her own words, "lost all hopes."

The small Third World stories of today will be the big stories of tomorrow. Opportunity lies hidden in the folds of other people's shortsightedness.

Integrative changes are happening all over the world from people who aren't asking what the 'correct path' is. They're not obsessing about the 'big picture'. The Controller sees himself standing outside the living world. He wants to grasp and manipulate it like a god. His ambition paralyzes him. The Integrator knows she's inside it, a part of it—that it is formed by a million unpredictable actions, of which hers is one. She trusts herself and those around her.

The Need for Integrative Thinking

In Chapter 1 I said that while the full emergence of Integrative Culture wouldn't automatically solve the world's problems, it would make those solutions possible, since there is no way they can even begin to be solved in the context of Control Culture. Integrative Culture is appropriate to an overpopulated planet made up of many interdependent nations with finite resources. Control Culture, with its value on belligerence, its tendency to construct artificial physical, conceptual, interpersonal, and psychological walls, its tendency to hide information and dis-empower people, its linear concept of perpetual (i.e., cancerous) growth, is a luxury the planet can no longer afford. This cultural metamorphosis is exactly what Jared Diamond had in mind when he said the societies that avoided extinction when faced with an ecological crisis were those that underwent a re-examination of basic values.

Self-Creating Coherence

David Bohm saw a vision of an ideal society in the freedom of movement of electrons within the organized collective system of the atom. Mathematician Michael Barnsley sees the same paradox in fractals—a unity in which every single component part is free.

Improvisation—both in theatre and in jazz—exemplifies this self-creating coherence. Each individual creates personal improvisations around a theme yet is utterly responsive to the improvisations of others, which creates a rich, integrated whole. No one dictates this. The order emerges from their collective creating. The emergence of these two art forms in the 20th century is another expression of the growth of Integrative Culture.

Alfonso Montuori points out that the Latin root of improvisation is *improvisus*, unforeseen, and suggests this form of creativity is particularly appropriate for our time:

> Our lives today are riddled with complexity, with the unfore-
> seen, the ambiguous, the uncertain—in science, in the
> economy, in ethics, and indeed just about every aspect of life.

He relates the emergence of improvisational phenomena to the cultural shift from a "fundamentally static worldview to one that is process oriented."

The transformation from Controller to Integrative Culture is taking place one connection at a time. As this happens we begin to realize that the relationships are all that really exist. That as we contribute to the changing of the world we're also groping our way into awareness that we're part of a whole—a whole that consists of an infinite number of perpetually changing connections.

Such a whole is never static, never suffocating, never oppressive, because it demands only that you be fully who you are, and that you appreciate and validate that same fullness in those around you.

Appendix
The Rise and Decline of Control Culture
A Brief History

> If others had not been foolish, we should be so.
> WILLIAM BLAKE

People have always quarreled, and in Paleolithic times there were no doubt skirmishes between one band and another. But most such conflict was handled—as in other primate bands—by separation. War as we know it did not exist for 99% of our history as a species. Pitched battles between standing armies began to occur only after people settled in villages, expanded their populations, and produced surpluses.

Before farming and herding there was little motivation for war. The human population was small and everyone was needed. There was no concept of territory or ownership and no spoils to be had.

The Beginning

Between 5000 and 3000 BC peaceful societies all over Europe and the Middle East were conquered one after another by waves of armed invaders who worshipped warlike sky gods. Before long, war became a way of life.

Robert O'Connell suggests that it began with animal-raising nomads, whose herds—their main source of food and clothing—were vulnerable to disease, droughts, and sudden freezes. When this happened they either had to raid other herds or starve to death. From raiding other herds it was only a short step to raiding villages.

Faced with aggression, O'Connell notes, there are three possible responses: flee, submit, or resist. Hunter-gatherers tended to flee, but sedentary groups didn't have that option, and since herdsmen had no interest in acquiring territory, there was little to be gained by submitting to them. Villagers began to build walls, form armies, and defend themselves.

Herdsmen may have begun it, but it was agriculturalists who carried war to the level familiar to us today—with trained standing armies capable of capturing and holding territory. By 3000 BC we find a full-fledged Control Culture in Sumer, with standing armies, centralized male power, social classes, hierarchies, slaves, and women reduced to mere property.

In Chapter 1 I stated that we were living through the greatest cultural upheaval in human history. This is true only because of the speed of it—that it's taking hundreds of years instead of thousands. The rise of Control Culture was otherwise just as shattering.

After a few millennia Control Culture had covered the globe except for a few isolated corners; and its domination continued into modern times with very little opposition. The short-lived Athenian democracy—barely more than an oligarchy, so much of the population was excluded from it—may have rejected Controller authoritarianism but it embraced all its other tenets.

Of course there have always been individuals—sages, mystics, prophets, and satirists—who attacked Controller values: Euripides, for example, was bitterly anti-war, sympathetic to women, mocked the rabid patriotism of his day, and was possibly the first to make fun of machismo—portraying Heracles as a muscle-bound buffoon and Achilles as a pompous narcissist. But for every Euripides portraying the horrors of war there were a hundred epic poets singing its glories. What we call the great literature of all major civilizations—Greek, Roman, Norse, Celtic, Judaic, Hindu, Moslem, Chinese, Japanese—is mostly about war.

Integrative Beginnings

The first seedlings of Integrative Culture appeared in the 18th century, which was also—ironically, but predictably—a peak for Control Culture. Efforts to purify Control Culture of non-

Controller elements were taking place, as we've seen, in politics, science, childrearing, and religion.

The 18th century was a time of ferment. Voltaire and Rousseau in France were widely read and praised, and Thomas Paine's *Common Sense* and *The Rights of Man* were best sellers, the former in America, the latter in England. People began to take seriously the idea that differences in social status didn't necessarily reflect differences in character, ability, or moral worth. People had complained about social injustice before, but as a sad fact of life, not as something that could be changed.

Even then, of course, it was only *men* who were "created equal." Few of the most radical egalitarians of the era thought women should be free and equal. Nor was pacifism popular—most radicals were enthusiastic about war, and their cries for freedom and equality were couched in military language. And radical thinking was still static—radical theorists loved to invent unchanging utopias in which every single detail of human life was rigidly scripted. Process thinking was far in the future.

Egalitarianism is one of those principles that, once stated, is hard to keep in bounds. Most of those who embraced it at the beginning never thought it would or should be extended to women. A century passed before it was.

Feminism

What's impressive about the earliest feminist writings is how mild they were and how bitterly they were attacked. Mary Wollstonecraft, for example, was only interested in women being educated. The vote wasn't even contemplated. It was another fifty years before women began to fight for adult legal status, and even longer before they sought the right to vote. The first women's gym was established in 1870 in Massachusetts, and was viewed with alarm—refined women were not supposed to be active in any way.

It wasn't until 1920 that women were able to vote in the United States. In France they had to wait till the end of World War II, in Switzerland until 1970. Men who have pursued egalitarian goals with revolutionary zeal have felt quite comfortable seeing women enslaved.

The modern women's movement was triggered by this very discrepancy: women during the civil rights and anti-war protests of the sixties noticed that in all these supposedly radical movements they were treated as second-class citizens.

And for decades after winning the vote, women tended to vote as their husbands did. The gender gap only began to appear when the women's movement became a major force in the 1970s. Today the gender gap is both large and clear-cut. On foreign policy issues men tend to be in favor of 'getting tough' with other countries, and are anti-UN. Women tend to be for establishing cooperative relations. More men also favor a competitive domestic agenda—pro-business, pro-wealthy, anti-tax, anti-government. Women are more likely to be pro-environment, pro-education, and for programs that benefit the poor and children. Women legislators, too, are more likely than their male counterparts to assign top priority to child-care programs, affordable health insurance, and care for the elderly, while male legislators are more focused on cutting taxes. The gap holds among both Democrats and Republicans.

To some extent the gap is due to the fact that women tend to be more future-oriented than men. They are more concerned with issues that will affect their children as they grow—education, health care, the environment, equal opportunity.

Romanticism

By 1800 Newtonian science—with its vision of a clockwork universe that would be entirely under human control once we got the hang of it—had become the dominant ideology of the age. But at that very same time the Romantic movement emerged, with its emphasis on feelings and mystery, and it maintained a strong hold on popular imagination throughout the 19th century.

The Newtonian vision had given us the feeling that we were in control of nature and this was comforting. But it was also boring. The Romanticists had a passion for nature and wildness, and a revulsion against man-made environments. Painters and poets were fascinated by wild, uncultivated landscapes. Even the rationalist John Stuart Mill was caught up in it:

> Nor is there much satisfaction in contemplating the world with nothing left to the spontaneous activity of nature; with every foot of land brought into cultivation . . . and scarcely a place left where a wild shrub or flower could grow without being eradicated as a weed in the name of improved agriculture.

But war was still popular. Its violence and passion appealed to the Romantics, and military men were often the heroes of their dramas. It took World War I to de-romanticize war. Only as war became increasingly 'purified' did it begin to lose its popularity.

Before the 1960s people had sought changes in one or two aspects of the Controller system, but the movements of the sixties constituted the first generalized challenge to it. By the late sixties and early seventies all Controller principles were under assault. For the first time every assumption of Control Culture was being called into question by a substantial segment of society, and everything of substance that the pioneers of that period began has endured and expanded.

A Return?

Some might see Integrative Culture as simply an undoing—a return to the archaic ways of pre-Control Culture. But Integrative Culture is not merely a revival. An illustration may make this clearer:

A child might show a talent for singing or dancing or painting. To channel and develop her gift she is provided with teachers in order to master the technical aspects of her art. At this point much of the spontaneity and feeling that were there at the beginning may be lost, as she struggles to achieve technical skill. That's the end of the story for some students, but for the truly gifted there's a return of that grace and spontaneity as technical facility is achieved. Yet we don't say that the mature artist has simply undone the intervening years and returned to childhood. On the contrary, the new spontaneity has been *added* to the technical skill—built upon it, in fact.

In the same way, Integrative Culture is built upon and incorporates Control Culture. No one would say that Western European culture is like that of the Pygmies and Bushmen. It has simply outgrown a few of the rigidities of the Controller system.

In Frank Herbert's novel, *Dune,* a character remarks that the goal of all life is "to maintain and produce coordinated patterns of greater and greater diversity." In other words, evolution is a process of integrating ever more dissimilar elements. A unity is created, then broken down as it tries to incorporate new, discordant components, then struggles to create a new unity. "Evolution is a continuous breaking and forming to make new, richer wholes."

It's this stage we're in now. We're like the child musician or artist trying to integrate her formal training with the spontaneity and feeling she once had. Integrators are trying to create a more complex unity out of the rich and dissonant elements introduced by the exuberant clashes of the Controller Age.

Notes

Introduction

1   —Elisabet Sahtouris: Scott London, "From Mechanics to Organics: An Interview with Elisabet Sahtouris" (www.scottlondon.com/interviews/sahtouris).

Chapter 1   *In the Middle of the Bridge*

5   —"willingness to reconsider core values": Jared Diamond, *Collapse* (Viking, 2005), 552.

7   —"that it wasn't always that way": Joel Arthur Barker, *Paradigms: The Business of Discovering the Future* (HarperCollins, 1993), 21–22. Barker mentions the growth of participatory management in industry, the acceptance of cohabitation as a substitute for marriage, gains in civil rights, the emergence of information as a key resource, the women's movement, the growth of terrorism, and environmentalism. Similarly, Warren Bennis contrasts the immediate post-World War II 'analog' decade with that of the 'digital' 1990s. The former features linear thinking, mechanical metaphors, authoritarian leadership, conventional warfare, specialists, and experience; the latter features nonlinear thinking, biological metaphors, democratic leadership, terrorism, generalists, and openness. See Warren G. Bennis and Robert J. Thomas, *Geeks & Geezers* (Harvard Business School Press, 2002), 11–13.

8   —two global cultural systems with opposing values and assumptions: We usually think of a culture as bounded by a society—French culture, American culture, Samoan culture—but cultures exist at many levels. There are subcultures within a society—urban culture, rural culture, youth culture, gang culture, rock culture, country-club culture. And every family has its own culture, too, as do friends who've been together a long time. At the other end of the scale we find patterns of behavior common to many societies. People talk of European culture, modern culture, and even Western culture—a term that not only embraces half the globe but three millennia. When I speak of Control Culture or Integrative Culture I'm casting an even

larger net, covering most of the globe, a kind of megaculture that transcends local variations. Despite huge differences, there are things common to Zulus, medieval Chinese, Aztecs, Biblical Israelites, ancient Greeks, New Guinea tribes, and 19th century Europeans, just as there are to hens, eagles, hummingbirds, and ostriches, all of which we call birds.

9   —that intelligence springs from organizational complexity: Gregory Bateson, *Steps to an Ecology of Mind* (Ballantine, 1972), 315, 460.

9   —"a critical mass, a quorum, and the thinking begins": Lewis Thomas, *The Lives of a Cell* (Viking, 1974), 12–13.

9   —self-creating coherence: Henry C. Metcalf and L. Urwick, eds. *Dynamic Administration: The Collected Papers of Mary Parker Follett* (Harper, 1942), 200.

12   —we were governed by very different habits and values: see, for example, Robert L. O'Connell, *Ride of the Second Horseman* (Oxford University Press, 1995); Riane Eisler, *The Chalice and the Blade* (Harper & Row, 1987).

12   —even fish . . . are less bound by instinct than we used to believe: closely related primate species can behave in diametrically opposite ways: female chimps prefer the most aggressive males, while females of the chimp-like bonobos prefer the *least* aggressive males. See Riane Eisler, *Sacred Pleasure* (HarperSanFrancisco, 1995).

12   —"can switch genes on and off": Jonathan Shaw, "Phenome Fellow" *Harvard Magazine* (Jan./Feb., 2003), 30–33. Even insects are capable of behavioral change. Entomologist Laurent Keller discovered an ant 'supercolony' stretching along 6,000 kilometers of coastline from Italy to Portugal. Highly belligerent Argentine ants imported to Europe in 1920 behaved amicably toward genetically diverse ants from nests a thousand miles away. Bijal P. Trivedi, *National Geographic Today* (4/18/02).

12   — self-organizing system that responds to events outside". Sidney Liebes, Elisabet Sahtouris, and Brian Swimme, *A Walk Through Time* (Wiley, 1998), 27.

13   —"the objective of understanding how nature organizes itself": Robert B. Laughlin, *A Different Universe* (Basic Books, 2005), 76, 200, 308.

13   —growing and evolving organically, without centralized control: Kevin Kelly, *New Rules for the New Economy* (Viking, 1998) 31, 83; see also Frances Cairncross, *The Death of Distance* (Harvard Business School Press, 1997); Stan Davis and Christopher Meyer, *Blur: The Speed of Change in the Connected Economy* (Perseus Books, 1998); Thomas L. Friedman, *The Lexus and the Olive Tree* (Farrar, Straus, & Giroux, 1999); William Knoke, *Bold New World* (Kodansha International, 1996); Virginia Postrel, *The Future and Its Enemies* (Free Press, 1998).

12   —Lovelock . . . Benyus . . . Ebert: J. E. Lovelock, *Gaia* (Oxford
     University Press, 1987); Janine M. Benyus, *Biomimicry: Innovation
     Inspired by Nature* (Morrow, 1997); John David Ebert, *Twilight of the
     Clockwork God* (Council Oak Books, 1999), 73.

14   —what Riane Eisler calls the "Dominator Model". See Riane Eisler
     and David Loye, *The Partnership Way* (HarperSanFrancisco, 1990.

17   —predicted in 1964 that democracy was inevitable: Philip Slater and
     Warren Bennis, "Democracy Is Inevitable", *Harvard Business Review*
     (March/April, 1964).

17   —"hierarchy and centralized control are collapsing": Knoke, *Bold*,
     162.

17   —informal networks responded quickly on 9/11: Duncan J. Watts, *Six
     Degrees: The Science of a Connected Age* (Norton, 2003), 292–299.

18   —worst possible way to deal with a crisis: Alfonso Montuori, "How
     to Make Enemies and Influence People: Anatomy of the Anti-
     pluralist, Totalitarian Mindset", *Futures* (2005), 18–38.

18   —"this at the peak of hurricane season": Erik Larson, *Isaac's Storm*
     (Crown, 1999), 102–103, 112–114.

19   —"from different sides of the room": Charles Handy, *The Age of
     Paradox* (Harvard Business School Press, 1994), 118–120. The
     classic Prisoner's Dilemma of game theory is based on the same
     inability to communicate.

19   —"competing to the point of lunacy": *Ibid.*

22   —it takes a network to fight a network: John Arquilla: *L.A. Times*
     (8/25/02). Plans for an invasion of Iraq were actually in place months
     before 9/11. The administration hoped the Iraqis would shoot down
     one of the American pilots patrolling the no-fly zone, providing a
     pretext. See Ron Suskind, *The Price of Loyalty* (Simon and Schuster,
     2004), 96–97.

22   —will go the way of other obsolete empires: As Charles Kupchan
     points out, American economic dominance is rapidly coming to an
     end. Charles A. Kupchan, *The End of the American Era* (Knopf,
     2002).

25   —"cooperative behavior would be favored by natural selection":
     Ernst Mayr, *What Evolution Is* (Basic Books, 2001), 131–132.

25   —what they wanted the child to do: Esther Herrmann, J. Call, M.V.
     Hernandez-Lloreda, B. Hare, M. Tomasello, "Humans Have
     Evolved Specialized Skills of Social Cognition: The Cultural
     Intelligence Hypothesis", *Science*, Vol. 317 (7 Sept. 2007),
     1360–1366.

25   —the toddler would ignore him: Felix Warneken and M. Tomasello,
     "Altruistic Helping in Human Infants and Chimpanzees", *Science*
     (3/3/06), 1301–1303.

Chapter 2 *The Way of Change: Purity Destroys*

29 —As Lewis Mumford once said: Lewis Mumford, "The Fallacy of Systems," *Saturday Review*, 32 (October, 1949).

30 —"escape self-asphyxiation": *Ibid.* Children brought up by rigid adherence to any kind of logical system are usually maimed by it.

30 —Paul stressed celibacy as a goal: see I *Corinthians*, 7.

30 —"but just the opposite": Mumford, *loc. cit.*

31 —"the most literal, unyielding interpretation of their sacred texts": Naomi Klein, "Baghdad Year Zero" *Harper's* (September, 2004), 53.

31 —"of the guiding logic behind deregulated free markets": *Ibid.*, 52.

33 —to make Christianity a more perfectly patriarchal religion, and desacralize 'Mother' Nature: see Rupert Sheldrake, *The Rebirth of Nature* (Bantam, 1991), 20–30.

34 —willing to sink it to prove their devotion: True conservatives want to preserve what exists, which is full of contradictions. Unlike al-Qaida, whose "ultimate objective is to 'purify' the world." Jessica E. Stern, "Caliphate of Terror" *Harvard Magazine* (July/August, 2004), 27.

35 —social eversion: For a fuller discussion of this concept see Philip Slater, *Earthwalk* (Anchor, 1974), 167–170. One might ask if we see these dimensions as straight lines only because we see such a narrow segment of their arc.

36 —the 'trends' that the media find interesting: Conservatives like the pendulum metaphor because it implies that nothing is really changing. It's in constant motion but never goes anywhere, thus providing novelty without threat—a media ideal.

Chapter 3 *On Gender Concepts: Is Stupidity Masculine?*

43 —men seem to be struggling to define themselves: See, e.g., Sam Keen, *Fire in the Belly* (Bantam, 1991), 48–51, 119–151, 180; Andrew Kimbrell, *The Masculine Mystique* (Ballantine Books, 1995), 235, 295–302.

44 —employed almost 13 million people: L. Wolfe, Trends and Statistics for Women in Business (About.com).

44 —"the majority are women": John Naisbitt and Patricia Aburdene, *Megatrends 2000* (Morrow, 1990), 220–226. This is true even in Asia. See Naisbitt, *Megatrends Asia* (Simon & Schuster, 1996), 199–229. For the impact of the Women's Movement see Ruth Rosen, *The World Split Open: How the Modern Women's Movement Changed America* (Viking, 2000).Leonard Shlain sees the Women's Movement as a result of the growing dominance of image over print. The causality is shaky, but the correlation with the spread of democracy, egalitarianism, pacifism, and nonlinear scientific theories is undeniable. Leonard Shlain, *The Alphabet Versus the Goddess* (Viking, 1998), 378–429.

45 —"lawyers and professors said": *The New York Times* (3/26/01). For women in academia, see Cathy A. Trower and Richard P. Chait, "Faculty Diversity", *Harvard Magazine* (March/April, 2002), 34 ff.

45 —women in positions of power as this cohort moves up: yet every few years the media ask if "feminism is dead." By 'feminism', of course, they aren't thinking of education, legal status, economic parity, day-care programs, battered women's shelters, women's health clinics, anti-discrimination battles, and other substantive issues, but bra-burnings and PC language, the superficialities that have always captured their interest.

45 —more than two-thirds female: Harbour Fraser Hodder, "Girl Power" *in Harvard Magazine* (January/February, 2008), 34–42.

45 —"the fireballs were mostly female": Tamar Lewin, *The New York Times* (7/8/06).

46 —they make up 70% of the graduates: Frances Harrison, BBC News, Tehran (9/19/06).

46 —correlation between gender attitudes and democracy: Ronald Inglehart and Pippa Norris, *Rising Tide: Gender Equality and Cultural Change around the World* (Cambridge University Press, 2003).

46 —denying the rights of women a major barrier to development: Jeffrey D. Sachs, *The End of Poverty* (Penguin, 2005), 60. Educating women also lowers birthrates.

47 —"found in herself the person she needed": James M. Kouzes and Barry Z. Posner, "Bringing Leadership Lessons from the Past Into the Future". In Warren Bennis, Gretchen M. Spreitzer, and Thomas G. Cummings (eds.), *The Future of Leadership* (Jossey-Bass, 2001), 82–83.

47 —Tara Church: John T. Boal, "The Tree Musketeers" *Creative Living* (Spring, 1998); *Los Angeles Times* (12/6/99).

49 —"sharing was the basis of our success as a species": quoted in Beryl Lieff Benderly, *The Myth of Two Minds* (Doubleday, 1987), 137. Male superiority in strength was in any case far less marked then than today. See Nancy Makepeace Tanner, *On Becoming Human* (Cambridge University Press, 1981), 61, 220–21, 271ff.

49 —decrease in sexual dimorphism: Mayr, *Evolution*, 245.

49 —gender equality in pre-historic times: Eisler, *Chalice*, 24–28. On women providing the most calories see O'Connell, *Ride*, 226. The fantasy of a primeval matriarchy is largely a projection of Controller fears onto the past.

49 —"even the hunt is a joint effort": Colin Turnbull, *The Forest People* (Simon and Schuster, 1961), 110, 154.

49 —Pygmy and Bantu reactions to menarche: *Ibid.*, 184–187.

51 —the rules rarely apply to men: See, e.g., J. D. Unwin, *Sex and Culture* (Oxford University Press, 1934).

51 —Hollywood and women's sexuality: Stephen Holden, *The New York Times* (5/3/98).

51   —propositioned in front of their patients: Frances K. Conley, M.D. *Walking Out on the Boys* (Farrar, Straus & Giroux, 1998).

52   —uselessness valued over utility: See Thorstein Veblen, *The Theory of the Leisure Class* (Modern Library, 1934).

52   —greater risk of violence from a husband then from a stranger: Elizabeth Rosenthal, *The New York Times*, 10/3/06.

53   —innovation comes from outsiders: Warren Bennis and Philip Slater, *The Temporary Society* (Jossey-Bass, 1998) Chapter 1; Handy, *Paradox*; Barker, *Paradigms*, 55–63. On the national level E. R. Service calls this "the Law of the Local Discontinuity of Progress": M. D. Sahlins and E. R. Service, *Evolution and Culture* (University of Michigan Press, 1960), 98: see also Jarod Diamond, *Guns, Germs, and Steel* (Norton, 1997), 247–254. A similar process may have occurred at the primate level. Janine M. Benyus, *Biomimicry: Innovation Inspired by Nature* (Morrow, 1997), 159.

54   —solving collective problems is not a form of hand-to-hand combat: When Afghanistan was invaded Afghani women in America organized to help both Afghan refugees and women still in Afghanistan, while the men engaged in political disputes. Dashka Slater, "Among the Widows", *San Francisco* (March, 2002), 78.

55   —"of pattern recognizers and meaning makers": Daniel H. Pink, *A Whole New Mind* (Riverhead, 2005), 50.

55   —women more apt to involve employees in decision-making: Deborah Tannen, *You Just Don't Understand* (Morrow, 1990), 181; Bennis and Slater, 131–134; Carol R. Frenier, *Business and the Feminine Principle* (Butterworth-Heinemann, 1997), 86ff. See also, Daniel Yergin and Joseph Stanislaw, *The Commanding Heights* (Simon & Schuster, 1998), 372; Knoke, 125.

55   —"all qualities that leaders need": Tom Peters, *San Francisco Examiner* (9/17/00).

56   —"guaranteed to be boundary-dissolving": Terence McKenna, in Ralph Abraham, Terence McKenna, Rupert Sheldrake, *Trialogues at the Edge of the West* (Bear & Co., 1992), 48.

56   —"do 11 things at a time and guys can't": Tom Peters. On being comfortable with chaos, see Kelly, *New Rules*, 109–116.

56   —a UCLA study showed women have another option: S. E. Taylor, L. C. Klein, B. P. Lewis, T. L. Gruenewald, R. A. R. Gurung, and J. A. Updegraff, "Female Responses to Stress: Tend and Befriend, Not Fight or Flight", *Psychol. Rev.* 107 (3) 41–429. The chemical agent in this response is oxytocin, the effects of which estrogen enhances and testosterone reduces. This may be why women outlive men, since people with social ties tend to have lower blood pressure, heart rate, and cholesterol.

57   —sees herself as "an individual in a network of connections": Tannen, *Understand*, 15, 24 ff., 43–47, 177, 218–224; Carol

Gilligan, *In a Different Voice* (Harvard University Press, 1982), 24–63.

57 —"We don't know what we want to be": Michael Kimmel, *The Boston Globe*, 5/17/98.

57 —"onto the scrapheap of evolutionary extinction": Lynn Margulis and Dorion Sagan *Microcosmos* (Touchstone, 1990), 18, 121–124.

58 —"men are marked by the warfare system and the military virtues": Keen, *Fire*, 37–38.

58 —"even in the cannon's mouth": Shakespeare, *As You Like It*, II, 7.

58 —Henry V at Agincourt: Act IV, Scene 3.

59 —"seemingly sadistic abuse and hardship": Lt. Col. Dave Grossman, *On Killing* (Little, Brown, 1995), 82. Abuse in boot camp serves the same purpose as hazing in fraternities. See Deborah Tannen, *The Argument Culture* (Random House, 1998), 189–191. Such rituals capitalize on the human reluctance to admit that a personal sacrifice was of no value. "If I subjected myself to degradation to join this group," people tell themselves, "it must be worthwhile." See Elliot Aronson, *The Social Animal*, 7th ed. (Freeman, 1995), 213–217. Other than as a hazing ritual, this aspect of military training is out of date. The ability to maintain a tough, unyielding stance is utterly irrelevant when a man's opponent can't even see him—a man firing from a tank or a plane or a missile silo. Mentally our soldiers are being trained to fight in Caesar's army.

60 —"men who have killed . . . tell a different tale": Grossman, *On Killing*, 3–4, 9–28, 34, 38, 51–56, 88, 97–108, 110, 118, 128, 158–165, 190–192, 237–244, 251–257, 306–308. The infamous gas chambers at Auschwitz were invented because shooting women and children was too disturbing to soldiers in Nazi firing squads. This same 'problem' was solved during the Vietnam War by making killing reflexive. Trainers used realistic models of humans that would pop up out of trenches and quickly pop down again, so the recruit had to fire without thinking or miss the tiny window of opportunity. The technique was effective—in the Vietnam War the firing percentage rose from 15% to 95%. So did the psychiatric problems.

60 —about 2% are sociopathic: Grossman, 44, 78–79, 180–189.

61 —some men see only threat in the women's movement: Robert Bly feels men have been weakened by feminism. Robert Bly, *Iron John* (Addison-Wesley, 1990); Michael Kimmel (ed.), *The Politics of Manhood* (Temple University Press, 1995), 19–22, 32–41. Bly claims a boy can't learn to be a man without a father figure, but a common characteristic of 'great' men is that they were maternally driven, with fathers dead, absent, inadequate, or despised. Dan Baum attributes the ingenuity of junior officers in Iraq (see Chapter 5) to being of a generation often brought up by single mothers (although he presents no data to support this assumption).

62 —"trying to hang onto certain masculine distinctions": Harrison G. Pope, jr., Katharine A. Phillips and Roberto Olivardia, *The Adonis Complex* (Free Press, 2000).

62 —three-fourths of the men wanted more time with their children: Warren Farrell, *The Myth of Male Power* (Simon & Schuster, 1993), 20; Kimbrell, *Mystique*, 12, 145–175, 181.

62–3—fathers doing more child-care: Kimbrell, *Mystique*, 150–151, 180–181.

63 —more boys than girls diagnosed with "Gender Identity Disorder": Phyllis Burke, *Gender Shock* (Anchor Books, 1996), 201 ff.

64 —the 'Boy Code': William Pollack, *Real Boys* (Random House, 1998); see also Elliot Aronson, *Nobody Left To Hate* (Worth Publishers, 2000), 97–98. The Boy Code may be the reason movies dealing with grownup situations are 'chick flicks', while movies with comic book heroes, gunfights, and car chases are considered appropriate male fare.

64 —eighty-five percent of teen suicides are boys: boys also commit 94% of juvenile murders and account for 84% of juvenile drunk driving arrests; and five out of six bullies are boys. See Daniel J. Kindlon and Michael Thompson, *Raising Cain: Protecting the Emotional Life of Boys* (Ballantine, 1999), 160, 183, 218–238.

64 —the search for genetic gender behaviors: David D. Gilmore, *Manhood in the Making* (Yale University Press, 1991); Deborah Blum, *Sex on the Brain* (Viking, 1997). See also Margaret W. Matlin, *The Psychology of Women* (Holt, Rinehart and Winston, 1987), 31–32; Alfie Kohn, *The Brighter Side of Human Nature* (Basic Books, 1990), 7–17, 26–27; Burke, *Gender Shock*, 189–219; Martine Rothblatt, *The Apartheid of Sex* (Crown, 1995), xiii, 107; Kimbrell, *Mystique*, 20–27. Despite negative scientific findings the media continue to push the genetic view. This led Beryl Lieff Benderly, a science writer, to write a book about "the new scientific findings" on gender differences, only to discover that none of them held up (Benderly, *Myth*, 1–3). For research on innate aggression see Alfie Kohn, *Brighter Side*, 181–204, 215–217. A recent study by Kurt Fischer and Malcolm Watson, funded by the National Institute for Child Health and Human Development found that adult violence in the home, including the physical punishment of children, was the best predictor of violence in the child. See also Kohn, 56; James Gilligan, *Violence* (Grosset/Putnam, 1996), 43–55.

64 —nurturance a masculine trait: The Teduray of Mindanao exemplified this. See Stuart A. Schlegel, *Wisdom from a Rainforest* (Univ. of Georgia Press, 1998), 109, 112–113.

64 —squelched in most boys by the Boy Code: Pollack, *Real Boys*, 11, 18, 20–51.

64 —Daniel Pink says: Pink, *Whole New Mind*, 166–167.

65   —workers continually trying to out-macho each other: Samantha Henig, *Harvard Magazine* (September/October, 2007), 16–18, reporting on an as yet unpublished study by Robin J. Ely and Debra E. Meyerson. To "take it like a man!" is one of the reasons workers are so easily exploited. Douglas Foley talks of young working class Mexicans in Texas "aspiring" to "dangerous, dirty, heavy work that only 'real men' did." Schoolwork was "boring, sissy stuff". *Learning Capitalist Culture: Deep in the Heart of Tejas* (University of Pennsylvania Press, 1990). Quoted in Janet L. Abu-Lughod, *Sociology for the Twenty-First Century* (University of Chicago Press, 1999), 253.

65   —Deborah Blum, *Sex on the Brain*, 68.

65   —"greater ability to read cues": Brizendine, *The Female Brain* (Morgan Road, 2006), 13 and *passim*. Brizendine made a notorious blunder by accepting as fact the unfounded rumor that women talked three times as much as men, when the first scientific study on the subject showed them to be equally talkative. See Matthias R. Mehl, Simine Vazire, Nairan Ramirez-Esparza, Richard B. Slatcher, and James W. Pennebaker, "Are Women More Talkative Than Men?" *Science*, 7/6/07, 82.

66   —confined to a mental hospital . . . for not being 'feminine' enough: Daphne Scholinski, *The Last Time I Wore a Dress* (Riverside Press, 1997).

66   —adult gender-typing of infants: H. A. Moss, "Sex, Age, and State as Determinants of Mother-Infant Interaction", *Merrill-Palmer Quarterly*, 1967 (13) 19–36; Kohn, *Brighter Side*, 29; Matlin, *Psychology of Women*, 33–41, 58ff.; Dane Archer, personal communication, 1997; Anne Fausto-Sterling, *Myths of Gender* (Basic Books, 1985).

67   —"models . . . have no relevance to today's world": Pollack, *Real Boys*, xxii, 10, 81–112.

Chapter 4   *On Thinking: Becoming a Verb*

68   —with Native Americans . . . the difference disappeared: Ian Marshall and Danah Zohar, *Who's Afraid of Schrodinger's Cat?* (Morrow, 1997), 15.

69   —"just as subject to fashion and whim": Paul Davies in his introduction to Richard Feynman's *Six Easy Pieces* (Addison-Wesley, 1994), ix.

69   —"as a codification of objective reality": Laughlin, *A Different Universe*, 13.

69   —"to be observed, conquered, and used": Marshall and Zohar, xxiv.

69   —this fantasy was laid to rest by Chaos theory: see James Gleick, *Chaos* (Viking, 1987), 18.

70   —"because his purpose is to integrate with it": Elisabet Sahtouris, in

Scott London, "From Mechanics to Organics: An Interview with Elisabet Sahtouris". www.scottlondon/interviews.

70 —as an indissoluble unity that incorporates yourself: see Fred Alan Wolf, *Taking the Quantum Leap* (Harper & Row, 1989), 128. Cf. Lovelock: "Our results convinced us that the only feasible explanation of the Earth's highly improbable atmosphere was that it was being manipulated on a day-to-day basis from the surface, and that the manipulator was life itself . . . The entire range of living matter on Earth, from whales to viruses, and from oaks to algae, could be regarded as constituting a single living entity, capable of manipulating the Earth's atmosphere to suit its overall needs and endowed with faculties and powers beyond those of its constituent parts." *Gaia*, 6–9.

70 —"everything is subtly connected to everything else": Marshall and Zohar, xxvii.

70 —to look at the universe as an undivided whole: David Bohm, *Wholeness and the Implicate Order* (Routledge, 1988), 11. Compare this with what Kevin Kelly says about the emerging network economy. "The net has no center . . . It is an indefinite web of causes." Kelly, *New Rules*, 9.

70 —mimicking the cellular structures of living systems: John Markoff, *What the Dormouse Said* (Viking, 2005), 143.

70 —the use of biological metaphors: Kelly, 31; David Brooks, "Cell Phone Naturalists" *Utne Reader* (March/April, 1999), 79; Knoke, *Bold New World*, 171–174.

71 —"people have been describing for millennia": Marilyn Ferguson, *The Aquarian Conspiracy* (Tarcher, 1980), 373. Jeremy Narby suggests that the animism of 'primitive' cultures is a recognition of the DNA, which animates all life. The double helix is everywhere in folk art, in the form of twin serpents, ladders, and so on: Narby, *The Cosmic Serpent* (Putnam, 1998), 67–72.

72 —"thinks in images, sees wholes, detects patterns": Ferguson, *Aquarian*, 78.

72 —"left hemisphere is the thousand words": Pink, *Whole New Mind*, 19.

72 —linear, mechanical thought processes were the only ones valued: *Ibid.*, 14.

72 —"right brain sees context, and, therefore, meaning": Ferguson, *Aquarian*, 297.

73 —"can't cope with paradox and ambiguity": Marshall and Zohar, xxv.

73 —"new scientific findings are always fraught with contradictions": Karl Pribram, quoted in Ferguson, *Aquarian*, 186.

73 —"union of two opposed principles": Narby, *Serpent*, 83. Sheldrake says dragon slaying symbolizes the "conquest of nature". *Rebirth of Nature*, 37.

74   —Modern science has torn down these walls, one by one: Academia is experiencing a similar challenge, although its innate conservatism will probably fend it off for the foreseeable future. A study found sharp contrasts in attitudes held by older and younger academics about the tenure review process. Older academics wanted it to be secret, saw merit as an objective concept, believed competition improved performance, thought research should be organized within disciplines, saw teaching as relatively unimportant, thought work and family should be kept separate, and felt faculty members should be autonomous. Younger academics thought the review process should be transparent, believed merit was a socially constructed, subjective concept, felt cooperation improved performance, felt research should be organized around problems rather than restricted within disciplines, thought teaching excellence should be rewarded, thought a balance between work and personal life was important, and thought faculty had a collective responsibility. The older academics, in other words, wanted to maintain rigid boundaries between individuals, between disciplines, between subject and object, between work and life. The younger academics were saying these boundaries were artificial, illusory, and harmful. Trower and Chait, "Faculty Diversity", 37.

74   —"seemed to be separate . . . are actually interwoven": Brian Greene, *The Elegant Universe* (Vintage, 1999), 51.

74   —Godfroi de Bouillon and Pope Innocent III: Malcolm Godwin, *The Holy Grail* (Viking, 1994), 189, 206–207.

74   —"convinced beyond doubt that they are right": Laurens van der Post: *The Lost World of the Kalahari* (Morrow, 1958), 155. Atrocities are made easier when a leader convinces his followers that some group is morally inferior. Eden Pastora, the American-backed Contra leader in Nicaragua, used to tell his troops: "If you kill a woman, you're killing a 'rabid dog' (the Contra term for Sandinistas), if you kill a child, you're killing a 'rabid dog.'" Quoted in Grossman, *On Killing*, 14. Germans under Hitler, Serbs under Milosevich, Hutus under Habyarimana and Bagosora, were told it was their patriotic duty to commit genocide against people they had lived with for generations. See, e.g., Alison Des Forges, *Leave None to Tell the Story* (Human Rights Watch, 1999).

75   —he often feels satisfied even if the conditions that produced the problem are unchanged: Controllers feel punishment is a deterrent to crime, yet in the days when most crimes led to capital punishment, pickpockets were particularly active during public hangings. And hellfire—which priests, nuns, and fundamentalist preachers never tire of describing in vivid detail—seems not even to deter priests and preachers themselves from sins that would supposedly condemn them to it.

75 —"auto-immune diseases such as AIDS": Fritjof Capra, *The Web of Life* (Anchor, 1996), 278; see also Conley, *Walking Out on the Boys*, 13–25. Healing—both physical and social—involves a recapitulation of infant care: "A sub-segment of a system is persuaded to stay in the system the same way an infant is persuaded to remain alive and join human society—by a kind of nurturant seduction." The animal licks the wound, the child says, "kiss it", the sick person is 'nursed'. Only when the ailing organ, limb, or individual is seen as beyond recovery do we decide to lop it off. See "Pleasure, Healing, and Conflict", in Philip Slater, *Footholds* (Beacon, 1977), 175–185.

76 —more visits to alternative practitioners than to traditional physicians: John Astin, in the *Journal of the American Medical Association* (May, 1998).

77 —"have something to give which we have not": Follett, *Creative Experience* (Longmans, Green, 1930), 39, 117, 156–163, 174. See also *The New State* (Longmans, Green, 1923); *Freedom and Coordination* (Management Publications Trust, 1949), 81–82. Frances Moore Lappé points out that conflict is an essential element in democracy. See Lappé, *Democracy's Edge* (Jossey-Bass, 2006), 275.

77 —also stem the continuing decline of small commercial fishing operations: Similar battles between labor and management are usually resolved by compromises that make no one happy. Management wants loyal and productive employees but wants to treat them like disposable diapers. Workers want a guarantee of work for reasonable wages and benefits even at meaningless and soul-destroying jobs. The Mondragon movement in Spain consists of 60 interconnected employee-owned companies employing 29,000 people, with revenues of six billion dollars and assets of fourteen billion. The highest-paid employee is not allowed to make more than six times the lowest paid. (This contrasts with the typical American corporation where the ratio is in the high hundreds.) Worker-owned businesses show higher rates of productivity, profitability, and job creation than other firms. They distribute wealth more equitably and create more responsible shareholders—for most investors today are interested only in short-term earnings, often at the expense of the long-term health of the company. This model is unlikely to make much headway in the West, but China is moving toward this kind of employee ownership as it begins to dissolve its huge centralized government operations. Greg MacLeod, *From Mondragon to America* (Univ. Coll. of Cape Breton Press, 1997); Joel A. Barker, "The Mondragon Model," in Frances Hesselbein, Marshall Goldsmith, and Richard Beckhard (eds.), *The Organization of the Future* (Jossey-Bass, 1997), 109–117. See also Roy Morrison, *Ecological Democracy* (South End Press, 1995).

78 —a chain, with no top, no bottom, just a circle of life: Remnants of the ranking habit persist today in the lists that bombard us daily: the ten best X's and the top twenty Y's and the hundred most sought after Z's. Books, films, athletes, restaurants, records, TV shows—nothing escapes the raters and rankers—a lingering nostalgia, perhaps, for the pecking orders of our feudal past.

78 —because he was looking for a "Boss cell": Tannen, *Argument Culture*, 13–15.

79 —"not by building but by self-assembling": Benyus, *Biomimicry*, 104.

79 —" a self-organizing universe of constant invention": Marshall and Zohar, xxvii.

80 —"foundation . . . upon which one could have built": quoted in Thomas Kuhn, *The Structure of Scientific Revolutions* (University of Chicago Press, 1970), 83.

80 —Marquis de Condorcet: quoted in E. Doyle McCarthy, *Knowledge As Culture* (Routledge, 1996), 86.

80 —a notion closer to religion than to science. See Rupert Sheldrake, *A New Science of Life* (Tarcher, 1981), *passim.*

82 —"expressing itself in its individual occurrences": F. David Peat, *Synchronicity* (Bantam, 1987), 58.

82 —stuck in rigid and limiting self-concepts: "John is joking" gives John a lot more leeway than "John is a joker".

82 —"corrected only by taking another step forward": George Soros, *The Crisis of Global Capitalism* (Public Affairs, 1998), 20, 227.

83 —"goal of a well-made network . . . to sustain a perpetual disequilibrium": Kelly, *New Rules*, 110–114.

83 —Mandelbrot set: See *Fractals: the Colors of Infinity* (Films for the Humanities and Sciences, 1997).

Chapter 5   *On Authority: Getting Out From Under*

85 —"as a means of conflict resolution": O'Connell, *Ride*, 6.

85 —"and highly mobile life styles": *Ibid.*

85 —no emblems of authority, no sign of 'chiefs': Steven J. Mithen, "The Mesolithic Age", in Barry Cunliffe (ed.), *The Oxford Illustrated Prehistory of Europe* (Oxford University Press, 1994), 37, 59–61, 79, 107, 116–117, 125ff.; James Mellaart, *Catal Huyuk* (McGraw-Hill, 1967); Eisler, *Chalice*, 25, 29–41; O'Connell, 206 ff.

85 —"usually for good practical reasons": Turnbull, *Forest*, 110, 124.

85 —Bushmen and Teduray: Laurens van der Post, *The Heart of the Hunter* (Morrow, 1961), 210; Schlegel, *Wisdom*, 111.

85 —"allowing for adaptation when the environment changes": Benyus, *Biomimicry*, 274.

86 —lords much taller than their peasants: O'Connell, 114–116.

87 —"years we spent as wanderers, hunters, and collectors": O'Connell, 232.

87 —For everyday frustrations the preferred scapegoats were women: And for some not-so-everyday ones as well. Susan Faludi observes that after 9/11 there was a surge in anti-female sentiment in the United States—some right-wing talk show callers even blaming feminism for the terrorist attack. See Susan Faludi, *The Terror Dream: Fear and Fantasy in Post-9/11 America* (Metropolitan, 2007).

88 —a cross-cultural study of family patterns: William N. Stephens, *The Family in Cross-Cultural Perspective* (Holt, Rinehart & Winston, 1963), 325–339.

88 —"virtual hunter-gatherer manifestos": O'Connell, 232.

88 —"without the rule of a king": Jack McIver Weatherford, *Indian Givers* (Crown Publishers, 1988), 127–129. My italics.

89 —institutions . . . that had nothing to do with fighting: The German sociologist Max Weber also saw bureaucracy as having its roots in warfare, though for somewhat different reasons. *Wirtschaft und Gesellschaft*, excerpted in H. H. Gerth and C. Wright Mills, *From Max Weber* (Oxford, 1958).

89 —traits of successful leaders: Warren Bennis and Burt Nanus, *Leaders* (Harper & Row, 1985).

89 —until they reach their "level of incompetence": Laurence J. Peter, *The Peter Principle* (Morrow, 1969). See also Warren Bennis, *On Becoming a Leader* (Addison-Wesley, 1990); Warren Bennis and Robert Townsend, *Reinventing Leadership* (Morrow, 1995).

90 —"they are holding the horses": Bennis and Slater, *Temporary Society*, 120.

90 —response to the Toyota disaster: *Ibid.*, 254–260.

91 —"becomes an ongoing necessity": *Ibid.*, 273, 274.

91 —Columbia disaster and American auto industry collapse: James Surowiecki, *The Wisdom of Crowds* (Doubleday, 2004), 173–184, 206.

92 —Circumventing it as much as possible: It's clear that Bush is clueless about democracy when he speaks of 'bringing democracy' to the Middle East. Democracy cannot be 'brought', much less imposed. Democracy arises from the people themselves or it is not democracy.

92 —"In Saudi, what can they do? Only use bombs": *Wall Street Journal*, 10/26/01. Whether democracy will take root in Bahrain remains to be seen (see above note). But Bahrain has at least been liberated from autocracy. Thomas Friedman points out that hostility toward America is strongest in authoritarian states like Saudi Arabia and Pakistan, and weakest in democratic, pluralistic societies like Bangladesh and India. *New York Times* (11/21/01).

93 —"without having to explain themselves constantly . . . enables rapid cognition": Malcolm Gladwell, *Blink* (Little, Brown, 2005), 102–111, 117–119, 143–146. The Pentagon handled the defeat char-

acteristically: after a couple of days in shock they turned back the clock, rewrote the rules so the game was completely re-scripted in the Blue Team's favor, and declared victory.

93 —their society was the most open and democratic: Sachs, *The End of Poverty*, 33.

93 —'bosses' too busy to hear new data: Bennis and Slater, *Temporary Society*, chapter one.

94 —Mao and Liu Shaoki: Roderick MacFarquhar, *The Origins of the Cultural Revolution. Vol. III: The Coming of the Cataclysm, 1961–66* (Columbia University Press, 1998).

94 —"an incentive to hide information and dissemble": Surowiecki, 209.

94 —"and ignoring all the rest": Kenneth M. Pollack, "Spies, Lies, and Weapons: What went Wrong", *Atlantic* (January/February, 2004), 88.

94 —"disinterested perspectives about what's real": Suskind, *The Price of Loyalty*, 263. Paul O'Neill, former Secretary of the Treasury, knew his days with the Bush administration were numbered when the President said to him, without smiling, "'You're getting quite a reputation as a truth-teller. You've got yourself a real cult following, don't ya?'" As criticism of the administration's Iraq policy increased, the White House began "making an example of anyone who had the temerity to speak truth to power" (323). Cf. also Richard A. Clarke, *Against All Enemies* (Free Press, 2004).

95 —didn't want anyone raining on their fantasy: James Fallows, "Blind Into Baghdad" *Atlantic* (January/February, 2004), 53 ff.

95 —the most serious defect was that it stifled creative thinking: Dan Baum, "Battle Lessons", *The New Yorker* (1/17/05), 42.

95 —"they are teaching themselves how to fight the war": *Ibid.*, 44.

96 —"no time to wait for carefully vetted and spoon-fed advice": *Ibid.*, 45. To its credit, the Army eventually recognized how important the independent web sites were and accepted them.

96 —"what life was like beyond their borders . . . are over": Friedman, *Lexus*, 54–55, 145–147, 179–182; Cairncross, *Distance*, xvi.

96 —"are the most democratic ones": Friedman, 182, 362.

97 —Hu Jintao holding open policy discussions: Howard W. French, "Letter From Asia", *The New York Times* (6/2/04).

97 —eighty percent practice some form of participatory management: E. E. Lawler, *From the Ground Up* (Jossey-Bass, 1996).Email has made it harder for authoritarian leaders to hoard data, and people are more willing to criticize bosses online. The Internet is "a powerful force for democracy . . . in the workplace." Cairncross, *Distance*, 148.

97 —number of levels its quaint hierarchy still maintains: In 2002 Web operator Jon Messner was able to get control of an Al-Qaida Internet communication site and offered it to the FBI, but the opportunity was lost in the quicksand of the agency's unwieldy bureaucracy.

97 —'amoeba-like' form of modern organizations: Knoke, *Bold*, 171–174. See also Bennis and Slater, 2, 6, 61–85; Frances Hesselbein, The Circular Organization" in *The Organization of the Future*, 81–83; Friedman, *Lexus*, 157–160; Naisbitt and Aburdene, *Megatrends 2000*, 218. Virtually all of Naisbitt's original *Megatrends* were examples of Integrative values replacing Controller ones. Naisbitt, *Megatrends: Ten New Directions Transforming Our Lives* (Warner Books, 1982).

97 —"not at the center": Friedman, 70–71, 74–76. See also Brooks, "Cell Phone Naturalists", 79; Bennis and Nanus, *Leaders*, 79 ff.; Friedman, 41–58, 72–81.

97 —"for the duration of the movie project": Kelly, *New Rules*, 111. See also Cairncross, *Distance*, xiii; Davis and Meyer, *Blur*, 231–232.

97 —small firms 24 times more innovative: W. Adams and J. W. Brock, *The Bigness Complex* (Pantheon, 1986).

98 —"a third of all new capital equipment is acquired through leasing": Knoke, 85.

98 —"centralizing power only makes mistakes more catastrophic": Postrel, *Future*, 30. Asked when an aviation accident had occurred that had not had a "precursor incident" the retired chief of the Aviation Safety Bureau replied, "basically, never." Memos alerting management to potential hazards are routinely ignored. See James R. Chiles, *Inviting Disaster: Lessons from the Edge of Technology* (HarperBusiness, 2001), 183, 286–293.

98 —"more fun, and cheaper to operate": Charles Handy, "Unimagined Futures", in Hesselbein et al., *Organization of the Future*, 381.

98 —men and women who felt information should be free and accessible to all: Markoff, *Dormouse*, xv–xix, 43, 78–80, 181–186.

99 —"to take decisions for themselves": Charles Leadbeater, *We-Think* (Profile, 2008), Chapter 4.

99 —"hard for corporations to make money from": *Ibid.* Chapter 3.

101 —male doctors on childrearing practices: Alice Ryerson, "Medical Advice on Childrearing Practices: 1550–1900." Unpublished Doctoral Dissertation, Harvard University Graduate School of Education, 1960; Ashley Montague, *Touching* (Columbia University Press, 1971), 122–137.

103 —"thoughts had no room to move in them": Elizabeth Taylor, *Angel* (Viking, 1957), 19.

103 —Lappé: Democracy's Edge, 255–256, 273.

103 —"inability to see relationships or detect meaning": Ferguson, *Aquarian*, 298–299. Her italics.

104 —"are personally developed rather than God-given": Jerold Starr, "The Great Textbook War", in Harvey Holtz, Irwin Marcus, Jim Dougherty, Judy Michaels, and Rick Peduzzi (eds.), *Education and the American Dream* (Bergin & Garvey, 1988), 96–97.

104 —ignorant of the issues that concern them most directly: *Ibid.*, 102–108.

104 —Hatch Amendment: *Ibid.*, 97.

104 —"that teach teamwork and tolerance for diversity": Aronson, *Nobody Left To Hate*, 91–92.

105 —"listen to the report of the person reciting": Aronson, 135–168. For a comprehensive look at education for tomorrow's world see Riane Eisler, *Tomorrow's Children* (Westview Press, 2000).

Chapter 6   *On Our Psyches: The Illusion of Control*

106 —Bacteria constitute 10% of our dry body weight: Margulis and Sagan, *Microcosmos*, 28.

106 —"these swarms of bacteria . . . keep us alive": Elisabet Sahtouris, *Gaia* (Simon & Schuster, 1989), 66–67, 85.

108 —wild animals doctor themselves: Cindy Engel, *Wild Health* (Houghton Mifflin, 2002). This ability hasn't been entirely lost to us, as Engel points out (230–231), but its signals are often ignored.

110 —"mammalian nervous system cannot self-assemble": Thomas Lewis, Fari Amini, Richard Lannon, *A General Theory of Love* (Vintage, 2000), 84–88.

115 —"apart from everything, relating to nothing": Donna Huse, "Restructuring and the Physical Context: Designing Learning Environments, *Children's Environment* (Vol. 12, No. 3, 1995), 290–311. Huse points out that the average school environment in which we train our children tends to be composed almost exclusively of metal, plastic, linoleum, glass, and concrete. Yet living in sterile boxes, scientists say, is a major cause of the rise in asthma. Children don't have enough dirt in their lives to get their immune systems working properly.

116 —obsessive control needs of our egos: Every tool is an extension of the human organism. The wheel an extension of the foot, the crane an extension of the hand, the telescope an extension of the eye, the telephone an extension of the ear, the computer an extension of the brain, and so on. And technology itself is an extension of the ego—its controlling and dominating tendencies. See Slater, *Earthwalk*, 9–12.

117 —Hughes disturbed by aquifers, etc.: James Phelan, *Howard Hughes: The Hidden Years* (Random House, 1976).

118 —Gated communities a growing phenomenon: See, for example, Gerald Frug, *City Making: Building Communities without Building Walls* (Princeton University Press, 2000).

119 —control over nature "almost synonymous with the scientific method": Fritjof Capra and David Steindl-Rost, *Belonging to the Universe* (HarperSan Francisco, 1991), 12.

120 —"a natural balance asserts itself": Masanobu Fukuoka, *The Natural*

Way of Farming (Japan Publications, 1985), 5–7, 15–23; Benyus, *Biomimicry*, 26.

120 —control . . . had little to do with garden's health: Dominique Browning, *Around the House and In the Garden* (Scribner, 2002).

121 —Pollan points out: *The Botany of Desire* (Random House, 2001).

121 —have to be . . . heavily medicated as a result: Cindy Engel, *Wild Health*, 129 ff., 221–223.

121 —"grass farming" in Midwest: Benyus, *Biomimicry*, 44–45.

121 —"everything affecting everything else": *Botany of Desire*, 241–242. Recognition of interdependence underlies the rapid spread of Community Supported Agriculture. In CSA, consumers and producers share the risks and benefits of farming, and free the farmers from the burden of marketing, allowing them to concentrate on quality.

122 —"no self-organizing allowed": Benyus, *Biomimicry*, 200–201.

122 —worrying about our ability to 'destroy' nature: Margulis and Sagan, 25–35. Bacteria can exchange up to 15% of their genetic material daily. In two billion years they "invented all of life's essential biotech-nologies." Capra, *Web of Life*, 228–230.

122 —"We have evolved to fit into a bacterial world, and not the reverse": Andrew H. Knoll, *Life on a Young Planet: The First Three Billion Years of Evolution On Earth* (Princeton University Press, 2003).

122 —"to do things for them they couldn't do for themselves": *The Botany of Desire*, xv–xxi. O'Connell calls it "co-evolution". *Ride*, 60ff.

123 —"the more valuable it becomes": Kelly, *New Rules*, 41–42. Controller and Integrative approaches are found within the world of computer systems. Cf. Surowiecki, 72–74.

123 —"feed back on themselves, creating unforeseen results": Charles Handy, "Unimagined Futures" in Hesselbein, et al., *Organization of the Future*, 380.

123 —failure-avoiders aren't respected: When covered up, a small mis-take tends to become a large one. Democratic leaders willing to admit their own mistakes create an environment in which errors are easily caught and corrected. See Amy Edmondson, "Learning from Mistakes Is Easier Said Than Done: Group and Organizational Influences on the Detection and Correction of Human Error" *Journal of Applied Behavioral Science*, Vol. 32, No. 1 (March, 1996), 5–28.

123 —"they weren't very effective": Adam Kahane, quoted in Nicola Phillips, *E-Motional Business* (Pearson, 2000), 83.

Chapter 7   *On Warfare: The Decaying Glory*

126 —McDonald's in Serbia: *The Wall Street Journal*, 9/3 /99.

126 —"borders among nations continue to erode": O'Connell, *Ride*, 240.

127 —'importing' from and 'exporting' to themselves: Knoke, *Bold*, 7, 153–155, 211.
127 —"told the nationalist Indian government to cool it": Thomas Friedman, *New York Times* (8/12/02).
127 —"than in any previous era in modern history": Friedman, *Lexus*, 197–198.
128 —highest per-capita income nations: Knoke, *Bold*, 211.
128 —and with little fear of retaliation: During the 20th century, in Latin America alone, "the United States invaded and occupied all or parts of nine sovereign nations", several repeatedly, and "actively sought the overthrow of another two dozen governments, seven of them installed by popular vote in competitive elections." John H. Coatsworth, "America and Latin America", in *Harvard Magazine* (Jan./Feb., 2002), 26. See also Willard C. Matthias, *America's Strategic Blunders: Intelligence Analysis and National Security Policy, 1936–1991* (Pennsylvania State University Press, 2001)
129 —"were rendered largely irrelevant": O'Connell, *Ride of the Second Horseman*, 235. Nuclear war is the ultimate in 'purity', for it kills without any element of bravery or skill.
131 —"are being settled more quickly": *The Wall Street Journal* (3/29/00).
131 —the two Koreas: *The International Herald Tribune* (6/21/00). Mine-clearing: *New York Times* (9/16/02).
131 —regional conflicts . . . being "ghettoized": Friedman, *Lexus*, 201–204.
132 —an economic context that was almost exclusively agrarian: O'Connell, *Ride*, 6, passim.
132 —"officials . . . have fewer places to hide these days": *The New York Times* (10/18/98). On the American overthrow of the democratically elected Allende, see Armando Uribe, *The Black Book of American Intervention in Chile* (Beacon Press, 1974).
133 —"the right to slaughter their citizens": Henry J. Steiner, "Securing Human Rights" *Harvard Magazine* (September–October, 1998), 45–46; *The New York Times* (10/18/98).
133 —"could not have been imagined fifty years ago": Steiner, 94.
133 —viewpoint of someone other than the traditional hero: John Gardner, *Grendel* (Knopf, 1971); Jean Rhys, *Wide Sargasso Sea* (Norton, 1982); Tom Stoppard, *Rosencrantz and Guildenstern Are Dead* (Grove Press, 1967); Marion Zimmer Bradley, *The Mists of Avalon* (Knopf, 1982); Jane Smiley, *A Thousand Acres* (Knopf, 1991); Valerie Martin, *Mary Reilly* (Doubleday, 1990); Gregory Maguire, *Wicked* (ReganBooks, 1995); Paula Vogel, *Desdemona* (Dramatists Play Service, 1994). Rebecca Reisert, *The Third Witch* (Washington Square Press, 2001).
134 —began in the sixties with Thomas Merton: Monica Furlong, *Merton* (Harper & Row, 1980), 321–330. Merton was active in the peace

movement, fought for racial integration, and wanted to work toward uniting the Americas (254–267). For ecumenicalism, see Alan Watts, *The Philosophies of Asia* (Charles E. Tuttle, 1995); Joseph Campbell, *The Masks of God* (Viking, 1968); Capra and Steindl-Rost, *Belonging to the Universe*, 3–8.

135 —hitchhiked safely from one end . . . to the other: see Karen Muller, *Hitchhiking Vietnam* (Globe Pequot Press, 1998).

135 —an enthusiasm for making connections with other species: See Konrad Lorenz, *King Solomon's Ring* (Crowell, 1952); Niko Tinbergen, *Animal Behavior* (Time, Inc., 1965); Jane Goodall, *In the Shadow of Man* (Houghton Mifflin, 1988); Dian Fossey, *Gorillas in the Mist* (Houghton Mifflin, 1983); Doug Peacock, *Grizzly Years* (Henry Holt, 1990); Timothy Treadwell, *Among Grizzlies* (HarperCollins, 1997); Farley Mowat, *Never Cry Wolf* (Little, Brown, 1963); R. D. Lawrence, *In Praise of Wolves* (Henry Holt, 1986); Katy Payne, *Silent Thunder* (Simon & Schuster, 1998); Jeffrey M. Masson, *When Elephants Weep* (Delacorte, 1995); Susan Chernak McElroy, *Animals as Teachers and Healers* (NewSage Press, 1996); John C. Lilly, *Man and Dolphin* (Doubleday, 1961); Roger Fouts, *Next of Kin* (Morrow, 1997); Francine Patterson and Eugene Linden, *The Education of Koko* (Holt, Rinehart & Winston, 1981); Keith Laidler, *The Talking Ape* (Stein & Day, 1980). See also Elizabeth Marshall Thomas, *The Hidden Life of Dogs* (Houghton-Mifflin, 1993) and Stanley Coren, *The Intelligence of Dogs* (Free Press, 1994).

136 —cultural differences . . . even among rats, birds, and fish: *The New York Times*, 1/2/03. The orangutan studies were led by Carel van Schaik at Duke.

136 —revolutionizing horse training: Monty Roberts, *The Man Who Listens To Horses* (Random House, 1997).

137 —which foods are healthy, which are poisonous, and which are medicinal: Benyus, *Biomimicry*, 147.

137 —"we watched the ways of animals to insure our own survival": *Ibid.*, 183.

138 —lights, greeting cards, parties, and gifts: Lee Gomes, *Wall Street Journal* (12/03/02)

138 —visible ties to everyone else on the planet: Yergin and Stanislaw, 369–370.

140 —stigmatize as wishy-washy . . . statesmanlike behavior from public figures: Tannen, *Argument Culture*, 8, 11–14, 28–35, 41–47, 54–94, 95–99, 114–121, 151–165, 277–278. See also Gordon Fellman, *Rambo and the Dalai Lama* (SUNY Press, 1998).

140 —with why these programs always fail: In the 1920s the 'war on alcohol' increased crime, enriched crime lords, and filled prisons with entrepreneurs tempted by the huge profits created, while failing to

reduce consumption. The 'war on drugs' has produced identical results.

140 —Johnson was trapped by his own machismo: Robert Dalleck, *Flawed Giant* (Oxford University Press, 1998) 239–249.

141 —the preemptive strike on the Soviet Union they were demanding: David Talbot, *Brothers: The Hidden History of the Kennedy Years* (Free Press, 2007), 85–174.

141 —"rigid", "closed-minded", "mulish", and "pig-headed": A headline in October, 2000, read: "ISRAELIS, PALESTINIANS STAND FIRM IN FACE OF LAST-DITCH PEACE EFFORTS". "Resolve" is also a favorite word of Controller politicians. It seems to mean the willingness to persist in a policy that isn't working.

142 —spent billions more trying to destroy them: This strategy was presented as 'realism': "He may be a vicious, brutal dictator", foreign policy experts would say about a Noriega, Shah, Somosa, Saddam, Pinochet, or Suharto, "but he's OUR vicious, brutal dictator." Yet these protégés eventually proved hugely expensive to us.

142 —degree to which it made trouble for the Soviet Union: see David Landau, *Kissinger: The Uses of Power* (Houghton Mifflin, 1972), 118. The shortsighted "Linkage" policy is a good example of how sophisticated-sounding foreign policy terms often mask the most primitive kind of sandbox behavior.

143 —"with bombs wired to garage-door openers or doorbells": Baum, "Battle Lessons", 43; see also George Packer, "Letter from Baghdad: War After the War", *The New Yorker* (November 24, 2003).It's not easy to act as peacekeepers and rebuilders in a country, city, or town that you've bombed into rubble, invaded, and occupied.

143 —"solving the wrong problem precisely": Ian Mitroff, *Smart Thinking for Crazy Times* (Berrett-Koehler, 1998), 6 ff. This anachronistic thinking has been applied to peacekeeping forces. In 2000 Staff Sgt. Frank Ronghi was convicted of raping and murdering an 11-year-old Kosovo Albanian girl. Investigation disclosed a host of brutalities by his battalion and concluded that the soldiers' training "failed to tone down their combat mentality". The 'peacekeeping' battalion's slogan was "shoot 'em in the face!"—an attitude encouraged by its commander, Lt. Col. Michael D. Ellerbe (*The New York Times*, 9/19/00). When asked by Afghan President Karzai for U.S. peacekeepers President Bush refused, saying, "the purpose of the United States military is to fight and win wars". But aside from foolish adventures like the invasion of Iraq, peacekeeping will be the primary purpose of future armies. Military training needs to shift from teaching men how to perpetrate violence to teaching them how to prevent it.

143 —expensive and unworkable missile defense system: See Frances Fitzgerald, *Way Out There in the Blue* (Simon & Schuster, 2000); Theodore A. Postol. "Why Missile Defense Won't Work",

Technology Review (April, 2002). When its missile trials failed the Pentagon simply rigged them so they wouldn't. In the Gulf War the army claimed Patriot missiles had shot down 45 Iraqi Scuds, when in fact they had missed every one.

143 —"it takes networks to fight networks": John Arquilla, *L.A. Times* (8/25/02). The absurdity of the 'rogue state' approach—used to justify military invasions of nations that have never attacked us—was captured by a friend of mine who suggested that since some Americans funded Jewish terrorists prior to the creation of Israel, and other Americans have funded the IRA; and since we 'harbored' Timothy McVeigh, we were a rogue state and should bomb ourselves.

144 —"true of terrorist organizations as well": John Arquilla, "How We Could Lose the War on Terror", *San Francisco Chronicle*, 9/7/03. Israel has pursued this policy for decades, a good indication of its futility.

Chapter 8   *On Religion: Back to Nature*

147 —crept back into the teachings, often reversing them entirely: Shlain, *Alphabet*, 176–177, 231–251. See also Robert Walter Funk, *Honest to Jesus* (HarperSan Francisco, 1996), 43 ff.; Laina Holzman, *Strange Birds from Zoroaster's Nest* (SUNY Press, 2000).

147 —distortions that Paul . . . brought to it: Romans 13; I Corinthians, 7:1–8, 11:1–16, 14: 34; II Corinthians 11:12–15; Galatians 1:6–9; Ephesians 5:21–24, 6:5–9; I Timothy 2:9–15, 5:11–13, 6:1–2.

147 —the only countries to want the death penalty for minors: *Mother Jones* (July/August 2006), 19.

148 —"to contradict their prophets or to start a new faith": Karen Armstrong, *Islam* (Modern Library, 2000), 6, 8, 10, 16–17, 21–23, 30.

148 —"intimations of the Unity which is God": *Islam*, 15.

150 —both books justify and promote homicide and genocide: Sam Harris: *The End of Faith* (Norton, 2005), 16.

150 —"he met on the way from birth to death": van der Post, *Heart*, 211. See also *Lost World*, 15–16, 19, 259.

150 —"little altars": Rebecca Wells, *Little Altars Everywhere* (HarperPerennial, 1996), 14.

150 —"we want it to share our happiness": Turnbull, *Forest People*, 92. This attitude was not shared by the Pygmies' Bantu neighbors, who worked plantations and had Controller values and customs. Misfortunes were attributed to witchcraft, or evil spirits who had to be placated.

151 —"They dwelt in ease and peace . . .": Hesiod, *Works and Days*, 109–201. My italics.

151 —Sahlins calls "the original affluent society": Marshall Sahlins, *Stone*

Age Economics (Aldine, 1972), 7–8, 13, 21–35. Hunter-gatherers could always find something to eat, but farmers and herdsmen, having committed themselves to certain animals and crops, were more at the mercy of the elements. During droughts and crop plagues the agricultural neighbors of scorned hunter-gatherer tribes often came to them for food. As Sahlins points out, both toil and hunger tend to increase with the advance of civilization. Sahlins, 27–28, 35–36; Richard B. Lee and Irven DeVore (eds.), *Man the Hunter* (Aldine, 1968), 39–40.

151　—"robust . . . even at older ages": Engel, *Wild Health*, 225–226. As Engel reminds us, we're genetically programmed for a hunter-gatherer diet: "At least one hundred thousand generations of people were hunter-gatherers; only five hundred generations have depended on agriculture; only ten generations have lived since the onset of the industrial age, and only *two* generations have grown up with highly processed fast foods."

151　—no present . . . would make their lives easier: *Lost World*, 276.

152　—"producing a range of sophisticated goods": Marija Gimbutas, *The Civilization of the Goddess* (HarperSanFrancisco, 1991), viii. See also *The Gods and Goddesses of Old Europe*, rev. ed. (Univ. of Calif. Press, 1982); J. Mellaart, *The Neolithic of the Near East* (Scribners, 1975); Merlin Stone, *When God Was a Woman* (Harcourt, Brace, & Jovanovich, 1976); Charlene Spretnak, *Lost Goddesses of Early Greece* (Beacon Press, 1981); Riane Eisler, *The Chalice and the Blade* and *Sacred Pleasure.*

152　—fifteen centuries with no sign of war: see, Eisler, *Chalice*, 13–14, 17–21; Gimbutas, *Civilization of the Goddess*, 9–10.

152　—"the earth . . . of herself gave all things needful": Ovid, *Metamorphoses* (Loeb Library, 1984) Book I, 89–10.

152　—"a process of decoupling ourselves from nature": Benyus, *Biomimicry*, 21.

152　—"they . . . were hard of heart"/"never rest from labour and sorrow": *Works and Days*, 109–201. Like many classifiers, Hesiod hated having things he liked and things he disliked in the same category, so he had to have two bronze races, the second described more positively because it included the Greek epic heroes.

153　—our own fear-obsessed nation: no country is more preoccupied with security—both national and personal. No nation has as many of its citizens in prison. No population is equipped with more weapons and security systems.

154　—"all traces of magic . . . were to be removed from the realm of nature": Sheldrake, *Rebirth of Nature*, 29.

155　—in the Controller age, a secret, forbidden, and even evil thing: *Sacred Pleasure.*

156　—"not only . . . local implications but global ones as well": William

McDonough and Michael Braungart, *Cradle To Cradle* (North Point Press, 2002), 122.

156 —doctrine of Original Sin spawned by Augustine: Matthew Fox, *Original Blessing* (Bear, 1983), 9–16. Andrew Harvey argues that any religious expert dilutes and contaminates spirituality: Andrew Harvey, *The Direct Path* (Broadway Books, 2000).

156 —spiritual experiences can be gained without abandoning rationality: Harris, End of Faith, 39–40.

157 —"billions of light-years away": Julia Butterfly Hill: *The Legacy of Luna* (HarperSan Francisco, 2000), 64–67, 142–143.

157 —"God the Father" has little appeal to many: Sally McFague, *Models of God* (Fortress Press, 1987.

157 —"a symbol of the unity of all life": Marija Gimbutas, *The Language of the Goddess* (HarperSanFrancisco, 1989).

158 —toward which we're gradually and fitfully moving: The phenomenal popularity of Eckhart Tolle reveals the strength of this need.

159 —"glorious outpouring of being." Brian Swimme, *The Universe Is a Green Dragon* (Bear & co., 1985), 40. Whereas to fundamentalists our blue planet is just a nasty trap set by a spiteful deity to send them to Hell should they enjoy this 'vale of tears'.

159 —"a single multiform unfolding of matter, mind, intelligence, and life": *Ibid.*, 28.

Chapter 9   *Is America's Decline Reversible?*

164 —"the freedom to focus on what it believed to be the most promising lines of investigation": Surowiecki, 160–163.

164 —2/3 of their mergers reduce shareholder value: *Ibid.*, 218–219.

164 —"While those in the South were vertical": Robert D. Putnam, *Making Democracy Work: Civic Traditions in Modern Italy* (Princeton University Press, 1993), 130.

165 —private organizations devoted to sports and cultural activities: The importance of such associations for democracy—so stressed by de Tocqueville—is reaffirmed in a new book by Theda Skocpol, who points out that they bring together people from different backgrounds. She sees the decline in such groups—and their replacement by what she calls "mailing-list groups" who don't actually meet together—as a blow to democracy in the United States. *Diminished Democracy: From Membership to Management in American Civic Life* (University of Oklahoma Press, 2003).

165 —"civics does predict economics, better indeed than economics itself": Putnam, *Democracy*, 157. An integrated democratic community fosters trust, which is essential for the expansion of trade. Economic development is impossible without a degree of trust, which is why vertically structured communities tend to be backward. See *Democracy*, 127–130, 170, 173–176.

165 —it was the individualistic southerners who wanted stricter law enforcement: *Ibid.*, 91–99, 102–106, 108–115.

165 —"carry water to your own": *Ibid.*, 144, citing examples from Carlo Tullio-Altan, *La Nostra Italia* (Feltrinelli, 1986). Alfie Kohn points out that—contrary to popular belief— cynicism is a sign of low intelligence, as well as rigidity, lack of curiosity, and reluctance to consider new ways of looking at the world. Kohn, *Bright Side*, 35–41.

166 —membership in egalitarian organizations of every kind: Robert D. Putnam, *Bowling Alone* (Simon and Schuster, 2000), 31–115, 218–220, 251–257.

166 —television . . . produces . . . an increase in aggression, cynicism, and ignorance: *Ibid.*, 228–237. Putnam was able to rule out working mothers and divorce as causal factors (267). As we might expect, women invest more time in associational life than men do (199), and "social capital" is weakest in our own South (292–294).

166 —seeing fur fly and trying to decide who "won": This makes peace news hard for the media to handle. The problem with peace is that everyone profits from it. How can you tell who's winning? So the outbreak of hostilities tends to get big headlines while peace negotiations wind up on the back pages.

167 —"having little or no control over their fate": David Jacobson; in Steve Perry, "An Interview with James Hillman" *Utne Reader*, January/February, 1997, 54–55. Some blame TV's fear-mongering on the fact that 95% of all media are owned by a few billionaires (see Ben H. Bagdikian, *The Media Monopoly*, 3rd. ed. (Beacon Press, 1990), 3–4.) But there's a simpler answer for TV. The ideal television viewer is agoraphobic. If people are convinced the world outside is unsafe, they're more likely to stay home and watch TV. Television couldn't survive if it had to depend on people who have a life.

167 —politics as another kind of consumerism: This democratic inertia is, of course, encouraged by those who find democracy an inconvenient restraint on their autocratic ambitions. Frances Moore Lappé observes that after 9/11, when there was "an outpouring of desire to help, President Bush told us that our real job was to go shopping." Lappé calls our system 'thin democracy'. See Lappé, *Democracy's Edge*, 6 ff.

167 —"we seem to be unlearning how democracy can work": Tannen, *Argument Culture*, 103.

168 —clinging to an old paradigm when a new one comes along: Barker, *Paradigms*, 155–156, 209–211.

168 —Michelle Cottle: "The Battle Is Over, but the War Goes On", *TIME* (12/6/2004), 128.

169 —a record 6.5 billion dollars keeping information away from its people: Rick Blum, "Secrecy Report Card" (8/26/04) OpenTheGovernment.org.

170 —American education ranks at the bottom of industrial societies: Knoke, 175. The No Child Left Behind act has been compared to weighing a lamb every day without feeding it.

170 —the single best index of a nation's future economic health: nations with the highest standards of living are those that spend the highest percentage of their national income on teacher salaries, and have the highest percentage of high school graduates. Friedman, *Lexus*, 176.

170 —At least 44 prisoners have been tortured to death: On October 24, 2005, the ACLU released U.S. military autopsies of prisoners tortured in Iraq and Afghanistan by Navy Seals, Military Intelligence, and the CIA. About half were listed as homicides, the others died of heart attacks. The Associated Press sent the report out to all news sources, but few bothered to print it—mostly small town papers, which, like the *Los Angeles Times*, buried it in the inside pages.

170 —the gap between rich and poor has ballooned: see, e.g., Friedman, *Lexus*, 250; *New York Times* (1/22/03). Eighty percent of the working men and women in America are putting in longer hours than they did thirty years ago, and making less money in real dollars.

170 —poorer majority and the future of the society as a whole: Diamond, *Collapse*, 421–440.

171 —now lags far behind other Western countries in foreign aid: Tony Judt, "America and the World" in *The New York Review* (4/10/03), 31. Twenty-nine dollars per capita in the US vs. seventy per capita for Europe.

171 —"what the United States has repeatedly promised, and failed, to give": Sachs, *End of Poverty*, 1.

173 —the European Union granted 40% more than the United States: Richard B. Freeman, National Bureau of Economic Research.

173 —Once the world's . . . leader, we're becoming an also-ran: Juan Enriquez, *The Untied States of America* (Crown, 2005), 63, 69–70, 81. Thomas Friedman, *The New York Times* (3/31/06).

173 —"education . . . a cost and never an investment": Handy, *Paradox*, 227. This is, in fact, the way anti-tax crusaders tend to see all government expenditures except the most wasteful one of all—military hardware.

175 —"let alone the 'big responsibility'": Friedman, *Lexus*, 350–351. The Bush administration tried to justify its unwillingness to contribute significantly toward the rebuilding of Afghanistan on the grounds that we had spent $4.5 billion destroying it.

175 —"inexperienced in the hard work of creative interdependence and international partnership": Benjamin R. Barber, *Jihad vs. McWorld* (Ballantine, 2001). Some congressmen actually boast of knowing no foreign languages and never having set foot out of the country. This seems to be a political manifestation of the 'Dumb and Dumber' concept of masculinity. The nation that led the world in the emanci-

pation of women now ranks 61st in the proportion of women in elected office—behind Rwanda.

175 —"I can't get it to be replicated": *The Los Angeles Times* (3/23/98). For multinationals, see Knoke, 142. The problem with the global economy is not that it exists, but that the international corporate network is not balanced by equally powerful international political networks, labor networks, and environmental networks.

175 —war and authoritarianism are Siamese twins: And since terrorism is not a time-limited event like a war, defining terrorism as a conventional war allows the presidential dictatorship to become permanent.

177 —"more intelligent decisions than even the most skilled 'decision maker'": Surowiecki, 32, 189–190.

177 —diverse, independent of one another, and decentralized: *Ibid.*, 20–22.

177 —"The organization with the smartest people may not be the best organization": *Ibid*, 31–32.

178 —"sometimes the messiest approach is the wisest": *Ibid.*, 30. There are, of course, different levels of democracy, from the "majoritarian' like our own, to the more truly democratic 'consensual' ones. See Arend Lijphart, *Patterns of Democracy* (Yale Univerity. Press, 1999).

179 —those firms with more women and minorities were more profitable: Knoke, 147.

179 —"the entrepreneurial . . . person who seeks to immigrate, the others stay home": Knoke, 64–65; see also Barker, *Paradigms*, 152–153.

180 —"we will feel that loss in America's standing around the world": Thomas L. Friedman, *New York Times* (4/23/04).

180 —"every time a foreign scientist can't attend . . . our security suffers": Bruce Schneier, *San Jose Mercury* (9/20/04).

180 —fiascos like the Bay of Pigs, the Vietnam War, and the invasion of Iraq: Surowiecki, 36–37.

181 —"the world is getting more integrated": Thomas L. Friedman, *The New York Times* (6/29/03).

181 —"are poorly adapted to the complexity of today's world": Tony Judt, "America and the World", 30. Jared Diamond observes that societies collapse when they cling to old, self-destructive values in the face of changing realities. Diamond, *Collapse*, 275–276, and chs 14 and 16.

Chapter 10 *Changing How We Change*

184 —Controllers on the left: here, as elsewhere, I'm using the terms 'Controller' and 'Integrator' as a kind of shorthand. All of us, as individuals, are a mixture of these two tendencies.

186 —"as much as $35 million by one estimation": McDonough and Braungart, *Cradle To Cradle*, 163.

186 —"that environmentalists who work with big business have sold out":

Ibid., 149.

186 —Lappé, *Democracy's Edge*, 67–75.

187 —"it won't be possible to solve the world's environmental problems": Jared Diamond, *Collapse*, 17.

188 —you'd better be doing it for its own sake: Kent M. Keith, *Anyway: The Paradoxical Commandments* (Putnam, 2001).

189 —every action we take causes change: This is also true of every action we *don't* take. The failure to vote, for example, has major consequences. In 1980 Ronald Reagan was elected by non-voters, who were for Carter 2 to 1, according to polls, and would have given him a landslide victory had they voted. Most were the lower income citizens who were most hurt by Reaganomics, and who complained most bitterly about it later. Democracy is like stone soup, it's only what people bring to it.

190 —"that did not appear in the traditional media": Rosabeth Moss Kanter, *Evolve!* (Harvard Business School Press, 2001), 30.

191 —"bringing forth the best from themselves and others": Kouzes and Posner, "Leadership Lessons", 82 ff.

191 —Dr. Charlie Mae Knight: Kouzes and Posner, 85–86.

192 —"were not able to accomplish in decades after spending millions of dollars": Anugerah Pekerti of World Vision, personal communication. Lappé points out that old-fashioned top down Alinsky-type community organizing is being replaced by more democratic approaches. *Democracy's Edge*, 156–262.

192 —"little successive victories . . . inspire confidence": Kouzes and Posner, 87

193 —"The new rule: tell everybody everything": Davis and Meyer, *Blur*, 232.

194 —"straight from a nomadic life on camels to a world of cell phones and faxes": Ken Ringle, "Dazzling Dubai", *Smithsonian* (October, 2003), 42.

194 —citizens can register their ideas and reactions online: Michael Tarm, "Estonia emerging as new e-topia" *San Francisco Chronicle* (4/21/03).

195 —you can work online anywhere: See Friedman, *New York Times* (10/31/07).

195 —solar power will easily meet the energy needs of computers: The cost per watt has already reached 'grid parity' in places like Hawaii, where there's plenty of sun and oil is expensive.

196–196 —microfinancing: Kelly, 158. Controller critics have attacked the Grameen Bank on the grounds that this is not the 'right way' to bring people out of poverty. The Integrator believes sincerely (unlike Mao) in 'letting a hundred flowers bloom'.

196 —freedom of movement of electrons . . . within the atom: in David Bohm and F. David Peat, *Science, Order, and Creativity* (Bantam, 1987), 5.

197 —a unity in which every single component is free: Michael Barnsley, in *Fractals*.

197 —"every aspect of life": Alfonso Montuori, "The Complexity of Improvisation", in *Human Relations*, Vol. 54 (2), 241.

197 —"one that is process oriented": Ibid.

Appendix

198 —waves of invaders who worshipped warlike sky gods: see, e.g., Eisler, *Chalice*, 42 ff.; O'Connell, *Ride*, 64–83. The same thing appears to have happened in China around 3000 BC (O'Connell, 162ff). For Old Testament conquests see *Numbers*, 31:33, *Joshua*, 6:21, 8:24, 10:36–40, 11:11–14. Shlain argues that literacy created patriarchy, but patriarchy was established well before literacy—the epics, after all, were based in oral traditions. See *Alphabet*, 3, 15–24, 39, 122, 362–429.

200 —*Common Sense* and *The Rights of Man* were bestsellers: Eric Foner's Introduction to *The Rights of Man* (Penguin, 1984), 10, 18.

200 —the vote wasn't even contemplated: Mary Wollstonecraft, *A Vindication of the Rights of Women*, ed. by Carol H. Poston (Norton, 1988), 147, 223–227.

202 —"without being eradicated in the name of improved agriculture": J. S. Mill, quoted in Sheldrake, *Rebirth of Nature*, 61–64.

203 —"produce coordinated patterns of greater and greater diversity": Frank Herbert, *Dune* (Chilton, 1965), 399.

203 —"a continuous breaking and forming to make new, richer wholes": Ferguson, *Aquarian*, 169.

Index

hellfire, 159, 215*n*
Henry V, King of England, 58
Heracles, 199
Herbert, Frank, 203
Herodotus, 163
Herzog, Werner, 137
Hesiod, 151, 152, 226*n*
hierarchical structures, 78–79, 86–87,
    89–91, 102
Hill, Julia Butterfly, 157
Hitler, Adolf, 18, 22, 87, 94, 177
Ho Chi Minh, 177
Holden, Stephen, 51
Hollywood films, 97
Holocaust, 74
Holy Grail, 53–54
horses, 136–137
Hu Jintao, 97
Hughes, Howard, 71, 117
human mind, 107–108
    see also ego
human nature, and Control Culture, 12
human organism, 106–108
    and the ego, 109–114
human rights, 132–133, 169
Human Rights Council, 171
hunter-gatherers, 11, 226*n*
    cooperation, 25, 54, 84
    as egalitarian, 12–13, 48–49, 84–86
    genetic-programming, 10
    and Nature, 19, 135, 150–151, 153
    as 'original affluent society', 151
    and religion, 150
    skills and abilities, 129
    see also pre-Controller world
Huntington, Samuel, 46
Huse, Donna, 220*n*
Huxley, Aldous, 84

Ibsen, Henrik, 103
Ice-Station Zebra, 117
imaginal cells, 1, 181
immigrants, 63, 179–180, 194
immunology, 75
improvisation, 119–120, 197
incivility, 8
India, 127, 137, 195
individualism, 163–164, 192–193
Indonesia, 74
industrial revolution, 17, 32
industrial societies, gender attitudes, 46
Inglehart, Ronald, 46
Innocent III, Pope, 74
innovation
    and outsiders, 53
    uniting of opposites, 77
Inquisition, 74, 135, 148
insects, 205*n*
instinct, 12
Integrative Culture, 15–26

adaptive capabilities, 22
beginnings of, 199–200
boundaries, 10, 14
and communication, 18–19, 81
compared to Control Culture, 10, 13,
    14–16, 19, 22, 25–26, 37, 202–203
competitiveness, 37
and concentrations of power, 99–101
and conflict, 76–77
and cooperation, 22, 25, 54, 192, 193
and diversity, 13
and ecological awareness, 16, 19–20
and the ego, 114
and ethics, 158
and interdependence, 10, 155–156, 189,
    196
and international trade, 126
and the Internet, 98–99
and medicine, 75–76
and men, 41–42, 57–58, 61, 62–63
need for, 196
needs, 188
and obsolescence of war, 20–22
and process, 79–83
reasons for growth, 16
right-brain thinking, 15
and science, 69–71
social change, 183–184, 188, 189,
    190–192, 193
sphere symbol, 78
and spirituality, 155–160
and technological change, 17–18
and women, 41–42, 53–57
Intel, 178
intelligence, 22, 103
    and complexity, 9
    creationism, 9, 149
interdependence, and Integrative Culture,
    10, 155–156, 189, 196
Internet, 36, 70, 98–99, 180–181, 190,
    193, 218–219*n*
intuition, 72, 113
Iran, 8, 21, 147
    higher education, 45–46
Iranian Mullahs, 147
Iraq, invasion of, 21, 30–31, 92, 95, 130,
    131–132, 206*n*
Ireland, 128
Islam
    authoritarian tradition, 9
    conflict within, 8
    and Control Culture, 147–149
    'culture war', 8
    democratic sentiments, 46
    inter-faith violence, 150
    see also Qur'an
Islamic fundamentalism, 8, 23, 147
Israel, 50–51
Italy, 164–165

Made in the
USA
Middletown, DE